Red Sox vs. Braves
in Boston

Red Sox vs. Braves in Boston

The Battle for Fans' Hearts, 1901–1952

CHARLIE BEVIS

McFarland & Company, Inc., Publishers
Jefferson, North Carolina

ISBN (print) 978-0-7864-9664-8
ISBN (ebook) 978-1-4766-2964-3

LIBRARY OF CONGRESS CATALOGUING-IN-PUBLICATION DATA

BRITISH LIBRARY CATALOGUING DATA ARE AVAILABLE

Front cover: George F. Graham (left) and Tris Speaker American
Tobacco Company baseball cards, 1911 (Library of Congress), 1914 Boston
Braves pennant head and 1915 Boston Red Sox Royal Rooters pin

Printed in the United States of America

*Box 611, Jefferson, North Carolina 28640
www.mcfarlandpub.com*

Table of Contents

Part Four: Red Sox Triumph, 1934–1945

Part Five: Braves Fight Back, 1946–1952

Preface

This is the first comprehensive work that examines Boston as a two-team major-league city, when the Red Sox and Braves both called Boston home from 1901 through 1952. Rather than review the games and ballplayers of the two teams during this 52-year period of co-existence, this book instead focuses on the development of Boston baseball fans, which is another fertile territory for new research and analysis.

This book examines the actions the two baseball teams took to compete for the allegiance of baseball fans as well as the obstacles that inhibited the teams from successfully attracting fans. By using the perspective of the fan to view the complex interconnection of the city of Boston and its two baseball teams, a deeper clarity emerges to explain why the Red Sox remained in Boston and the Braves moved to Milwaukee. The reasons are not nearly as straightforward as the existing rationales postulated by researchers.

Several baseball-related factors foster fan support. At the top of the list is a winning team. While this is an obvious factor, it does not explain everything. Other relevant factors include star players, ballpark quality, game scheduling, and the team's style of play. Beyond the baseball-related factors, there are also numerous broad trends that impact the ability to build a fan base, such as transportation, geography, communication, population, and employment.

Fans were central to baseball club economics in the days before the advent of television, yet we have only a very limited understanding of the nature of the people who inhabited the ballparks and listened to radio broadcasts in that era. This book fills a significant research void in the literature of baseball fans, where knowledge has progressed only minimally beyond the work of Steven Riess in his book *Touching Base: Professional Baseball and American Culture in the Progressive Era*. While I have woven as much granularity as possible into my analysis to explain how the two Boston teams developed fans, this book is an initial deep dive into this subject area to serve as a foundation for additional future research.

Researching fans is challenging, since there is limited directly on-point research material available for a virtually virgin topic such as baseball fans; ballpark attendance numbers are one exception to this general rule. Digitized databases of newspapers and periodicals have made the research into understanding the nature of fans a bit easier, although it often involves separating the 98 percent of the material that is associated with games and players to parse out the 2 percent related to fans and spectators. Being able to mine the digitized files of the *Boston Globe* and *The Sporting News* was essential to my learning about baseball fans in Boston.

This project took five years to come to fruition, even with a good foundation formed by my previously published work about Sunday baseball, doubleheaders, and the 1901 formation of the American League team in Boston. New research in these three areas provided not only greater clarity about how these elements evolved in Boston, but also revealed new insights into their impact in general and, in particular, their role in the development of Boston baseball fans. One prominent example is the 1933 sale of the foundering Red Sox club to new ownership.

When researching the past, it is always a challenge to suppress the bias that how things work in the present is the same way they did in the past. One of the big obstacles in my research process for this book was an initial belief there were always two distinct camps of "Red Sox fans" and "Braves fans." Nothing could have been farther from the truth, as it turns out.

While trying to comprehend some contradictory (to me) research findings, I asked my older brother Bob, who, as a young boy, along with our father, who died back in the 1970s, had experienced Boston baseball as a two-team city (I was born just after the Braves left Boston for Milwaukee). I asked Bob whether Dad had been a Red Sox fan or a Braves fan. "Neither," he replied. "He was a baseball fan." This was the "a-ha" moment for this book. Suddenly that contradictory research, and many other pieces of research, now made perfect sense in a world of "Boston baseball fans" who were not highly partisan for one team or the other.

This revelation gave birth to my general thesis to explain the overall evolution of baseball fans in Boston and the creation of a three-tier hierarchy to categorize Boston fans during the two-team era. This hierarchy, which is used throughout this book, is explained in the Introduction.

Introduction

One of the most elemental ways to categorize baseball fans is to group them by levels of interest, such as high, moderate, and low. This was the pioneer approach postulated in a 1993 article by Daniel Wann and Nyla Branscombe which was published in the *International Journal of Sport Psychology*. These two authors laid the foundation for more elaborate work to understand the nature of fans of all sports.[1]

A more robust classification method groups baseball fans into three tiers of enthusiasts, such as intense, shared, and casual. This was the approach articulated by John Davis and Jessica Zutz Hilbert in their 2013 book *Sports Marketing: Creating Long Term Value*. Intense enthusiasts are "the most loyal, characterized by ongoing support of their favorite sport, team, and athletes, irrespective of success." Shared enthusiasts also love their favorite team, but are less intense since they prefer a shared community experience over an individual one. Casual enthusiasts "pay occasional attention if time permits and doing so is convenient." This three-tier approach is a simple, yet broadly representative way to examine baseball fans.[2]

Similar to the Davis–Hilbert hierarchy, this book utilizes a three-level classification to categorize Boston baseball fans—dedicated, general baseball, and intermittent—when analyzing the period when there were two professional baseball teams in Boston between 1901 and 1952. While the highest and lowest tiers are similar in both taxonomies, the middle tier used in this book differs significantly, since it is the linchpin to explaining the nature of fans in Boston when it was a two-team city.

Dedicated baseball fans were highly partisan and thus followed just one of the two Boston professional teams to the exclusion of the other. General baseball fans enjoyed professional baseball no matter which of the two teams was involved; while general fans could, and often did, have a leaning to one team or the other, they had no qualms about following both teams. Intermittent baseball fans viewed either team as simply an entertainment option; when one team performed especially well, they might "jump on the bandwagon," but that interest was merely temporary.

This examination of baseball fans in Boston when it was a two-team city is organized into five parts. This structure best facilitates an understanding of how fans jockeyed between the two teams and ultimately how more fans gravitated to the Red Sox to relegate the Braves to second-class status. The resulting exodus of the Braves from Boston to Milwaukee in 1953 was never a foregone conclusion, though, as the pendulum of fan preference swung back and forth between the two teams in five meaningful segments of time.

Part One (1871–1900) provides the nineteenth-century backdrop to the two-team city of the twentieth century. During this period, the Braves (then known blandly as the Boston National League team) had a monopoly for the most part, which fostered a solid body of general baseball fans. In the 1890s this weakened as a result of a variety of factors, most prominently transportation improvements and population shifts.

Part Two (1901–1920) examines the reasons why fans quickly favored the Boston team in the newly formed American League (soon to be called the Red Sox) and how the National League team (to be known as the Braves) failed to adequately respond to the competition. While fans were largely dedicated Red Sox fans, they soon reverted to being general baseball fans, although many were Sox-leaning fans. Both clubs needed to build new ballparks, Fenway Park for the Red Sox and Braves Field for Braves, to handle the explosive growth of baseball fans.

Part Three (1921–1933) reviews how the Braves used initiatives relating to Sunday baseball and radio broadcasts to achieve an edge over the Red Sox during an era when both teams compiled dismal won-lost records on the field. With the Braves on the cusp of achieving a monopoly on Sunday baseball, because the new law didn't allow Sunday games at Fenway Park, politics intervened to force the Braves to rent Braves Field to the Red Sox for Sunday games. During the three years from 1931 to 1933, the Braves had their most visible fan preference over the Red Sox, but it evaporated soon after the Red Sox secured a new law in 1932 that permitted Sunday games at Fenway Park and thus provided a future to the foundering Red Sox club.

Part Four (1934–1945) covers the refurbishing of the Red Sox and Fenway Park by its new owner, Tom Yawkey. These improvements resulted in a rapid shift of dedicated and Braves-leaning general fans to the Red Sox, due to a preference for the power-hitting style of play in the American League compared to the more strategic small-ball style of play in the National League. However, the Braves planned a postwar comeback to use night baseball to recapture fans and create new fans.

Part Five (1946–1952) analyzes how the Red Sox maintained their fan dominance in the face of stiff competition from night baseball at Braves Field. The Braves were also leaders in the adoption of televised ball games beginning in 1948. The demise of the Braves was actually caused by radio, not television, because the Red Sox in 1951 initiated radio broadcasts of road games. Many general baseball and intermittent fans that followed the Braves, who mostly lived in the suburbs, became dedicated Red Sox fans because they preferred to listen to Curt Gowdy broadcast a Red Sox road game on the radio rather than attend a Braves home game or listen to Jim Britt broadcast that home game on radio or television. Ideas to ease travel by suburban fans, such as a new ballpark in the suburbs and limited-access highways into Boston, did not move forward fast enough to deter the Braves from leaving Boston after the 1952 season.

PART ONE:
NATIONALS HAVE MONOPOLY, 1871–1900

◆ 1 ◆

Merchants as Spectators

In 1868 there were three top-flight amateur baseball clubs in the Boston area, the Harvard College, Tri-Mountain, and Lowell clubs. Several hundred people routinely devoted part of an afternoon to watch the ball games played by these amateur clubs. Most of these spectators were merchants or aspiring businessmen, who had both the means and, more importantly, the time flexibility to attend ball games by leaving their place of business in Boston's central business district.

Competition, not money, was the motivation for these three Boston baseball clubs, unlike some clubs in other cities who practiced sham amateurism by paying their players sub rosa through a limited-appearance job or an "expense" subsidy. In December 1868, though, the National Association of Base Ball Players, ostensibly strictly an all-amateur organization, voted at its annual meeting to recognize the existence of professional ballplayers within its ranks. The already pseudo-professional baseball clubs in New York City, Brooklyn, and Philadelphia could now openly compensate their players.

Although none of the three Boston-based amateur clubs converted to professional status, the Tri-Mountains and Lowells did play their games on a new ball grounds in 1869. This established the foundation for a possible profit-making venture in the future, since the existing ball fields used by the two clubs were not suitable for a professional environment. Staunchly amateur Harvard did have its own ball field on campus, but the college did not wish to share its facility with the other two baseball clubs to tarnish its amateur tradition of sportsmanship.

Before 1869, the Tri-Mountains played at Riverside Park while the Lowells played their games on the Boston Common. Neither was an ideal site for baseball. Riverside Park was a horse-racing venue, located three miles west of the center city in the town of Brighton. The Boston Common, while adjacent to the central business district, had an uncertain sporting future. Just a few years earlier, the Common had been an isolated waterfront property, with its western edge fronting the foul-smelling tidal basin of the Charles River. Because the tidal basin was now a landfill-in-progress, the city was issuing fewer permits to play baseball on the Common, to cut back on activity that might impede the sale of house lots in the emerging elite neighborhood known as the Back Bay.

The model for the new Boston ball grounds stemmed from an excursion the Tri-Mountains had made to Brooklyn, New York, in 1868. In their games played there at the Union Grounds, the Tri-Mountains noticed the functionality of having a ball field that was shared by multiple clubs. In the spring of 1869 a group of Boston businessmen met to discuss the feasibility of establishing such a collaborative ball grounds in Boston. This group, "by the liberality of several gentlemen connected with the various clubs," secured a vacant five-acre lot next to the tracks of the Boston & Providence Railroad in a marshy area of the Roxbury neighborhood of Boston. The land was leased from its owner, Philadelphia coal merchant Barnabas Hammett.[1]

Although two miles from the central business district, the Hammett lot was spacious enough for baseball games and reasonably convenient for both players and spectators, as a horse-drawn streetcar line passed nearby on Tremont Street. The resulting baseball facility on this land was dubbed the Union Grounds, honoring the Brooklyn facility of the same name. This location, soon to be known at the South End Grounds, was used by the Boston franchise in the National League for its ball games until 1914.

While the Hammett lot in 1869 was within the borders of the city of Boston, just a year and a half earlier the land had been part of the city of Roxbury. At the beginning of 1868, Roxbury was annexed to Boston, relinquishing its independent status to become a neighborhood of Boston. The Hammett lot was ideally situated to draw patrons from two nearby upper-income neighborhoods, the South End to the east and the Back Bay—expanding westward as the mudflats of the Charles River were filled and houses erected—to the north.

In 1869, the South End was the key area from which to draw baseball patrons. The neighborhood was built largely on landfill around the original neck of land that connected central Boston with Roxbury. Streets in the new South End neighborhood were laid out with adjacent parks. Brick townhouses were constructed to attract wealthy residents who were seeking refuse from the Irish immigrants who were taking over the center city, where large homes were replaced by commercial buildings. By 1869 the South End was a very fashionable neighborhood. With the Back Bay slowly developing as an up-and-coming neighborhood, things looked optimistic for high-level baseball at the Union Grounds.[2]

Despite its proximity to these upscale neighborhoods, the Hammett lot was located in a gritty area on the fringe of Roxbury's industrial district, dominated by foundries and breweries, and ringed by working-class housing. "This was a working class area," one historian described this area of Roxbury during the 1870s, "a small drab section of two- and three-story wooden houses and barracks such as could be found in any New England mill town." This was one reason why a five-acre parcel of undeveloped land within two miles of downtown Boston in 1869 was available for lease.[3]

Another reason that this land was undesirable was its restricted access, because the Hammett lot was nearly landlocked. The parcel was bounded on the north by the Boston & Providence Railroad tracks, on the east by marshland, on the south by houses on Berlin Street, and on the west by Franklin Place. However, Franklin Place provided the only entrance to the land, but, unfortunately, this roadway consisted of two disconnected sections. The big problem was that there was no direct access between Tremont Street, where the horse-drawn streetcar line was located, and the northern portion of Franklin Place where the entrance to the land was located; the southern section of Franklin Place did, in fact, intersect with Tremont Street. The bifurcation of Franklin Place resulted from a house owned by Robert Booker, at 24 Franklin Place, which divided Franklin at its intersection with Berlin Street. The Booker house would be an albatross for two decades before unrestricted access along that roadway was finally negotiated to simplify access for baseball fans.[4]

Since the complications with the layout of Franklin Place made it awkward for spectators to easily reach the Union Grounds, newspaper advertisements specified its location as "Milford Place, off Tremont St." Milford Place was the next street west on Tremont Street from Franklin Place. Because the Booker house blocked direct travel on Franklin Place from Tremont Street to the Union Grounds, people had to instead travel west on Tremont, north on Milford Place, east on Grinnell Street, and cross the northern section of Franklin Place to enter the ball grounds.[5]

Because the Union Grounds was not ready when the all-professional Cincinnati Red Stockings came to Boston in early June, Cincinnati played Harvard at its campus field, the Tri-Mountains at Riverside Park, and the Lowells on the Boston Common. True to form, Cincinnati easily trounced all three amateur clubs, but the trip was a financial disaster for Cincinnati. The game at distant Riverside Park attracted only a meager crowd. While 2,000 people attended the game on the Boston Common, only a few people paid for the opportunity to sit in a small, roped-off bleacher area as everyone else stood and watched the game for free on the city's public land. These two games validated the decision to secure new ball grounds, if Boston had any chance to field a professional team that would be able to turn a profit.[6]

After the first ball game at the Union Grounds on June 19, 1869, when the Tri-Mountains took on the Atlantic club from Brooklyn, most matches at the Union Grounds that summer pitted one of the three Boston amateur teams against local amateur competition, with little professional competition until the Eckford club from Brooklyn arrived in October.

During the winter of 1870, Ivers Adams became convinced that professional baseball had a future in Boston and began to form Boston's first professional baseball club. Adams, who worked as a clerk at John Pray & Company in the central business district, was one of the few members of the nascent middle class, living in a large house in the suburban Boston Highlands area of Roxbury with his wife, three children, and three servants.[7]

Adams was not just an avid sportsman, but also a savvy businessman, as a carpet mogul in training at John Pray & Company. He realized the potential that a professional baseball team could do for the Boston business community, to elevate Boston into the same economic realm as New York City and Philadelphia. Boston's stature in the world of commerce had steadily slipped over the previous 20 years, moving from being the nation's third largest city in 1850 to fifth largest in 1860 and down to seventh largest in 1870. The popularity of a winning professional baseball team could help elevate the overall prospects for all businessmen in Boston, not just the investors in the baseball club.

Improvements were made to the formative Union Grounds for the 1870 season, to encourage more spectators to make the trek to the ball grounds, which was advertised as being "accessible from the heart of the city by horse cars running to and from them every five minutes, and taking thirty minutes only to make a trip." More seating was added to the small stand erected for the 1869 season, to hold 2,000 spectators but still allow sufficient standing room along the sidelines. The field itself was "thoroughly graded and turfed" and a higher fence was erected to discourage free viewing from the houses along neighboring Berlin Street.[8]

During the five-week period from May 24 to June 29, four top-notch professional teams appeared at the Union Grounds in 1870. The Athletics of Philadelphia, the Red Stockings of Cincinnati, the Mutuals of New York, and the White Stockings from Chicago all easily defeated the three Boston amateur teams. The verdict was clear that amateur baseball in Boston had little future in the face of stiff professional competition. While the inability to secure a victory on the ball field was disappointing, the Union Grounds facility was a winner regarding the ability to generate a profit. Five thousand spectators jammed the Union Grounds on Saturday, June 4, to watch Harry Wright's Cincinnati team dominate the Harvard College team. Several thousands also watched each game played by the Tri-Mountains and the Lowells against the professionals. Baseball followers were more than willing to pay 25 cents to see a ball game at the Union Grounds.

Although the game results do not indicate it, the Tri-Mountains may have been Boston's first professional baseball club. While the evidence is meager, the Tri-Mountain club apparently did pay a player or two, but the money was not well spent, since the Tri-Mountains lost games to professional clubs by lop-sided margins and a few times barely defeated avowed amateur clubs. The futility of the Tri-Mountains as a professional enterprise, both on and off the field, may have spurred Adams to insist upon experienced business managers to operate his proposed fully professional club in Boston.[9]

Professional baseball in Boston did not flow directly from either the Tri-Mountains or the Lowells, but rather was formed from the ground up by Adams, who served as the first president of the new baseball club. While Adams could provide the legal and finance elements, he obviously needed someone to handle the baseball aspects with a sound business perspective. Adams hired Harry Wright, who was one of the best in the nation at organizing and managing the affairs of a touring baseball club, having performed those duties for the undefeated Cincinnati club in 1869 as well as its 1870 incarnation. Wright brought not only his management wisdom but also the name "Red Stockings" that the baseball team was informally called during its formative years. What the Tri-Mountains and Lowells did provide was the spectator base for the ball games.

In 1870 most baseball followers in Boston, like Adams, were equally likely to watch a ball game contested by any of the three top amateur teams, since few were exclusive followers of just one club. For example, the Lowell club had only about 100 members (both players and dedicated fans) while their ball games typically attracted 1,000 to 2,000 spectators at the Union Grounds.[10]

Therefore, the composition of the original audience for professional baseball in Boston was upper-income merchants and the brokers and clerks (apprentice businessmen being groomed to be partners in firms) of the "old" middle class. Other people were welcome to attend ball games, but they were not a high priority. To say the desired audience was "middle class" is an oversimplification, and doesn't adequately allow for an examination of how the nature of baseball followers changed over the ensuing decades.[11]

In antebellum American society, there were essentially two social strata, non-manual workers—merchants who worked with their head—and manual workers—mechanics who worked with their hands. There were distinct economic ramifications, as the merchants (owners) were the "haves" and the mechanics (laborers) were the "have-nots." There was a "middling sorts" category, which Stuart Blumin in his book *The Emergence of the Middle Class: Social Experience in the American City, 1760–1900* defined as sole-proprietor shopkeepers, intermediaries between merchants and shopkeepers, and clerks being groomed to be merchants. These people were the bulk of the "old" middle class.[12]

In the evolving social structure of postbellum America, a more sizeable middle tier emerged between the two polar groups of upper-class merchant and lower-class mechanic. This "new" middle class was not one homogenous category, but rather, as outlined by Sam Bass Warner, Jr., in his book *Streetcar Suburbs: The Process of Growth in Boston, 1870–1900*, consisted of three distinct segments: upper, central, and lower. The upper middle class was the antebellum "old" middle class, who were large storeowners, successful manufacturers, brokers, wholesalers, and prosperous lawyers. The central middle class consisted of small-store owners, successful salesmen, lawyers, school teachers, and large contractors. The lower middle class were skilled artisans (whose craft hadn't yet been eliminated by industrialization) and better-paid salaried office workers and sales personnel.[13]

Eventually, the new middle class would outnumber the old middle class, but in 1870 the older version dramatically outnumbered the newer one by a six-to-one margin. It was the old middle class that Adams expected to be the bulk of the audience for the games of the new Boston professional team.[14]

Manual workers were not even a consideration at the dawn of professional baseball in Boston. Because they worked a 60-hour work week, ten-hour days for six days a week, they had no time to attend a baseball game.[15]

At the founding meeting of the Boston Base Ball Association in January 1871, the 32-year-old Adams formally established the strategy of attracting spectators to watch the baseball games, namely "shareholders, members of the club and those of our friends who may take sufficient interest in the success of this enterprise." Essentially, the original desired spectators for professional baseball in 1871 were either men who purchased one of the 200 available season tickets or upper-income merchants and businessmen who would regularly attend games.[16]

The nature of expected spectators was indicated by the few number of home games played each season, only two to three dozen, all erratically scheduled. There was also a distinct lack of games played in August, when the baseball club often took extended road trips, since most businessmen were away at the shore or mountains to escape the summer heat. With no schedule of games, spectators needed broad flexibility to attend the games. Since about 40 percent of the American workforce was self-employed in the 1870s, this was not a particular problem.[17]

One example of an early baseball fan was George Appleton, a rabid fan of the old amateur Lowell club who was equally interested in following the new Boston professional club. In 1871, Appleton was a clerk at Bradford & Anthony, a hardware store that specialized in fine cutlery and fishing tackle, located in Boston's central business district. The other men watching ball games in the grandstand were a natural clientele for his firm's high-end goods. In 1883 Appleton opened his own business, Appleton & Litchfield, which he operated until 1901, last as Appleton & Bassett where he served as a ticket broker for the games of the National League team. When he died in 1921, the *Boston Globe* characterized Appleton as "one of the oldest baseball fans in Boston, his interest dating from the origin of the game, back in the '70s."[18]

Adams initiated a number of policies that were the foundation of Boston professional baseball for the next quarter-century. He chose to name the new baseball club "Boston," after its city location, not by a nickname that most other clubs of the era used, such as the Mutual club in New York or the Athletic club in Philadelphia.

Perhaps most importantly, Adams established the baseball club as a corporation, to enable financial funding through stock purchases where the stockholders had limited liability for future debts. The Boston Base Ball Association received its legal standing as a corporation on March 24, 1871, after a protracted effort to marshal a bill through the Massachusetts legislature. In 1871 only entities engaged in specific business activities could be organized as a corporation under the general laws, such as a manufacturer, hotel, or printer. Adams needed a special act of the legislature to establish his baseball corporation.[19]

Adams turned to George Monroe, a state senator representing the Roxbury district, who published a small weekly newspaper. Monroe introduced a bill in early March to incorporate the baseball club, which was referred to the Education Committee. Since Massachusetts was a commonwealth, not merely a state, laws needed to have a "common good" purpose, not simply to benefit a few people. The bill had several bumps in the legislative process, as some lawmakers failed to see how the proposed corporation would promote commerce rather than just enrich a few individuals. After several rewrites, the bill that finally became law defined the new corporation as having "the purpose of promoting physical culture, and for the encouragement and improvement of the game of base ball."[20]

The Union Grounds was now officially known as the Boston Ball Base Grounds, although it was informally called simply the Boston Grounds. The seating strategy for the Boston Grounds was to erect "a covered building capable of seating about a thousand people," with reserved seats for the shareholders, members, and friends. The grandstand provided fans with modest comfort, a simple wooden plank to sit on with a wooden backrest, but there was a roof for protection from the elements, an important improvement over seating at the old Union Grounds configuration. Bleacher seating was soon added along the baselines. However, the grandstand was physically separated from the bleachers, which served, in effect, to segregate spectators by income class.

Admission to the games was 50 cents, double the 25 cents that the amateur clubs had been charging. Seating in the grandstand cost an additional 25 cents, for a total cost of 75 cents to watch a game from the best vantage point at the Boston Grounds. Tickets could be purchased within the central business district at the Wright & Gould sporting goods store, owned by George Wright, brother of Harry, and Charlie Gould, who both were ballplayers for the Boston team.[21]

This physical segregation practice was consistent with the values of the time, according to Richard Butsch, author of *The Making of American Audiences*. Restraint and self-control were part of the defining character of the emerging middle class of the 1870s, where there was an insistence on "separation from coarseness, rowdiness, and other forms of emotional outlet that characterized the lower classes." In Boston, the segregation was more than merely social class, though, but also due to religious and ethnic snobbery, since the "better class" of baseball followers then were almost exclusively of the Protestant faith and Anglo-Saxon heritage even though the majority of the Boston population was Catholic and of Irish heritage.[22]

Ball games were played Monday through Saturday, but never on Sunday, in accordance with the Massachusetts law that provided that no person "do or exercise any labor, business or work of their ordinary callings, nor use any game, sport, play or recreation on the Lord's Day." The Sunday laws were a vestige of the state's Puritan heritage, dating from the 1692 when Sunday was strictly for religious observance and a day of rest as decried by the fourth commandment of the Bible. While not an issue with the primary baseball audience of the nineteenth century, the inability to play ball games on Sunday became an increasingly significant impediment to expanding the fan base during the twentieth century.[23]

Game time was normally 3:00 or 3:30 in the afternoon, so that businessmen could be home for dinner at 6:30, whether they lived nearby in the South End or commuted to the city from a railroad suburb such as Newton on the Boston & Albany Railroad or Dedham on the Boston & Providence Railroad. Both train terminals were not far from the Boston Grounds.

With the ball grounds, fan base, and corporate structure all in place, the Boston Base Ball Association competed in the 1871 season of the fledgling National Association of Professional Base Ball Players, a loose confederation of professional clubs that had splintered from the national amateur association to focus on the game as played by professional players. There were "championship" games played against other clubs in the National Association, as well as sporadic exhibition matches versus other clubs.

The spectator strategy worked reasonably well for the inaugural 1871 season, as 36,000 people paid to watch 19 home games, or about 2,000 per game. To stimulate greater interest in grandstand seating for the 1872 season, though, the club sold season tickets to the general public ($10 for a single person and $15 for a gentleman and lady) and advertised the availability of single-game grandstand tickets.[24]

When a significant increase in patronage didn't materialize in 1872, the Boston Base Ball Club was formed (not to be confused with the Boston Base Ball Association, which was the actual baseball club) to actively recruit new season-ticket buyers, which resulted in 108 new patrons. Advertising expenditures were also increased for 1873 (to $1,350, nearly three times the $500 rent paid for the ball grounds) by employing Henry McGlenen, an Irish-American who was the business agent for the Boston Theatre, to drum up new spectators to augment the horsecar signage and handbills previous used to promote ball games.[25]

Games were also played on three holidays during the 1873 season, May 30 on Decoration Day, June 17 on Bunker Hill Day, and two games (morning and afternoon) on the July 4 Independence Day. As a result, the baseball club experienced a 50 percent increase in attendance in 1873 (to 52,000), with the sizeable crowds on the holidays comprised of many working-class spectators, who could finally watch a ball game. This was the high-water-mark for seasonal attendance for many years, though.

Carte de visites, such as this one of ballplayer Dave Birdsall, were distributed to drum up interest among Boston businessmen to purchase season tickets for 1873. The photographs, taken by George K. Warren, showed the ballplayers in business attire, rather than baseball uniforms, to portray them as part of the Boston business community (New York Public Library, Digital Collections).

By 1874, the population growth patterns of the Greater Boston area already had exposed a flaw in the location of the Boston Grounds regarding the ease that the club could draw desired middle-class spectators to ball games. Boston had 250,000 residents in 1870, about 40 percent of the 635,000 people who lived in the entire Greater Boston area. While most men still worked in the Boston business district, the prosperous ones increasingly lived not in the better areas of "old" Boston, such as Beacon Hill and the South End, but rather in areas three to five miles distant from downtown Boston that were served by railroad or horsecar lines, especially in the annexed towns. By 1880, the population of the suburbs of

Greater Boston grew at a faster rate than the city itself, a trend that never reserved itself over the next 75 years.[26]

The Boston Grounds enjoyed just a brief two-year stint as an ultra-prime location for professional baseball. The Great Boston Fire in November 1872 destroyed a large part of the Boston business district, which radically changed the complexion of the South End. The neighborhood became less gentrified and more rundown, as low-income residents of the burned-out waterfront district moved into the South End, driving existing residents into the new Back Bay or out to the suburbs. Real estate values declined in the South End as a result. One example of the exodus from the South End was Nicholas Apollonio, who was the president of the Boston Base Ball Association from 1874 to 1876. While Apollonio had lived on Sharon Street in the South End in 1872, by 1875 he was living on Hancock Street in the fashionable Savin Hill section of Dorchester.[27]

Prospects for patrons from the emerging Back Bay neighborhood also declined. Few roadways connected the South End with the Back Bay, since the two neighborhoods were bifurcated by the Boston & Providence Railroad tracks. The closest connecting thoroughfare in the 1870s was Dartmouth Street, located a half-mile from the Boston Grounds. West Chester Park (now Massachusetts Avenue) and Ruggles Street were connecting roadways closer to the Boston Grounds, but these two streets only led to marshland until those sections of the Back Bay landfill operation were completed. Sizeable patronage from the Back Bay never really could materialize at the Boston Grounds.

Replacing the downtown merchants as spectators at the Boston Grounds were shopkeepers who could walk to the ball grounds from the commercial areas of nearby Roxbury Crossing and Dudley Street. Interest was also sparked within local businessmen in Dorchester and West Roxbury, which were contiguous to Roxbury. Dorchester and West Roxbury were both former independent towns, which were annexed by Boston in 1870 and 1874, respectively. Annexation was a growing trend in the Boston area, because town residents wanted cheap access to water, sewer, street lights, and schools that Boston could provide, while city residents wanted to forestall political control by the growing Irish-American population, then about one-quarter of Boston's population. The towns of Brighton and Charlestown were also annexed to Boston in 1874.

Expanded horsecar service to neighborhoods in northern Dorchester and the Jamaica Plain section of West Roxbury, all within three miles of the central business district, created new patrons for the Boston Grounds. Because these areas "became prime locations for professionals and businessmen who might not have been able to afford or gain social entry to Brookline or Newton," Dorchester and West Roxbury were the first substantial enclaves of middle-class Irish-Americans, known as "the bastion of the central middle class," in contrast to Roxbury that was "the land of the lower middle class."[28]

These new baseball followers had lower incomes than the merchants who no longer went to the ball games, though, as well as less time flexibility. While they were not grandstand patrons for the most part, they were at least ticket buyers. This group of baseball followers formed the foundation for the "baseball public" in Boston, which Terry Furst, author of *Early Professional Baseball and the Sporting Press: Shaping the Image of the Game*, defined as "a collection of individuals who consumed baseball, both directly and indirectly, through a common informational background which included attendance at games, the playing of baseball, knowledge of baseball matters through reading newspapers, sporting journals, baseball guides, and discussion with others." For the next several decades in Boston this distinct community of baseball followers was the heart of the "general baseball fan" category, following major-league baseball without an exclusive partisanship to one specific team.[29]

By 1875 there were more lower-income spectators and fewer businessmen at the Boston Grounds, which caused the baseball club to publicly apologize for the "many unruly and disorderly persons in the Boston assemblages ... [whose] behavior is distasteful to the larger and better portion of the spectators who attend the matches in Boston." In its first year of play in the National League, which was established in 1876 to improve upon the loose organization of the National Association, a huge crowd at the Decoration Day game, estimated to be 12,000, exemplified the changed nature of the spectators from the admirable spectator policy of 1871. "As early as 2 o'clock the vast range of plank seats extending down the sides of the field were black with people, and a large throng of restless spirits roamed about over the field," the *Boston Globe* described the scene. "Every southbound street-car on the Shawmut Avenue and Tremont Street lines came loaded with living freight and a constant stream of humanity poured along the sidewalks and roadways towards the grounds for two hours."[30]

One disgruntled patron at that game complained to the *Globe* that he had purchased a reserved seat several days before the game but then found the grandstand filled with squatters, "a crowd of men and boys, not one in fifty of whom had any monetary claim to such a privilege." He could not find anyone "who seemed to pretend to authority," whether policeman or guardian of the grandstand, to take action on his situation or a broader concern that the "crowd swarmed over and through the fences, and in many instances paid the policemen, who were stationed to prevent their entry, a price of entrance." He admonished the baseball club that "this is not the way to increase its popularity or the popularity of its grounds."[31]

As lower-income patrons became the staple of the baseball audience at the Boston Grounds, the baseball club struggled to survive during the latter years of the 1870s. The club put Boston on the national map, but the businessmen expected to support the club no longer had the time to watch the games, as industrialization fundamentally changed the Boston economy in the 1880s.

◆ 2 ◆

Emerging Middle Class
at the Ballpark

After the 1876 baseball season, another up-and-coming capitalist, like Adams six years earlier, took charge of the Boston Base Ball Association, the official name of the city's National League baseball club. Arthur Soden, then 33 years old, would serve as president from 1877 to 1906.

Soden was the owner of Chapman & Soden, a roofing manufacturer that made pine-tarred roofing felt and a variety of other waterproof roofing material. Following the Great Boston Fire in 1872, there was a large demand for roofing material to rebuild buildings in the burned-out section of Boston. The ball games at the Boston Grounds were a good place to associate with prospective roofing buyers among the businessmen sitting in the grandstand. Soden lived in upscale Newtonville, one of Boston's first railroad suburbs, and took a Boston & Albany train to get to his office on Water Street in the central business district. Soden subscribed to the devout Methodist belief in strict prohibition from alcoholic beverages as well as other temperate aspects of a respectable lifestyle at the time, which informed many of the baseball club's policies.[1]

Soden came into the fold of the Boston Base Ball Association around 1873 through the companion Boston Base Ball Club, which had been formed to drum up spectator interest in the baseball team. Soden initially bought a club membership, then purchased some stock in the association (reportedly at the urging of George Appleton), became one of the club's directors, and eventually its president in December 1876. His presidency of the spectator group was short-lived, though, since his first act was "to dissolve the club and turn over its effects to the association."[2]

With this merger of the club and the association, the stockholders of the association now completely controlled the baseball operation. This made perfect sense to Soden, the consummate businessman. There were no "members" at Chapman & Soden who were interested in watching the workers make roofing material at the manufacturing plant in Chelsea, only "customers" for that eventual roofing material. Soden applied this focus on the product, not the artisan (worker) who physically made it, to the baseball diamond as part of the burgeoning industrialization of American society. From a business perspective, Soden looked to appeal to a new generation of businessmen in Boston to watch baseball games at the Boston Grounds.

Soden tried to polish the image of the ball grounds by asking baseball writers to refer to the location as the South End Grounds, to impart a greater cachet to the Boston Grounds that many people still associated with Roxbury, a decidedly drab step-sister of an area that had been annexed to the more urbane South End. While the grounds were commonly called the South End Grounds beginning in 1878, the cachet of the South End neighborhood rapidly dwindled over the next dozen years. Mortgage foreclosures on newly built houses on Columbus Avenue (which at the time stopped at the former Boston city line with Roxbury) caused land values to plummet throughout the South End, which accelerated its economic decline. By 1890 the South End was known as a lodging-house district; by 1900 it had transformed into a slum area.[3]

The introduction of a fixed 30-game home schedule in 1877 helped to stem disinterest among spectators, who could now plan ahead to attend games at the Boston Grounds. However, attendance peaked in 1877, as spectators were not impressed with the competition from far-flung small cities like Milwaukee, Indianapolis, and Buffalo, which had replaced big-city clubs in New York, Philadelphia, and St. Louis that had been expelled for violating league rules. Two local rivalries were created when Providence, 50 miles south in Rhode Island, was added to the league in 1878, and Worcester, 40 miles west of Boston, was added to the league in 1880. However, annual attendance continued to plummet, even after the schedule was expanded to 42 home games in 1879.

By 1880, the old model of reliance on merchants and other members of the "old" middle class to fill the grandstand at the South End Grounds was no longer viable. An attendance analysis published by the *Boston Globe* indicated that the average game attendance of 1,000 people was comprised of just 100 people in the grandstand with the other 900 people seated in the bleachers.[4]

However, there was increased interest in baseball among lower-income men. Soden could not have missed the attendance spike at the team's games played on a holiday. At this time there two national holidays during the baseball season, Decoration Day on May 30 (now known as Memorial Day) and Independence Day on July 4. To evenly divide the lucrative holiday dates, the

National League generally scheduled Decoration Day games on the grounds of the eastern clubs and Independence Day games on the grounds of the western clubs. Boston, though, had its own local holiday, Bunker Hill Day on June 17, which gave Boston baseball fans two holiday dates during the season. Attendance swelled for these holiday games because it was the only time that most working-class men could attend a ball game, since they typically labored ten hours a day for six days a week and rested on Sunday. Because Sunday baseball was prohibited in Boston, mill workers and other laborers traveled to the South End Grounds for a holiday game, as did lower middle-class patrons, often packing the grounds to its capacity.

A large number of the holiday throng in the bleacher sections were no doubt Irish-Americans, who held laborer jobs where they "eked out a miserable existence" in Boston's discriminatory environment where "the Yankee response to Irish immigrants was mostly hostile and intolerant." The derisive atmosphere in Boston had ethnic and religious considerations, not just social class, whose foundation was eight centuries of Anglo-Saxon Protestant rule over Catholics in Ireland, capped by the insensitivity of the meager response to the Great Famine of the 1840s that led many Irish to leave Ireland for America. Interest in baseball among lower-income Irish-Americans was sparked by the several of their brethren who had played for or against the Boston team, including Jim O'Rourke and Tommy Bond in Boston uniforms, Mike Kelly on the Chicago team, and Tim Keefe on the Troy team. These Irish-American ballplayers were ascending into the middle class through their much higher salaries compared to the average manual laborer.[5]

With larger crowds on holidays and certain other dates, Soden had to tackle the issue of better access for horsecar-traveling patrons to get to the South End Grounds, since the Booker house at the corner of Franklin Place and Berlin Street still blocked direct access between the horsecar line on Tremont Street and the South End Grounds bordering on the isolated portion of Franklin Place. In 1879 and 1881 Soden arranged for petitions to be made to the Board of Street Commissioners for an extension of Franklin Place via the city's taking of the Booker land by eminent domain. However, in both instances, the petitions were denied; in 1881 the explicit concern was the lack of a release by "certain lands owned by parties in Philadelphia."[6]

The Boston baseball club did not own the land under the South End Grounds, which was becoming more problematic for Soden. The land owner, Barnabas Hammett, had died in 1873, but there were complications with his estate, which resulted in lawsuits that would reach the Pennsylvania Supreme Court in 1883. While the baseball club continued to rent the land, the problems with the settlement of the Hammett estate impaired Soden's ability to improve spectator access. The best resolution that Soden could negotiate with the city, at this time, was to change the name of the street from Franklin Place to Walpole Street, to align with the many streets in the South End that were named for towns in Massachusetts (such as Northampton Street and Dover Street) to try to expunge the Roxbury image from the minds of horsecar patrons. In November 1881, the section of Franklin Place between Tremont Street and the Booker house was officially renamed Walpole Street; however, the section of the street that ran from behind the Booker house to the South End Grounds continued to be known as Franklin Place and was not renamed Walpole Street until 1890.[7]

Soden eventually negotiated an easement through the Booker land for days when a ball game was to be played. The club paid the Bookers $150 a year to use the small strip of private land—basically to have the Bookers open a gate in their fence at the end of Walpole Street—to enable spectators to walk directly from the horsecar line to the South End Grounds. While not a perfect solution, this did help dissuade potential spectators from taking advantage of a cut-rate opportunity to watch the game from access points a few houses down on Berlin Street as an alternative to walking the circuitous route from the horsecar line to the grounds. There was a cottage industry among Berlin Street residents of charging ten or 15 cents to watch the games from their rooftop. By 1879 there were sporadic newspaper reports that the fences at the South End Grounds were raised to block the view of these free-loaders. The most famous viewing spot was the so-called Sullivan Tower behind the home of Michael Sullivan.[8]

After attracting less than 1,000 people per home game in 1880 and 1881, the lowest points in franchise history, attendance perked up a bit in 1882 when 50,000 spectators watched the ball games. Soden did several things to attract more people to the South End Grounds. He spent some money to provide regular maintenance to the grounds by hiring carpenter John Haggerty to be the groundskeeper and all-around fixer-upper of the facility. A new grandstand was erected (privately financed by "a few gentlemen interested in the club"), which had a special section for newspaper writers. The "pen," as the special section was called, was perhaps the most important of the improvements. There had been only brief coverage of the team's games in the Boston newspapers, led by the *Boston Herald* and the *Boston Daily Advertiser*, which both appealed to businessmen. While Soden no doubt sought more coverage to encourage upper-income merchants and businessmen to the ball games, the larger impact occurred among central and lower middle-class baseball enthusiasts, as the *Boston Globe* took a greater interest in covering sports.[9]

The 1883 season was the turning point when the Boston baseball club firmly established a nearly two-decade-long monopoly among general base-ball fans in Boston. The combination of a strong product on the field, which captured the National League pennant that year, and the emergence of the

Boston Globe newspaper as a catalyst to stoke interest in the baseball team resulted in a massive increase in attendance at the South End Grounds.

Under the leadership of Charles H. Taylor, the *Boston Globe* was one of only two Democratic newspapers (the other was the downtrodden *Boston Post*) in a city dominated by several partisan Republican newspapers, led by the *Boston Herald*. Beginning publication in 1872, the *Boston Globe* was "a new Boston newspaper seeking a new readership [that] would find a natural clientele in the new Irish," who were quickly becoming the majority of the city's population. "In supporting the causes of labor and the underdog element, it would naturally form association with Democratic politicians, who were chiefly Irish." Taylor targeted more than just men and the Irish, though, as he addressed issues of interest to women and children and "encouraged coverage of baseball" by appointing writers to specialize in sports reporting. Ingeniously, Taylor targeted children who began to insist that their father buy the *Globe* so they could read the expansive coverage of sporting news, especially in its Sunday edition. By 1887, the *Globe* had the highest circulation number of any newspaper in Boston, topping the *Herald* that had been the most-widely-read paper in the city for many years.[10]

Attendance in 1883 more than doubled from 1882, reaching 128,000, the first time the Boston club had experienced six-digit attendance figures. One reason was the return of clubs from New York and Philadelphia, which replaced the small cities of Worcester and Troy, to resume these big-city rivalries. The second reason was that Boston occupied first place in July, which coincided with the arrival of William D. Sullivan as a full-time baseball writer for the *Boston Globe*. Sullivan joined the staff following his graduation from Harvard College that spring. Sullivan produced novel reporting during the 1883 season, writing a special section in the October 1 issue with biographies of all the ballplayers, augmented by woodcut images of the players. He also interviewed Soden for his reflections on the season in the September 30 issue.[11]

Sullivan was part of the emerging middle class in Boston, a man with Irish heritage but who was well educated and held a salaried job. Most of the new followers of the baseball team came from the emerging central and lower middle classes in Boston, comprised essentially of second-generation Irish-Americans. Newspaper coverage of boxer John L. Sullivan had sparked interest among Irish-Americans, after Sullivan won the heavyweight boxing title in February 1882. That interest increased a notch in July 1883 when Soden promoted John Morrill to be the first Irish-American to be the manager of the Boston baseball team.

Historically, the descendants of the Puritan settlers in Boston had sought to perpetuate their conservative Anglo-Saxon Protestant values through the function of government and operation of business in the face of increasing immigration of the Irish Catholics who had different ideas of how government and business should operate. While the Irish had initially been merely "cogs in an economic machine" for prosperous Boston merchants, "through the 1880s, successive levels of conflict between the two groups showed that the Irish had developed ... [a] growing assertiveness which challenged Brahmin domination." The future result was that "the submerged conflict between the Anglo-Saxon employer and the Celtic employee, which was the normal condition of the relationship, was about to erupt into a political revolution," in government, business, and baseball fandom.[12]

The seeds of that revolution were the children of Irish immigrants who made the ascent from the working class into the emerging middle class. Landing in the central or lower segments of the nascent middle class, these Irish Catholics initially imitated

John Morrill, an Irish-American, managed the 1883 Boston team to first place in the National League standings, which encouraged emerging middle-class Irish Catholic businessmen to become baseball fans in Boston's largely Anglo-Saxon Protestant business community (New York Public Library, Digital Collections).

the lifestyle of the dominant Anglo-Saxon Protestants (earning the somewhat derisive moniker "lace-curtain Irish") and "achieved affluence by making links with the economic power of the Anglo-Saxon elites." Examples includes Thomas Fitzpatrick, a dry goods merchant; James Phelan, a banker; James Prendergast, a cotton broker (who would later play a key role in 1901 in the establishment of the American League baseball club in Boston); and Hugh O'Brien, a politician and the first Irish-American mayor of Boston (in 1885). Other Irish-Americans thrust themselves into the central middle class as self-employed businessmen (grocery and liquor retailers, contractors, and undertakers) and white-collar workers (lawyers, doctors, and journalists) who "relied on the working-class Irish for their clientele."[13]

The South End Grounds was one area where the opposing two groups could commingle, with only the economic barrier of an additional fee to the grandstand section differentiating them from the adjacent, though non-connected, bleacher seating areas. Central middle-class Irish-Americans had aspirations for grandstand seats at the South End Grounds, while lower middle-class Irish-Americans (e.g., storekeepers and a few salaried clerks) were content with bleacher seating. Soden sought to fill both the grandstand and the bleachers, using strategies to attract fans to both sections, although he was more concerned with those of traditional Protestant values—or at least those that aspired to those values independent of religious affiliation. Having a higher income or living in a wealthy neighborhood was not the important consideration, but rather aspiring to those elements of higher social status. If you dressed well and could afford a grandstand ticket, you could mingle with those of a higher social standing. In this way, baseball assisted ambitious Irish-Americans to elevate themselves in Boston social circles.

Given the demonstrable demand among lower middle-class men (Protestant or Catholic) for one game on a holiday, Soden scheduled two games for the Decoration Day holiday in 1883, one in the morning and the other the traditional afternoon game. To differentiate the two games of a holiday match in order to maximize potential attendance, Boston played one team in the morning game and a different team in the afternoon game. To make this happen, the nearby Providence club also adopted the same pattern.

On Decoration Day in 1883, Boston and Providence hosted two-game sets where their respective opponents, Cleveland and Buffalo, shuttled by train between the two cities. After a morning game in Boston, Cleveland took the train to Providence for an afternoon game there. Likewise, Buffalo played a morning game in Providence and took the train to Boston for an afternoon contest at the South End Grounds. The maneuver worked, as attendance in Boston for both games in 1883 exceeded that of its single holiday game in 1882. "A crowd that occupied every seat on the South End Grounds assembled yesterday morning," the *Globe* reported the next day. In the afternoon, "the spectators began to gather by 1:30, and the [horse] cars were replete with them, in some cases affording the poor conductors only the precious foothold the brake could give."

Boston and Providence continued to employ the different-opponent strategy on Decoration Day in 1884, with New York and Philadelphia serving as the traveling opponents, to the delight of huge crowds at the South End Grounds. New York and Philadelphia also served as alternating opponents in a second holiday match in Boston that year on Bunker Hill Day on June 17. With the exodus of Providence from the National League after the 1885 season, though, Boston reverted to playing the same team in both games of a holiday twin bill in 1886.

In 1884 Soden actively sought to take advantage of the increased interest in baseball by raising season-ticket prices for National League games (now 56 home games) and establishing a "reserve team" to stage games at the South End Grounds when the league team was on the road. He also installed better seating in the grandstand, chair seats to replace numbers on a plank, since "those now employed are scarcely fit for a second-class stable," for which he raised the incremental price to sit in the grandstand to be half a dollar rather than a quarter.[14]

Attendance rose again in 1884, even in the face of competition for the first time from a Boston club in the newly established Union Association. The Boston Unions were the first attempt to overtly attract lower middle-class and working-class spectators to professional baseball games in Boston. Admission was just 25 cents to the Dartmouth Street Grounds, half the fare at the South End Grounds. However, the newly constructed ball grounds in the Back Bay didn't siphon many fans away from the South End Grounds, nor attract many new ones, since having the time flexibility to attend ball games in the mid-afternoon was still the primary consideration rather than the admission price. "I always was a firm believer that Boston would support a twenty-five cent team, but there is no use talking," Tim Murnane, manager of the Unions, later said. "Boston people want the best ball playing to be had anywhere, and they are perfectly willing to pay well for it. Look at the way they turned out at the Boston League games when the team was losing right along." The Union Association lasted just one season before folding, so the National League club reverted to having a monopoly in 1885.[15]

With attendance topping 100,000 for two consecutive seasons, Soden moved forward in late 1884 to purchase the land underneath the South End Grounds. The land was finally available for purchase ten years following the death of Barnabas Hammett, because the Pennsylvania Supreme Court had ruled on the legal issues impeding the settlement of Hammett's estate. Soden paid a hefty price for the five acres, since the land had a significant value if it were to be cut up into house lots. Soden paid $100,000 for the land, $35,000 in cash and the remaining $65,000 through a mortgage. It was a mistake, though, to purchase the Hammett lot and not find a new location for the ball grounds that would be more favorable to longer-term factors such as transportation access and population growth patterns. Remaining at the South End Grounds limited the geographic area from which the Boston baseball club could draw spectators.[16]

Most of the spectators for ball games worked in Boston, and they lived either in the city itself or within five miles of Boston's central business district. This was a problem in the making, since the growth rate of Boston's population began to slow down during the 1880s from its pre–1880 levels, relative to the population growth rates of the suburbs within Greater Boston; the suburbs began to grow at a faster rate than the city itself, a trend that would not dissipate for the next eight decades. The fastest growing suburban towns were the railroad suburbs located five to ten miles distant from the central business district, at double the city's growth rate, while the horsecar suburbs were a close second in growth rate. The population trends would not have been a huge problem were it not for the unequal transportation access to the South End Grounds from the various suburban areas.[17]

Residents in the more populous and faster grower towns within five miles north and northeast of Boston had a much more challenging effort to get to and from the South End Grounds than those people who lived in communities south and west of the ballpark. This was a vital consideration to entice businessmen working in downtown Boston as well as those who worked in those communities, since they needed to traverse the central business district, either via horsecar back to their community or to one of the railroad terminals (most importantly, the Boston & Maine terminal) located north of downtown to take a train home. Cambridge and Somerville were particularly troublesome, since all horsecar lines originating in Cambridge and Somerville (except those lines to Brighton) crossed into Boston near the central business district, forcing passengers to suffer a slowdown through the busy downtown area to get to the Tremont Street horsecar line to go to the ballpark. This restricted access from the northern suburbs was a problem.

Southern and western suburbs did have decent railroad access to the South End Grounds, since the terminals of the Boston & Albany, Boston & Providence, and Old Colony lines were within easy reach from the ballpark. However, horsecar access to the South End Grounds from southern and western suburbs was only good if the suburbs were within two miles of the ballpark. Thus there was good horsecar access from the adjacent neighborhood of Jamaica Plain and the northern parts of Dorchester (Grove Hall, Meetinghouse Hill, and Codman Square). However, the Emerald Necklace, authorized by the Park Act of 1875, became a barrier to suburban access to the South End Grounds from suburbs more than two miles distant. Franklin Park and the Arnold Arboretum blocked horsecar lines extending to West Roxbury and the creation of crosstown lines to southern portions of Dorchester. There was also meager horsecar access from Brookline to the west, since the town had voted against annexation to Boston and remained a rural area.[18]

The hemming in of the South End Grounds from suburban growth in all directions was not a huge problem for the remainder of the 1880s, but the electrification of the horsecar system beginning in 1889 did severely stunt spectator growth, as the streetcar suburbs that emerged five to eight miles from downtown Boston exacerbated inconvenient access to the ballpark. Thus, while he had navigated the baseball club through the turbulent early years of the National League and built a solid foundation for the next several years, Soden mortgaged the future of the club—figuratively and literally—by the location decision made in 1885, which crippled the club's ability to compete with the American League baseball club to be established in 1901.

By the mid–1880s, newspapers began to identify certain spectators at the ball games. Baseball followers were not yet called "fans" during this period; instead, they were known as "cranks," high-spirited baseball followers who were "obsessed with baseball." The term had gained popularity in 1881 during the trial of Charles Guiteau, the crazed assassin of President James Garfield. However, baseball writers in Boston were equally apt to characterize baseball followers as "base ball enthusiasts" or "lovers of the national game" as they were to use the term "crank."[19]

One of the earliest profiles of Boston baseball fans was published by the *Boston Globe* in a Sunday edition in 1885: "There are a goodly number of base ball enthusiasts, or cranks—call them which you please—whose faces are almost as well known on the grounds as the players themselves … who attend as many of the League contests as his business will permit." The non-attributed piece, presumably penned by Sullivan, reported that a man named Captain Jones was the patriarch of the enthusiasts. Others named were Arthur Dixwell, George Appleton, Dr. Pope, and G.H. Lloyd. While ostensibly intense fans of the Boston National League team, they were, in reality, general baseball fans with no specific allegiance to the team. This article noted that both Jones and Dixwell had attended more Union Association games in 1884 than National League games due to a dispute over higher season-ticket prices.[20]

Dixwell was the pre-eminent Boston baseball rooter of the late nineteenth century, as measured by newspaper reportage of his activities. His Brahmin upbringing (his father was a bank president, who at death left him a large trust fund to live on) gave him ample time to follow baseball and mingle with the more prosperous businessmen who sat in the grandstand at the South End Grounds. Sullivan often noted that Dixwell was one of the "familiar faces" or "regulars" in the grandstand, since he conspicuously sat at the front near "the pen" where the newspaper writers sat. "There may have been earlier baseball rooters, but there were not any firmer ones," John Morrill said at Dixwell's death in 1924. "He was Bostonian in every way and he was a good man for a 'Boom Boston' campaign."[21]

One of the first non-grandstand accounts of a baseball spectator appeared in an 1887 edition of the *Boston Globe*. "Going out to the grounds an hour before the game a gentleman jumped on the same [horse] car I was on," baseball writer William Harris recounted. "He wore a tall hat. He had been having a good time with himself and was very happy. Added to this he was a crank of cranks. 'Yes,' said he, 'I'm going to see the game. I don't mind standing up, either. I've seen lots of ball games, too. Talk about standing up, I'll bet you 5 to 2 that we won't get a seat now.'" Indeed, many in the audience needed to stand that day, as 10,000 jammed into the ballpark that accommodated only 7,000 with seating. The other 3,000 stood in the outfield or in front of the stands.[22]

There were few direct references to Irish-American fans in the audience at the South End Grounds during the 1880s. However, widespread institution of a half-holiday in business during the summer months (closing for an afternoon during the work week) enabled lower middle-class men to attend ball games more often. Also, the working class finally had a greater chance to view a ball game on the typical Saturday half-holiday when mill and factories closed at noon that day during the summer.

With a solid spectator base, hubris set in to Soden and the two other members of the so-called Triumvirs, James Billings and William Conant, who had consolidated power within the Boston Base Ball Association around this time. These three men held a majority of the stock in the baseball club, which enabled them to hold all three officer positions and reduce the number of directors from five to three. This negated the interests of minority stockholders and eventually worked against Boston baseball fans.

Interest among baseball fans accelerated in 1886 and 1887, both to watch games in the ballpark and to know game results outside the ballpark. There were lots of games to observe at the South End Grounds in 1886. In addition to the expansion of the National League schedule to 63 home games, up from 56 each season, the South End Grounds also hosted the minor-league Boston Blues of the New England League when the major-league team was on the road. "The lovers of base ball in this city who think the League price of admission is too high, and have long felt that twenty-five cents is the proper fee for a ball game, will have no chance to complain this season," the *Boston Globe* reported in March about the minor-league team to play in Boston, which adopted the nickname Blues to distinguish it from the city's major-league product. However, the quarter-ball experiment was a failure, as the Blues relocated to Haverhill midway into the 1887 season.[23]

People wanted a cheap view of the major-league product, which they increasingly exercised from the rooftops of houses along Berlin Street. At one game in July 1886, about 5,000 people watched the clash between Chicago and Boston, "3900 of whom gave up half a dollar, the balance filling the observation stands outside the grounds at ten and fifteen cents a head." For the reduced fare, baseball fans obtained "the privilege of balancing on the edges of flat roofs and rough stagings and in that precarious manner witnessing the efforts of Captain Kelly and his men." The baseball writer added that "anyone, man or boy, who would climb up into the air eighty feet to see a base ball game, no matter if it costs him only a dime and a half, must be a base ball crank." Frugal fans even gathered in numbers on the Northampton Street bridge over the Boston & Providence Railroad tracks to watch ball games for free from a quarter-mile distance.[24]

By now the National League had a contract with the Baltimore & Ohio telegraph company to wire the game results of each inning, so that interested parties external to the ballpark and across the nation could be informed. One day at the South End Grounds, when a telegraph operator from Western Union was denied entrance, he stationed himself on a pole overlooking the ballpark to wire the results. Telegraph reports of the games in progress served an important function in Boston, since the newspaper offices on Washington Street, known as Newspaper Row, posted the in-progress scores on a chalkboard in their front windows along with other breaking news of the day. This allowed businessmen who were not able to get away from the office for an entire afternoon to follow the ball games, often times sending a messenger down to Newspaper Row to relay the game scores back to the office.[25]

Interest accelerated in the Boston baseball team in 1887 when Mike Kelly was purchased from the Chicago club for the then exorbitant price of $10,000. Kelly had been the batting champion in the National League in 1886, but he clashed with Chicago ownership over the amount of his pay. Kelly's play interested both the grandstand crowd, as part of a community supporting a championship team, as well as his fellow Irish-Americans on the bleaching boards. For the first time, Soden used a star player to hype baseball games in Boston.

The expanded National League schedule to 63 home games introduced a new wrinkle for baseball fans, since there were far fewer open dates on the calendar in which to make up games that were rained out. The two-for-one doubleheader was popularized in 1887 after the heated 1886 pennant race between Chicago and Detroit demonstrated how unfair the haphazard technique of rescheduling rainouts was. Fans could now see a game for "free" as part of a two-for-one doubleheader that materialized to make up a rained-out game.[26]

Boston staged its first doubleheader in August 1887. "The Bostons and Washingtons will play two games on Saturday," the *Boston Globe* reported the day before. "There will be one admission charged. Fifty cents will entitle a man to see both games." On the day of the doubleheader, the *Globe* reported: "The entire grandstand will be reserved for today's games. Reserved seats can be obtained at Brock's Cigar Store, Water Street, up to 1 o'clock. After that they can be had at the grounds." Many people liked the idea of seeing two games for the price of one, and paid 50 cents to sit in the bleachers. But this first experiment with a two-for-one doubleheader also resulted in greater sales of reserved grandstand tickets. To avoid sitting in the bleachers with a new glut of lower middle-class spectators, many people who would have otherwise sat in the bleachers paid $1 to sit in the grandstand, effectively paying twice to see two games, albeit with a better view of the game.[27]

After more than 260,000 people watched the ball games at the South End Grounds during the 1887 season, Soden moved forward with his plan to build a new ballpark to replace the ramshackle South End Grounds. The new South End Grounds opened in May 1888 as a regal palace for the community to congregate for baseball, sporting a double-decked grandstand, spires atop the grandstand, and tall walls to block pirated views of the ball games from the rooftops of houses on Berlin Street. There was triple the seating in the grandstand, and increased bleacher seating. The grandstand con-

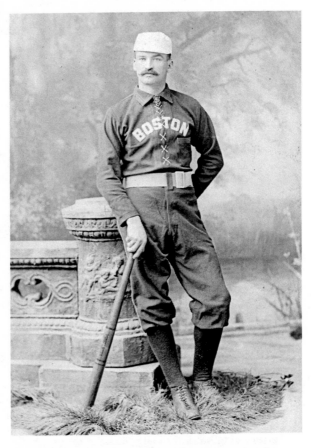

Mike Kelly joined the Boston team in 1887, when his contract was purchased from the Chicago club. Kelly's feats on the baseball diamond increased interest among his fellow Irish-Americans to attend ball games at the South End Grounds (New York Public Library, Digital Collections).

tained 2,800 seats, with nine sections in the lower section seating 2,028 and seven sections in the upper balcony seating 772 people.[28]

In addition to the new ballpark, Soden also added another star player on the playing field, purchasing pitcher John Clarkson from the Chicago club, to encourage more patrons to attend the ball games during the even longer 70-game home schedule in 1888. A third holiday was added to the Boston schedule, as Labor Day was now an official state holiday, which added two more games that catered to lower-income fans.

The old and new middle classes intermixed in the expanded grandstand

Spectators in the grandstand at the South End Grounds were primarily prosperous businessmen, such as the man in the lower left of the photograph who sports a business suit and bowler hat. There was a strict demarcation between the grandstand and the third-base bleachers (upper left of photograph), where lower-income fans often had to watch the ball games.

of the new South End Grounds, as the longstanding Anglo-Saxon Protestant patrons crossed paths with the emerging Irish Catholic middle class amid "a feeling of community with anonymous neighbors in an imitation of a pastoral setting." The more "democratic" crowd at the ball games was attested to by a July article in the *Boston Globe* that listed ten fans by name, including one obvious Irish-American, Thomas Shannon, "a well-known South End businessman," as well as an out-of-town fan, Manzy Hayes, "a Brockton enthusiast who comes in to about all the games." The latter signaled an increasing presence of suburban men in the baseball crowd.[29]

Baseball fans could read about the details of the game in one of several daily Boston newspapers, many of which had an evening edition in addition to the next day's morning edition. Following the Boston team in detail when it was on the road was more difficult, though, since the Boston newspapers printed basic dispatches written by local reporters in the visiting city. This changed in 1889 when the *Globe* and *Herald* began sending baseball writers to travel to road games on a regular basis, to telegraph back to Boston more intimate game accounts to baseball-hungry readers, providing detailed coverage of the ball games for the entire season, not just the one-half that was played at home.

Sullivan of the *Boston Globe* hired former ballplayer Tim Murnane to replace Harris, who left to write for the *New York Press*. While Murnane added depth of knowledge and an Irish-American connection to readers (he was born in Ireland and came to America as a toddler), Sullivan added an "e" to his last name that had been spelled "Murnan" and substituted "T.H." for his first name "Tim" to lessen the Irish tinge of his byline to appease Anglo-Saxon Protestant advertisers.

Another communication innovation in 1889 was the telegraphic recreation of road games, which were produced at the Music Hall beginning in June 1889. These "bulletin boards" were elaborate recreations of the actual ball game, providing as much detail as could be transmitted through the telegraph lines from the city where the game was actually being played. The inaugural bulletin-board game was the June 10 game in New York City, which the *Globe* reported "an immense crowd of spectators" attended and "was willing to testify to the completeness of this latest feature for reporting the results of the national game." Admission to the Music Hall was ten cents, with an extra dime to secure a reserved seat.[30]

In 1889 the new ballpark and two star players (Kelly and Clarkson) combined with a championship-contending team to encourage 283,000 spectators to visit the South End Grounds, which established a new high-water-mark for attendance in Boston. However, competition for Boston baseball enthusiasts was just over the horizon as the long-rumored Players' League announced its intention to conduct business in the 1890 season.

The label "base ball enthusiast" characterized the underlying nature of most followers of the National League team in Boston, which sportswriters continually reinforced in their newspaper accounts. That enthusiasm stemmed from an intrinsic interest in the sport itself and a desire to be part of the sporting community in Boston. If there was any difference among these general baseball fans, it was the frequency of attendance at the ballpark, either very often or just occasionally. Because the National League club had a monopoly on high-level professional baseball in the 1880s, Soden seemed to confuse those motivations with a direct attachment to *his* club. Partisanship in Boston would be tested during the 1890 season, when the general baseball fans needed to choose teams, which became a choice between management (Soden et al.) or the ballplayers (Kelly et al.). To the chagrin of Soden, many fans chose the players.

◆ 3 ◆

Two-Team City
for Two Years

For the 1890 season, Boston baseball fans had their first serious choice of another team to follow other than the established National League team. That other team was the Boston entry in the Players' League, formed by a mutiny of National League ballplayers who were members of the Brotherhood of Professional Base Ball Players. The Brotherhood was an early players association, not a union per se, which fought for player rights, especially the elimination of the reserve clause and the league's attempt to restrict salary levels. After making only minor headway with the National League owners, the Brotherhood enlisted the help of some capitalists to form its own league, which provided for profit sharing among the ballplayers and limited-duration contracts.

The Boston Players' League team played its games at a new ballpark built on Congress Street extension, across the Fort Point Channel from Boston's central business district, in the sparsely developed South Boston section of the Boston waterfront. The Congress Street Grounds, an ornate, double-decked facility with four entrances and two towers, resided on five acres of land leased from the Boston Wharf Company. The ballpark was designed to seat 4,000 people in the grandstand, with bleachers along the first-base and third-base foul lines to hold another 6,000 people; bleacher seating was later expanded to accommodate another 4,000 people, to bring the total seating capacity of the Congress Street Grounds to 14,000. Since the grounds were half a mile (and a 15-minute walk) from the central business district and no streetcar lines served the isolated area, private firms operated "land barges" to transport spectators from the business district to the ballpark.[1]

Unlike the financing of the other seven clubs in the Players' League, the investors in the Boston club were baseball fans first, not primarily capitalists looking to turn a quick profit. Stockholders included Arthur Dixwell (who had the largest stake), Julian Hart, Charles Prince, John Haynes, Charles Corey, George Wright, and John Morrill. All these investors in the Boston Players' League club had been regular spectators for the National League games at the South End Grounds in 1889.[2]

What made these investors a formidable lot was the resolve of several (e.g., Hart and Haynes) who were disgruntled former minority stockholders of the Boston National League club, having been denied an accounting of the club's financial condition so that the value of their shares could be reasonably determined. The minority stockholders filed a lawsuit in October 1888 that sought to force the majority stockholders to provide an accounting. Rebuffed by the court, they sold their shares to the three majority stockholders, likely at much lower than fair market value.[3]

When the Players' League coalesced as competition for the 1890 season, the timing seemed auspicious for Hart and Haynes to launch a competitive strike against the National League club. With a significant financial investment in a new ballpark at the South End Grounds and two expensive player acquisitions in Mike Kelly and John Clarkson, Soden might not be able to spend enough money to sufficiently thwart the competition from the Boston Players' League club.

The Players' League team not only gave Boston baseball fans a choice, but often forced them to choose by scheduling numerous games on the same date as the games of the National League team. "The lovers of base ball in this latitude are likely to have splendid opportunities during the coming season for enjoying their favorite pastime," the *Boston Globe* wrote in a January 1890 editorial. "Boston can support two good clubs, and events may prove that she will be glad to do so in a handsome and profitable manner." When the season was about to open, Tim Murnane of the *Globe* put it more bluntly: "You can pay your money and take your choice, and the patrons of the game are likely to drift around where they can see the most fun for their money." When many baseball fans initially gravitated to the Congress Street Grounds, they were motivated to watch a highly skilled ball game and thus supported the ballplayers, not the management of the National League club. This was the first foray to attempt to divide the general baseball fans in Boston.[4]

Virtually all the ballplayers on the 1889 National League team jumped to the 1890 Players' League team; only Clarkson and catcher Charlie Bennett stayed with the National League team. Kelly led the exodus to the Players' League team, which created an extraordinary product to attract baseball fans to the Congress Street Grounds, in comparison to the diluted product on the field at the South End Grounds.

At the season-opening games played on April 19, 1890, the Players'

League game drew a reported crowd of 10,000 people to the Congress Street Grounds, while only 3,800 reportedly attended the National League game at the South End Grounds. The Players' League team regularly outdrew the cross-town rival National League team in head-to-head games. That is, if newspaper reports of attendance numbers can be believed. Both Boston clubs fudged their attendance figures, either by rampant distribution of complimentary tickets or by exuberant inflation of turnstile counts. The accepted season-long attendance numbers show a combined attendance of 344,000 spectators, with 50,000 more people having watched the Players' League games (197,000) than the games of the National League team (147,000).

While the exactness of attendance figures for 1890 are suspect, the relative comparison of reported same-day numbers does indicate that the epicenter of professional baseball in Boston was the Congress Street Grounds for the first part of the 1890 season. However, interest in the Players' League waned by mid-season due to the sizeable number of high-scoring games. The new league sought to encourage more hitting by lengthening of the pitching distance (57.5 feet compared to 55 feet in the National League) and using the Keefe ball that had more spring in it than the deader ball used in the National League.

Rather than spark more spectator interest, these modifications produced less interesting games. On April 26 the game score at the Congress Street Grounds was 14–10 while the National League game at the South End Grounds produced a tighter 3–1 score. It was not at all unusual to see 22–4 and 19–0 scores for games played at the Congress Street Grounds. Gradually, fans lost interest in the Players' League games, despite the superior ability of the ballplayers. Even the telegraphic reproductions of road games, which began on May 4 at the Music Hall, experienced a similar decline. By early June, the *Globe* noted,

The Boston teams in the Players' League in 1890 and American Association in 1891 played games at the Congress Street Grounds, which provided Boston baseball fans with their first competitive choice of baseball teams to follow besides the established National League team (Boston Public Library, Print Department, McGreevey Collection).

"Brotherhood supporters are generally in the majority, but the forces were about equally divided yesterday."[5]

Fading attendance at the Congress Street Grounds spawned the first Ladies Day promotions for professional baseball in Boston. The Players' League club initiated the promotion for its July 11 game at the Congress Street Grounds by providing free admission to females. About 350 women took advantage of the promotion, within a reported crowd of 1,350 spectators. The National League club responded in kind, however, and attracted 500 women within an audience of 4,100 people by offering not just free admission to the grounds but also to the grandstand.

The custom of Ladies Day was at least half a dozen years old by 1890 (often attributed to a New York Giants game in June 1883), which was designed to soften the rowdy masculine atmosphere at the ballpark as well as fill grandstand seats. "Many professional teams thought it wise to offer women free admission," author Jean Hastings Ardell wrote in her book *Breaking into Baseball: Women and the National Pastime*, "in hopes of converting them to regular fans as well as consumers of food, drink, and souvenirs." In the competition for general baseball fans in Boston in 1890, Ladies Day served as a monetary incentive for men to buy a ticket to the grandstand to accompany a woman on her complimentary pass, and thus express an explicit opinion as to whether they supported management of the League club or the renegade ballplayers.[6]

Boston had no problem winning the pennant in the first and only year of the Players' League. Had the Boston Players' League club only been competing against the local National League club, it may have forced Soden out of business. However, it was competing against the cartel of National League owners, who were bound and determined to destroy the Players' League and do whatever was necessary to save the National League. Soden was part of the consortium to bailout the New York Giants, when that club teetered on bankruptcy after the local Players' League team had decimated its attendance.

The Players' League began to crumble soon after the playing season ended when the financial backers of the New York club deserted the new league to buy out the financially desperate owners of the New York Giants. Unfortunately, profit-maximizing capitalists controlled most of the Players' League clubs, with the exception of the Boston club, which made these clubs easy targets for a buyout by the National League owners by the end of the 1890 season.

When Charles Prince, one of the stockholders in the Boston Players' League club, became the president of the Players' League in November 1890, he tried to negotiate with National League owners to keep the Players' League alive. When those prospects faded, Prince arranged for the transfer of his Boston team to the American Association, a major league on its last legs

(1891 was its last year of existence). Prince became president of the Boston club.

Soden had at first objected to the transfer, but then agreed to accommodate the move under several conditions. All the former ballplayers of the National League team had to be returned and could not play with the Association team. Admission to the Association games must be 50 cents (the same as for National League games). The Association team could not bill itself as "Boston," but rather "must have a distinct name, like the Blues." Soden seemed to be confident that the Association, which in its other cities allowed Sunday games and the sale of beer at games, would not last in Boston where such déclassé mores were not tolerated.[7]

Prince agreed to abide by all the conditions. He chose the name "Reds," rather than adopt the suggested "Blues" name of the former minor-league club in Boston, to rekindle memories of the original Red Stockings club of the 1870s. As it turned out, Soden was mostly interesting in having Kelly returned to the National League team, so many of the former National Leaguers continued to play for the Association team. Kelly, though, balked at returning to the South End Grounds and he joined the Cincinnati team in the Association.

With all the commotion about transferring the Players' League team to the American Association, Dixwell sold his stock to Prince and distanced himself from major-league baseball in Boston. "Now that the Players' League is a thing of the past," the *Globe* reported in March 1891, "Mr. Dixwell will not be quite so enthusiastic this season as last, as he intends starting on a three months' tour in Europe the first week in May." While he wasn't observed in the stands during the 1891 season, Dixwell did become a more fervent follower of minor-league baseball in New England, in keeping with his persona as a general baseball fan not solely dedicated to any one team.[8]

Prince introduced three changes to the Boston baseball landscape, which had lasting future implications for broadening the audience for professional baseball.

In March Prince awarded the scorecard concession for the Reds games to Harry Stevens, a Columbus, Ohio, businessman, who had a similar arrangement with the Columbus club in the Association. Stevens would later achieve widespread fame for his food concessions in baseball ballparks, particularly for the hawking of hot dogs.[9]

In early June Prince announced that the Reds would play Sunday games at the Rocky Point resort in Rhode Island, a notorious "island of illicit professional baseball on Sunday within the vast New England ocean of strict Puritan observance of a Sunday day of rest." The games would be exhibition games, though, rather than championship games that counted in the league standings. While Prince had concerns about alienating some of his base audience at the Congress Street Grounds, a larger concern was that several players, notably Paul Radford, refused to play in the Sunday games due to their devout Sabbatarian beliefs. The first Sunday game was played at Rocky Point on June 21 against the visiting Athletic team from Philadelphia. The Reds won, 15–5, before 2,500 spectators, as the Boston players "had a hearty shore dinner about an hour or so before the game and those clams seemed to be just full of base hits." Prince's team played three more exhibition games at Rocky Point on the following three Sundays before abandoning the experiment.[10]

Despite the previous agreement not to undercut admission prices, the Reds implemented a 25-cents admission policy at the Congress Street Grounds at the game on Saturday, July 18, since Prince believed "it pays to cater to the masses." Hundreds of lower-income people saw their first major-league baseball game on July 18, when a half-holiday was observed by many employers on that Saturday during the sweltering summer months. On Monday, July 20, the Reds further undercut the pricing for National League games not only by continuing the 25-cents "popular price" admission at the Congress Street Grounds but also allowing free admission for women via a Ladies Day promotion, permitting boys to sit in the bleachers for 15 cents, and anyone to sit in the grandstand for an additional 25 cents. On August 5, the "popular prices" policy was instituted for the remaining home games that season. However, Prince was ahead of his time when it came to professional baseball for the masses in Boston.[11]

Since the American Association was weak, the Boston Reds waltzed to the 1891 pennant. The National League team also finished in first place, following a controversial 18-game winning streak in September. Although Prince wanted to stage a postseason series between the two teams to determine the best Boston team, Soden refused to consider it.

The two-year competitive environment changed the nature of baseball followers in Boston, by diminishing the number of general baseball fans as many fans chose to dedicate themselves as partisans to one team or the other. "I have always contended that one club was enough for any city," Soden said during the 1891 season. "With two clubs the interest is divided and the people lose their enthusiasm for the home team. We have a great many people who attend the League games that will not go to Association games, and no doubt a great many people who attend the Association games feel the same way. The patrons of the sport have too much base ball anyway in seeing it every day."[12]

When the American Association merged with the National League before the 1892 season, the Boston club in the National League bought out the owners of the Boston Reds to regain its monopoly position in the Boston baseball market. As part of that transaction, Soden acquired the Congress Street Grounds.

By the end of the 1891 season, Prince was no longer associated with the Association club, having stepped down as its president in August, since he was by then more interested in speculating in railroad stocks. Prince gave a banquet for the Boston Reds on October 18, to honor their championship season. If paying for a few lavish meals was Prince's only financial vice, he might have enjoyed a wealthy, if unheralded, life of leisure in the United States. But he wanted the fame and fortune that he did not get from investing in baseball.

During 1892, Prince inserted himself into a power struggle at the New York & New England Railroad, as the financially weak company struggled to survive in the consolidating railroad industry. He was part of a cabal that ousted two company presidents and in March 1893 installed noted railroad executive Archibald McLeod, who was also president of the Boston & Maine Railroad. Expecting McLeod to merge the two Boston-area railroads that he was chief executive of, Prince swindled people into giving him money to purchase New York & New England Railroad stock. When McLeod abruptly resigned as president of the Boston & Maine Railroad in mid–May 1893 (indicating that a merger was not to be), Prince's financial scheme collapsed, as the price of New York & New England Railroad stock dropped precipitously. On June 1, 1893, Prince left the United States before he was publicly disgraced when his embezzlement was discovered.[13]

The *Boston Daily Advertiser* pieced together the embezzlement story that led to the departure of such a prominent Boston citizen and "boomer of the Brotherhood baseball scheme in 1890." In an article entitled "Mr. C.A. Prince: His Absence Likely to Be a Long One," the newspaper reported that Prince had "borrowed" money from friends, who politely said they didn't remember signing any loan documents, and that several men made good on Prince's fraudulently obtained loans with the proviso that he leave the country. According to a *Sporting Life* account of the scandal entitled "Prince Exiled: The Ex-Magnate Will Never Come Back to America," Prince reportedly spent between $1 million and $2 million more than his income as a lawyer in the previous few years. He "spent a few thousand on the Brotherhood ball team," a few thousand more on a half-built house in Manchester and lavish dinners in New York and Boston. These were the only tangible purchases with his embezzled funds; the rest was put toward stock speculation, as Prince "made $1,000,000 disappear, absolutely, with nothing but a half-built house to show for it."[14]

Prince lived the rest of his life in exile on the island of Noirmoutier, off the coast of France. He died there during World War II, when France was occupied by Nazi Germany.[15]

Fueled by Prince, the two-year competitive environment for baseball spectators created the basic outline of future baseball fan composition in

Boston—some dedicated to only one team, but most as general baseball fans who would crossover between teams or lean to the best product on the playing field. Soden, though, didn't seem to take to heart the lessons of the two-year competition. Rather Soden believed that monopoly trumped competition and thus the disposition of fans did not matter. This attitude would come back to haunt Soden by the end of the decade.

In the interim, the competition dampened interest among many baseball fans after the 1891 season. It took several years, and improvements in transportation and shifts in population, for the enthusiasm of baseball fans to rebuild in Boston.

♦ 4 ♦

Rise of Irish-American Fans

For the 1892 season, there was once again just one baseball team in Boston. Many general baseball fans returned to focus on the National League team, no longer torn between rooting for the new team playing at the Congress Street Grounds or the longstanding team at the South End Grounds. However, the enthusiasm of many other such fans waned, after the ruthless efforts of the National League club to eliminate the competition for baseball spectators.

In an article entitled "All the Cranks Were Out," the *Boston Globe* described about 50 attendees who sat in the grandstand at the South End Grounds for the 1892 season opener, seemingly going to great lengths to portray a peaceful array of baseball fans. Naturally, there were many politicians, from the State House and the Boston City Hall, as well as other governmental officials. George Appleton, the dedicated National League fan "whom all sporting men know," was singled out, juxtaposed against John Haynes and Julian Hart "of the old Brotherhood team," the latter who "moved about the crowd and smiled on those of his old clientele." Among numerous "city businessmen who left their office for the sport were Eugene Coleman of Fiske, Coleman & Company, Charles Phipps, Charles H. Hollins, and the silk industry was well represented by such devotees as John Turner and J.D. Warner." A few Irish-Americans were noted, including Dennis Sullivan and Edward Donnelly, "bill posters who shut up their desks to go to the grounds," and Harry McGlenen, who had promoted the team in the 1870s. Notably, Arthur Dixwell was not mentioned, as the longtime fan had soured on the owners of the National League club.[1]

Two enhancements to traveling to the South End Grounds helped to encourage attendance. Both had been inaugurated two years earlier, but it wasn't until the 1892 season that they demonstrated their full potential now that the National League team had regained its monopoly on major-league baseball.

The Tremont Street streetcar line was now electrified, which enabled baseball fans to get to the ballpark faster from the central business district. Electrification came to the Tremont Street line in November 1889, as part of the West End Street Railway's plan to eliminate horses and speed up transport of passengers. Streetcar electrification was just the first of many transportation improvements that would be instituted in the city of Boston over the course of the next two decades that impacted baseball fans.[2]

Once baseball fans riding on a Tremont Street streetcar reached Walpole Street, they could now walk directly up Walpole Street to the South End Grounds without having to squeeze through the narrow passageway on the Booker property that for many years had divided Walpole Street from the Franklin Place roadway in front of the entrance to the South End Grounds. In the fall of 1889 the City of Boston took a portion of the Booker property by eminent domain to connect Walpole Street with Franklin Place. In the process, this last vestige of Franklin Place was renamed as Walpole Street, which now spawned the informal reference to the South End Grounds as being the Walpole Street Grounds.[3]

It took more than a year to usher this change through the Boston Common Council, once Soden finally changed his mind to pay the city for this improved access to the ballpark. In June 1888, the Council took up a request for "the street commissioners to extend and lay out Walpole Street, and authorizing the city treasurer to receive $3000 from the Boston Base Ball Association to pay the cost thereof." However, the Council rejected the request, since there were allegations that "an old lady owning premises on the street objects to the extension and wishes to be paid," since she claimed the baseball club was a "giant monopoly."[4]

Three months later the Common Council again took up the Walpole Street matter, emphasizing the benefit "to those who attend the ball games, as by its adoption better means of access and egress to the ball grounds would be afforded." However, once again the Council defeated the motion because the baseball club "refused to pay the price asked for the building which stands in the way of the extension," which the owners asked $5,000. The *Boston Daily Advertiser* reported that when one of the councilmen later asked one of the baseball club's directors why they didn't pay that amount, the reply given was "well, that old thing [referring to one of the land owners] wants too much money for it." Given the revenue generated by the Boston baseball club, the councilman didn't believe the price asked was all that steep.[5]

With a healthy composition of Irish-Americans, the Common Council was no longer a friendly environment to Anglo-Saxon Protestant businessmen like Soden who were seeking inexpensive solutions to their problems. In December 1888 the *Boston Globe* reported in an article entitled "The Price Too High: Triumvirs Will Not Be Called Bribers" that the baseball club had low-balled an offer to buy the Booker land. More damagingly, though, there were allegations that the club had offered a $1,500 bribe to a councilman to get approval for the street extension.[6]

After the petition was withdrawn from the Common Council, Soden sought a less public forum to accomplish his goal of improved access to the South End Grounds. In September 1889 an innocuous public notice from the Board of Street Commissioners was printed in Boston newspapers notifying the citizenry that "the public necessity and convenience require that Walpole St. should be extended as a highway of the city from Berlin St. to Grinnell St. ... and that notice be given to the heirs of Robert Booker ... that the board intend[s] to extend the highway before mentioned, and to take therefore a portion of their land." The Boston Base Ball Association reportedly paid $2,000 to the Booker heirs to enable "opening a good driveway to the ball ground through Walpole Street."[7]

Despite the greater ease of getting to the South End Grounds from the streetcar line, attendance was dismal for most of the 1892 season, as only

Electrification of streetcar lines in Boston in 1889, and during the 1890s on suburban lines such as this one in Holbrook, allowed more fans to attend ball games at the South End Grounds. However, the composition of the audience changed when middle-class businessmen moved to more-distant suburbs from downtown Boston (Library of Congress, Prints and Photographs Division, LC-USZ62-14246).

146,000 fans paid to watch the ball games, about the same level as back in 1884. The National League had lengthened its playing schedule to 154 games for the 1892 season, to handle the new 12-team league (following the absorption of four teams from the now-defunct American Association) and enable the owners to recoup losses from the competition with the Players' League. In an attempt to maintain spectator interest over such a long season, the league devised a split-season format, dividing the season into two halves of 77 games each, with the winners of each half to meet for the championship in a postseason playoff. Boston had little problem maintaining the interest of fans during the first half of the season, as the team played good baseball to finish in first place. However, that accomplishment served to depress attendance during the second half, since the team had little to play for as it awaited the October playoff for the championship.

The expanded 154-game schedule was feasible only through the inclusion of Sunday baseball in the western cities where it was legally permitted. Otherwise, the schedule would have to make deeper inroads into the cool weather months of April and October, when spectators were much less inclined to go to the ballpark. Soden refused to permit Boston to play road games on Sunday, though, since he feared even this minor bending of the Puritan Sunday doctrine would alienate grandstand patrons from attending home games at the South End Grounds.

A positive outcome of the club's Sunday abstinence was that Boston received preferential treatment in the scheduling of national holiday dates during the 1890s, with at least two holiday home dates each year between 1892 and 1899, usually Decoration Day and Labor Day, while Sunday-playing teams like St. Louis rarely had holiday dates. Boston, of course, also had Bunker Hill Day as a third holiday on its schedule each year. Lower-income patrons at the morning and afternoon games on the three holidays helped to stem some of the attendance decline. Bleacher seats for 25 cents were quietly added at the South End Grounds, at the farthest end of the first-base line, to accommodate a growing number of lower-income fans.

Boston, the first-half winner, defeated Cleveland, the second-half winner, in the first postseason playoff in National League history. While Boston easily defeated Cleveland to take the championship, interest in the series was tepid in Boston, especially since the series didn't begin until October 17. The first game in Boston on October 21 drew a respectable 6,547 fans, but the next game attracted just 3,466 "genuine lovers of the national game" and third a paltry 1,812 in the cold autumn weather more suitable to football. Soden was opposed to the series. "The public to a certain extent will say that it was all a put up job," Soden said in early October. "I would have given considerable to have the games postponed until the spring when there would be some interest in the sport."[8]

After Boston repeated as champions in 1893, when the unpopular split-season format was dropped in favor of a 132-game full-season schedule, the club inaugurated a new tradition in 1894 with its season-opener played on the new state holiday of Patriots Day, which was celebrated on April 19. Because the club now had three holiday dates within a span of nine weeks, the club elected to play two games only on Decoration Day and just a single game on the two Boston-specific holidays of Patriots Day and Bunker Hill Day.

The fortunes of the Boston club took a negative turn on May 15, 1894, when a fire destroyed the South End Grounds. A cigar dropped by a fan under the all-wood bleachers in right field during the ball game with Baltimore set off the conflagration. The Great Roxbury Fire destroyed not only the ballpark but also 200 buildings in the immediate neighborhood, which left 1,900 people homeless.

While the ballpark was rebuilt, the team played its games at the Congress Street Grounds. By mid–July the new South End Grounds were in place, with just one of three sections of the new grandstand, now fire-resistant with a brick foundation and iron columns, and wooden bleachers along the first- and third-base lines. For the remainder of the 1894 season, there was far more seating in the bleachers (7,000) than in the grandstand (800); in 1895 the other two grandstand sections were completed to accommodate a total of 2,400 people with preferential seating.[9]

Attendance spiked to 242,000 for the 1895 season, close to the levels experienced in the club's heyday of the late 1880s. However, the nature of the spectators at South End Grounds began to change in 1895, with fewer upper-income businessmen who worked downtown and more Irish-American middle-class men. Clues to this transition appeared in printed descriptions of the crowds at the season-opening games in the late 1890s, which included names of veteran fans but sprinkled in an increasing number of Irish-American surnames.

One reason for this change in fan complexion was that this third vintage of the South End Grounds was much less regal than the second vintage that had burned down, which dissuaded businessmen from attending ball games and thus opened the door to greater participation by men in the lower reaches of the middle class. A more complex reason was, ironically, the electrification of the streetcar system, which had a detrimental impact because it extended the range of reasonable commuting to work into Boston's central business district. Unfortunately, the distance from the ballpark to the suburbs that developed around the expanding streetcar lines was inversely related to the income level of the suburban inhabitants.

As Warner detailed in his book *Streetcar Suburbs*, during the 1890s the upper middle class now lived in a 5- to 15-mile radius from downtown Boston, more distant than its previous living space in the 1870s that was within a 3.5-to 5-mile radius. The central middle class now resided in that 3.5- to 5-mile radius, more distant than its previous 2.5- to 3.5-mile radius in the 1870s, which the lower middle class had now moved into. Because land was more expensive the closer it was to Boston, builders constructed three-story tenement houses in the 2.5- to 3.5-mile radius, which became known as a three-decker. As Warner concluded, "The interaction of the growth of the street railway and class building patterns had produced class-segregated suburbs." Dorchester (southern sections) and West Roxbury were bastions of the central middle class, while Roxbury, where the South End Grounds were located, "underwent a shift from lower middle class to a working-class district … and was becoming a slum."[10]

From a baseball patronage perspective, transportation time to the ballpark was the key factor. A 15- to 30-minute commute home from the ballpark on an electric streetcar was reasonable, while a 45- to 60-minute commute was less tolerable. The National League club, under its current management and ballpark location, was doomed to a shrinking, lower-income base of fans, those who lived in the lower socio-economic neighborhoods closer to downtown Boston than higher-income fans that lived more distant and had much longer commutes on the streetcar.

Streetcar electrification, while permitting workers to live at a greater distance from their jobs in downtown Boston, also exacerbated the transportation congestion within the central business district. Very quickly transportation planners began to investigate the prospects of putting streetcar tracks above and below ground to enable "rapid transit" of passengers from the suburbs to their destinations in downtown Boston. A new law passed by the Massachusetts legislature in July 1894 called for a subway to be constructed under Tremont Street in downtown Boston as well as three elevated railway lines. The mission of all four transportation enhancements was to get streetcars off the roadways. This initial plan was advantageous to the prospects of the Boston National League club.[11]

The Tremont Street subway was two miles long and had three portals, one north at Haymarket Square leading to the North Station train terminal (which had consolidated the Boston & Maine and other railroads running north and west), one south at the intersection of Tremont Street and Pleasant Street, and one west at Boylston Street. The subway would provide a faster exit from the central business district for businessmen seeking to get to a ball game in the mid-afternoon, since the ballpark was located near the Tremont Street streetcar line that directly connected to the subway.[12]

The elevated railways were designed to transport suburban workers into the central business district on a faster and more efficient basis. One elevated line was designed to go from Sullivan Square in the Charlestown neighborhood at the edge of Somerville, through Boston, down Dorchester Avenue in the Dorchester neighborhood, to the city line with the town of Milton. A second elevated line would go from Union Square in Somerville, through Boston, down Washington Street in Roxbury, to Franklin Park in Dorchester, to the city line with the town of Hyde Park. The third elevated line would go from Harvard Square in Cambridge, through Boston, down Tremont Street in Roxbury, to the neighborhood of Jamaica Plain. The third proposed elevated railway line would pass close to the South End Grounds, providing convenient direct access to baseball fans from the northern suburbs of Cambridge and Somerville and via branch lines to the nearby towns of Everett, Chelsea, and Revere. Cambridge and Somerville were then the most populous, and fastest growing, suburbs of Boston.[13]

Residents in these northern suburbs had a difficult journey to reach the South End Grounds via streetcar lines, since until 1893 nearly all streetcar lines originating in Cambridge and Somerville crossed into Boston near the central business district, and thus passengers had to suffer a slowdown to pass through downtown to get to the Tremont Street line to go to the ballpark. Once a streetcar line was extended over the Charles River in 1893 to West Chester Park in the Back Bay (renamed as Massachusetts Avenue in 1894), Cambridge residents had a somewhat easier trek. However, the streetcar line ended at Boylston Street, leaving baseball fans another circuitous streetcar ride to get to the South End Grounds. This was enhanced in 1896 when a streetcar line opened to run directly from Harvard Square to Dudley Street in Roxbury, which stopped on Northampton Street, where fans could walk a few blocks to the South End Grounds.[14]

The new elevated railway line along Tremont Street would enable more baseball fans to get to the South End Grounds. Unfortunately, it was never built. Once the subway was completed in 1897, the elevated railway plan changed. The two proposed lines beginning at Sullivan Square and Union Square were merged into one line, to run from Sullivan Square, through Boston, down Washington Street, terminating at Dudley Street in Roxbury. The third elevated line, of most interest to Boston baseball fans and the Boston National League club, was deferred, pending completion of a new bridge between Cambridge and Boston, to be called the Longfellow Bridge. Because the construction gave Cambridge residents time to rethink whether they wanted an elevated railway or a subway, eventually Cambridge opted for a subway.

The elimination of the Tremont Street elevated railway line severely hurt the future prospects for the Boston National League club. The general impact on ballpark spectatorship at the South End Grounds during the 1890s was decreased patronage among two groups, older dedicated baseball fans and upper middle-class general baseball fans. New followers developed among burgeoning central and lower middle-class Irish-Americans, whether they worked in downtown Boston or were shopkeepers and artisans that provided services in the developing suburbs.

These new followers became a large portion of a new "baseball public" that sought community at the ballpark where, according to David Nasaw, author of *Going Out: The Rise and Fall of Public Amusements*, "they were able to offer men and boys a male-only alternative to the 'mixed' entertainments that were proliferating on the streets of the city." In the virtual absence of women, the men at the ballpark were allowed to act in ways that were prohibited in the vaudeville halls, theaters, and amusement parks. They could gamble, smoke, spit, shout, curse, and evil hurl abuse at the umpire, although at the South End Grounds no alcoholic drinks were served. Because Soden was fundamentally opposed to a Ladies Day promotion, this encouraged even more emotional-charged rooting at the ballpark.[15]

Soden and his other officers of the baseball club apparently never considered a permanent relocation to the Congress Street Grounds, the temporary home of the baseball team in 1894, or abandoning the South End Grounds to build a new ballpark in a more favorable location to attract spectators. "I can assure you that we have not even thought of moving from the South End Grounds for several years to come," William Conant, the man who oversaw the real estate end of the baseball business, said at the time."[16]

Soden seemed to be convinced that the plan for the forthcoming subway and elevated railways would benefit the baseball club in the existing location of the South End Grounds. Any hope to use the Congress Street Grounds vanished in the fall of 1896 when the Boston Wharf Company dismantled the ballpark to make room for buildings to respond to the expected business demand arising from the completion of the South Station railroad terminal in 1898. Given the earlier impact of North Station, Soden failed to anticipate the substantial impact of the consolidation into South Station of the railroad terminals of the Boston & Albany, Old Colony, and the New York, New Haven and Hartford (formerly the Boston & Providence) lines. This would have improved the perceived desirability of the Congress Street Grounds, especially given how the public transportation system in Boston eventually developed.

One immediate impact of the 1894 Great Roxbury Fire that destroyed the South End Grounds was that the city moved forward in 1895 with an extension of Columbus Avenue to replace Berlin Street, which was now bereft of houses. Columbus Avenue had ended at Camden Street at the former city line with the town of Roxbury before Roxbury was annexed to Boston in 1868. With so many burned-down buildings in the neighborhood, the city could now easily execute its plan to build a thoroughfare from downtown through Roxbury to provide an easier route to get to Franklin Park.[17]

With the extension of Columbus Avenue changing the texture of the

While the opening of the Boston subway in 1897 improved access to the South End Grounds, ultimately the subway's connection to the Back Bay streetcar line, as shown in this photograph, and the scuttling of planned elevated railway lines, hindered the National League club when the new American League club emerged in 1901 (Library of Congress, Prints and Photographs Division, LC-DIG-det-4a17211).

neighborhood around the South End Grounds, Soden did try to get the Board of Aldermen to extend Walpole Street over the railroad tracks to connect with Huntington Avenue, in order to improve access to the ballpark from the northern suburbs. However, that request was never approved.[18]

As the nature of baseball fans in Boston changed in the late 1890s, newspaper writers gave the National League team the nickname of "Beaneaters," presumably to drum up more interest among readers than by continuing to use the bland "Bostons" term (the "Nationals" was not used very often until the American League team existed after the turn of the century). The Boston writers also now used the term "fan" to describe an "enthusiastic follower of baseball," as crank had fallen out of favor. There is an uncertain etymology of this term, according to Paul Dickson, author of the *Dickson Baseball Dictionary*. Often believed to be a shortened version of the word "fanatic," it also plausibly is related to how a talkative person blows wind.[19]

The dismal future of the National League club in Boston was masked during the 1890s by the five championships the team won in the eight-year period between 1891 and 1898. The most visible symbol of the future, the emergence of the "Royal Rooters," has been viewed by baseball historians as a positive impact, whereas this group of predominately lower middle-class fans was actually the leading edge of a downturn in baseball followers of the National League team.

Charley Lavis was leader of the Royal Rooters at this time. As an Irish-American that ran a billiard room, Lavis aspired to greater achievements beyond his lower middle-class rank at the time in the Boston social spectrum.[20]

Mike McGreevey was not the ringleader, as is often asserted by baseball chroniclers. For example, Stephen Hardy wrote in *How Boston Played: Sport, Recreation, and Community, 1865–1915*: "This season also brought the birth of Boston's first organized fan club, the Royal Rooters. At the head of this marvelous collection of baseball kranks was one Michael T. McGreevey, who had recently opened a saloon called The Third Base near the National League grounds." However, McGreevey was neither the head of the group in 1897 nor was his saloon "near" the South End Grounds. His liquor emporium in 1897 was at 17 Linden Park in Roxbury Crossing, a block off Tremont Street and about a half-mile from the South End Grounds. There were many saloons on Tremont Street in between McGreevey's place and the ballpark, including one owned by Michael J. Quinn at 1153 Tremont Street, at the corner of Ruggles Street, where McGreevey had clerked before opening his own establishment in 1894. Once the Columbus Avenue extension was completed, McGreevey relocated to 940 Columbus Avenue, near Quinn's saloon, about a quarter-mile from the ballpark.[21]

As the Boston team marched toward the National League pennant in 1897, the Royal Rooters gathered steam as a crowd of baseball followers who routinely sat in bleachers on third-base line near Boston third baseman Jimmy Collins and left-fielder Hugh Duffy, both Irish-Americans who were favorites of the predominately Irish-American Royal Rooters. The influx of intermittent fans to follow the pennant contenders and join the Rooters resulted in a crowd of 16,000 at the Saturday, August 7, game at South End Grounds, to watch Boston tangle with second-place Baltimore. The *Boston Globe* called the crowd "one of the largest non-holiday crowd ever seen at the grounds."

The Royal Rooters gained everlasting fame for the boisterous road trip they took to Baltimore to watch the games against Boston in late September. The 125 Rooters in the traveling party included "many businessmen, a clergyman, physicians, seven women, and several others who daily occupy seats on the bleachers back of third base." The key phrase of "bleachers" instead of "grandstand," tacitly recognized the changing mix of spectators from the "old standbys" like Dixwell who had regained interest in the Boston team.

Even the names listed in the traveling party indicated an increased presence of Irish-Americans among Boston baseball fans with Congressman John Fitzgerald topping the list that included many with surnames such as Doherty, O'Brien, Murphy, Doyle, Donahue, and Mahoney.[22]

Fans who couldn't take the time off to travel to Baltimore could vicariously enjoy the excitement of the ball games in Baltimore by attending bulletin-board recreations at the Music Hall or standing outside the newspaper offices on Washington Street to hear men shout inning-by-inning results off the telegraph wire. A thousand people reportedly paid to attend the telegraphic recreations at the Music Hall, while several thousand were said to congregate on Newspaper Row.[23]

After edging Baltimore for the National League pennant, Boston played Baltimore in the postseason Temple Cup series, a contrived match to generate additional pay to the ballplayers for their regular-season success. Because it was a meaningless series of exhibition games, since the championship was awarded based on the regular-season results, the ballplayers didn't take the games very seriously from a competitive standpoint,

About 10,000 spectators paid to see the Temple Cup opener at the South End Grounds on Monday, October 4, but most fans were there more to honor the Boston ballplayers for winning the National League pennant rather than to celebrate the first game of the Temple Cup series. Although Boston won the first game, 13–12, the team's star pitcher, Charley Nichols, pitched only the first five innings, in a clear indication that Boston was not taking the Temple Cup seriously. Nichols never pitched another inning in what turned out to be a five-game series, as Baltimore proceeded to rattle off four consecutive wins to cop the Cup. Some of the spectators went on to join the Boston ballplayers at the main event on October 4, the presentation of a pennant that evening during intermission of the play *The Swell Miss Fitzwell* at the Tremont Theatre.[24]

After the third game on Wednesday, October 6, called after seven innings allegedly due to darkness but more to player indifference, the Boston team was honored at a banquet that evening at Faneuil Hall. About 250 fans attended the banquet, where Congressman (and Royal Rooter) Fitzgerald was the toastmaster. "The congressman got a rousing reception and made an address of welcome and congratulations which aroused the wildest enthusiasm," the *Boston Globe* reported, before he then talked about each ballplayer. Mayor Josiah Quincy then presented each player with a diamond pin and a watch charm inscribed "Boston champions."[25]

Total attendance at the South End Grounds during the 1897 season was 334,000 people, the highest level since the club was formed in 1871. However, that attendance level also remained the club's high-water mark for another 17 years.

Boston repeated as champions in the 1898 season, which the league owners had elongated to 154 games, which in Boston depressed attendance and fan interest due to the number of cool-weather games as well as doubleheaders to make up rainouts. To celebrate the 1898 championship, a testimonial was held at the Music Hall on October 20. After the musical portion of the program, the ballplayers, dressed in their uniforms, were introduced to the audience and received a hearty ovation. The ballplayers were then presented with a check for $2,500 from the ballclub's ownership, which was parceled out at $235 per player. "We trust this gratuity will be accepted as evidence of our high appreciation of the united and successful efforts of the Boston team in again winning the championship," the accompanying letter from Soden read. "Great praise is due the team for its correct deportment and clean, manly ball playing. Skill, intelligence, and harmony have won a well-deserved victory."[26]

There was just tepid interest during the 1899 and 1900 seasons among "the army of baseball enthusiasts" and "genuine followers of the game." The *Boston Globe* even noted for the last game of the 1900 season that "Grand Master Charley Lavis has ordered out every member of the royal rooters for this afternoon" to try to produce a decent sized crowd. Soden had alienated the Royal Rooters, who were not just a cut below the more gentlemanly audiences of the 1880s economically and politically (the Rooters were affiliated with the Democratic Party), but more importantly the Rooters enjoyed drinking alcoholic beverages. To a staunch prohibitionist like Soden, this was anathema.[27]

Additionally, many of the traditional patrons had moved to the suburbs. "It is a fact that about half of the patrons of the games played here come from the suburbs," Soden told the *Boston Daily Advertiser*. "As soon as a game is over they want to make quick connections for trains to their home." While the Tremont Street subway had certainly facilitated this transfer, particularly to North Station for fans going north, the new South Station was more inconvenient to fans going south and west than the previous railroad-specific terminals that had been closer to the ballpark.[28]

In addition to the transportation issues, Soden remained convinced that larger audiences paying a lower admission price could not result in a profitable baseball operation. "From what I have seen of baseball I should say that the question of time affected patrons more than whether they had to pay 25 or 50 cents for an admission," Soden argued. "Here in Boston the patrons want the best there is and they won't take anything else. When a lover of the sport thinks that he wants to see a game of baseball, he doesn't say, 'Will this cost me 25 or 50 cents?' but 'Can I spare the time to see a good game?'"[29]

Both of these considerations would be put to the test during the 1901 season.

◆ 5 ◆

American League
Enters Boston

In the fall of 1900, Ban Johnson was building a national footprint for the minor-league American League to elevate into a major league. By November, the new American League consisted of the four existing western teams in Chicago, Cleveland, Detroit, and Milwaukee balanced with the three new eastern teams in Baltimore, Washington, and Philadelphia that complemented the existing Buffalo franchise. The city of Boston was not even in the American League's plans at the time.

When Johnson was rebuffed by the National League owners at their meeting in mid–December, he decided to exact revenge on the National League by locating a franchise in Boston. Johnson was able to outfox the National League, and its apparent vastly superior position in Boston sporting circles, through the use of Irish-Americans, which Soden had dismissed as unimportant to the success of the National League club in Boston. When a ballpark location had been secured in Boston in mid–January, Boston replaced Buffalo as the eighth team in the soon-to-be-major-league American League.

The ball grounds for the fledging Boston club in the American League was located on the "shoot the chutes" circus grounds on Huntington Avenue, just west of Massachusetts Avenue, which the club rented from the owner of the land, the Boston Elevated Railway Company. The lease announcement signaled the end of the National League's monopoly on Boston baseball fans, although this conclusion was not nearly as clear at the time as it would be five months later.

By deploying Connie Mack and Hugh Duffy, both successful middle-class Irish-Americans, Johnson chose an innovative strategy to get a new business off the ground in conservative Anglo-Saxon Protestant business circles in Boston. Mack, who lived in East Brookfield, Massachusetts, about 60 miles west of Boston, was the former manager and part-owner of the Milwaukee club in the minor-league American League in 1900, and current manager and part-owner of the Philadelphia club in the major-league American League in 1901. Duffy had been the captain of the Boston team in the National League in 1900 and would replace Mack as the Milwaukee manager in 1901.

Mack and Duffy were the front men for the lease transaction to secure the Huntington Avenue Grounds, which was funded by Cleveland business-man Charles Somers, since Johnson was unable to locate a Boston investor that was willing to go up against Soden and the supposedly entrenched National League club. Mack and Duffy worked with several other successful middle-class Irish-Americans in Boston, including Jack Dooley, who was instrumental in a behind-the-scenes role in the transaction. Dooley worked as a broker in cotton goods at J.M. Prendergast, which was owned by James Prendergast, who was a highly successful Irish-American and also a trustee of the Boston Elevated Railway. Prendergast was the only trustee who was an Irish Catholic, as all the others were solidly college-educated Anglo-Saxon Protestants. His cousin, Daniel, was the real estate agent at the Boston Ele-vated. Dooley served as middleman between Daniel Prendergast and Connie Mack.[1]

"The railway people were anxious to let the property for baseball pur-poses, as it meant traffic for their road," according to lawyer Michael Moore, another Irish-American, who assisted Mack and Duffy with the transaction. "The American League people were pleased with the rent agreed upon as they were anxious to give Boston some lively ball for 25 cents admission."[2]

Officials of the National League club, whose ballpark was situated just the other side of the New York, New Haven, and Hartford Railroad tracks from the Huntington Avenue Grounds, scoffed at the proposed competition. "Billings thinks there is no doubt that the American League will be starved out in short order," Jake Morse of the *Boston Herald* wrote. "He quotes the fate of the brotherhood [in 1890], and says the death of the American League will be far more rapid, a case of quick consumption, as it were."[3]

Once the Boston franchise was officially part of the American League, Johnson turned to yet another Irish-American to manage the new Boston team. Jimmy Collins, the third baseman of the Boston National League team in 1900, agreed to leave the Nationals to lead the Americans as player-manager. Collins was the pivotal link in the success of the new baseball ven-ture in Boston.

The historical timeline of events has usually been generally accepted as (1) the Huntington Avenue ballpark location was selected in mid–January, (2) the Boston franchise was established in late January, (3) Collins was secured as manager in early March, and (4) the Boston baseball fans (including the

Royal Rooters) switched their allegiance from the National League to the American League by the time of the Americans' first game of the 1901 season. However, Collins and the Boston baseball fans undoubtedly entered the picture at the beginning of this timeline, before the ballpark location was even secured.

Johnson would not have moved forward on a lease for the Huntington Avenue Grounds without some reasonable expectation that spectators would materialize to watch the ball games there. Deep in the background was Arthur Dixwell, one of Boston's top baseball fans in the 1880s, who had soured on the National League club during the 1890s after the Players' League folded in 1890. Although he was rarely mentioned in contemporary newspaper accounts, Dixwell was instrumental in convincing the American League boosters that there was an unfulfilled demand for baseball among emerging middle-class Irish-Americans, whom the National League club had snubbed. That Dixwell was a very key component to the establishment of the Boston club in the American League is backed up by two significant pieces of evidence: (1) Dixwell was the honored dignitary to shovel the first spade of dirt at the ground-breaking ceremony for the Huntington Avenue Grounds, and (2) Dixwell threw out the ceremonial first ball at the opening game at the Huntington Avenue Grounds.[4]

Somers was in Boston in early January, ostensibly to investigate leasing ball grounds, but more likely to assess the Boston baseball market. Duffy easily could have set up Somers to talk with Dixwell to get a better understanding of the likely spectatorship situation for the new club. Dixwell, part of the dwindling old guard of baseball patrons and part-owner of the Boston franchise in the ill-fated 1890 Players' League, was certainly not averse to improving the status quo. Dixwell would have candidly told Somers that there was no love lost between many of Boston's general baseball fans and the management of the Nationals. If a popular player or two could be convinced to jump from the Nationals to the Americans, then many of those fans would very likely abandon the Nationals and support the Americans.

Dixwell would have also been familiar with the geography that would be favorable to the new baseball club, particularly the scheduled opening of the Boston Elevated Railway system in June 1901. This above-ground trolley system connected the downtown subway with both railroad stations, North Station and South Station, to more easily allow suburban spectators to get to the Huntington Avenue Grounds than to the Nationals' South End Grounds. Crosstown streetcar lines unloaded passengers at the nearby corner of Huntington and Massachusetts Avenue, where they could transfer to a streetcar running directly to the Huntington Avenue Grounds.

The discussion of a popular player to draw the allegiance of Boston baseball fans would have quickly led to Collins topping the list of spectator-favorite ballplayers among the Boston Nationals. It appears that in early January Collins was approached to consider switching leagues, probably by a telegram from either Dixwell or Duffy, and encouraged to talk with Somers. Both Dixwell and Duffy knew that Collins was motivated by money and would consider taking the risk of switching over to the Americans, since he was very displeased with his recent salary negotiations with the Nationals. Collins's relationship with the Nationals had soured because Collins had no success in convincing Soden to increase his salary above the informal $2,400 salary limit. Compounding the situation was that Collins had little leverage to counteract that position, because no other baseball club in the league would hire him due to the reserve clause contained in the standard league contract. Because Collins was a bachelor with non-baseball economic interests in his hometown of Buffalo, New York, he could afford to take the risk of switching clubs, unlike most other ballplayers on the Nationals.

The 30-year-old Collins was not a run-of-the-mill ballplayer, since he had begun to actively plan for his life beyond baseball. He had earned a sizeable salary as a major-league ballplayer with the Boston Nationals the previous five summers, although less than his perceived value. While his baseball income was more than enough to fuel a comfortable bachelor lifestyle, Collins did have designs on eventually marrying and raising a family. He had also saved a portion of his earnings, which he could use to support his post-baseball, married future in Buffalo. During the winter of 1900, Collins made an investment to take advantage of the explosive future growth he saw in the South Buffalo neighborhood, where many Irish-Americans were moving to flee the deteriorating inner city. Collins purchased a house lot on Seneca Street in South Buffalo and made plans to build a rental unit on it. No longer would Collins work for someone else in the offseason; he was going to be self-employed as the landlord of his own real estate. If everything worked out well, he could also pursue this occupation in his post-baseball years.[5]

In the American League, not only could Collins be a manager, but former ballplayers could also be part-owners, as exemplified by Mack in Philadelphia. The ownership opportunity intrigued Collins. The league was going to adopt the Players Protective Association proposals, which included stipulated contract lengths, so the open-ended reserve clause in National League contracts would not be an issue. The clincher was that Collins could help topple the National League owners and inflict some pain on tight-fisted owners like Soden. Because people such as Mack and Duffy saw the leadership potential in Collins that had escaped the attention of the Boston Nationals' ownership, they convinced Johnson that Collins could handle the on-the-field duties of manager and quickly learn the other responsibilities.

Collins verbally agreed with Somers in early February to the broad outline of a deal to join the Boston Americans, where he would be paid $3,500 per year for three seasons to be the team's third baseman, captain, and manager, with the freedom to negotiate with other clubs after that three-year period. This was nearly a 50 percent increase to his $2,400 salary for the 1900 season. This $10,500 package was a key aspect of the deal for Collins, so that he'd have sufficient capital to invest into his Buffalo real estate business.[6]

In a mid–February article entitled "Are After Jimmy Collins: American League Would Like Him to Manage," the *Buffalo Express* reported that "Collins is a strong Protective Association man and it is believed that in case of an outbreak he will either be manager or captain of the Boston American League team." As rumors of his departure swirled, Collins told Tim Murnane of the *Boston Globe* that he "is with the league who gives him the most money, with a preference for the crowd who make it look the surest."[7]

Collins never bothered to negotiate with Soden of the Boston Nationals, whose posi-

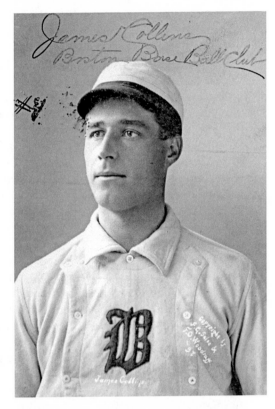

Jimmy Collins, a bachelor with real-estate development interests in Buffalo, New York, was willing to take the risk of leaving the Boston National League team to become player-manager of the Boston team in the new American League. Many fans, especially Irish-American ones, chose to follow the Americans exclusively (Library of Congress, Prints and Photographs Division, LC-DIG-ds-04690).

tion was that the reserve clause in his current contract legally bound Collins to the National League club for the 1901 season. Soden publicly said that he would pursue legal action against any ballplayer, e.g., Collins, if he signed with an American League club. Collins used Soden's legal threat to get Somers to improve his offer to Collins, since he didn't want the risk of being a legal test case. Although Collins never divulged who his lawyer was in these contract negotiations, Harry Taylor would have been an obvious choice, given his expertise in player contracts from his work with the Players Protective Association (he developed the group's legal opinion that the existing reserve clause in player contracts had no legal value) and the location of his law office in downtown Buffalo. Somers agreed to add a personal guarantee concerning the payment of the salary amounts in the deal with Collins. Somers also agreed to make Collins a nominal owner in the new Boston baseball club. While the few shares of stock in the baseball corporation weren't worth much, symbolically the shares were priceless to Collins.[8]

The personal guarantee by Somers was a key point for Collins, since this provision made the venture virtually risk-free to him. Not only would the $10,500 in salary over three years go a long way toward expanding his real estate business, but it could also possibly allow him to retire as a ballplayer at the end of the three-year duration of his contract. As Morse explained about the "cast-iron personal contract with Mr. Somers," Collins would receive "a fat salary, for three years" because even "if the Boston League [club] succeeds in enjoining him from playing, he will, according to his contract, manage from the bench."[9]

On March 2 Somers held a meeting in Cleveland with sportswriters to announce that Collins had signed to be manager of American League club in Boston. "This is only the beginning. Similar announcements may be expected to follow shortly," Somers told the newspapermen who had congregated in his office. "We are not asking players to break any legal contracts with the National League. But we hold that the option clause in the National League contract is not valid, and therefore practically all players are free to sign American League contracts if they so desire."[10]

Taylor made a lasting, but unsung, contribution to baseball history through his legal services that helped to elevate the American League to major league status in 1901. As the lawyer for the Players Protective Association, Taylor issued the crucial legal opinion to his ballplayer constituents that it was his belief that the reserve clause in the National League's standard player contract had "no legal value." Taylor's legal analysis set the stage for Jimmy Collins, Napoleon Lajoie, and dozens of other ballplayers to jump from the National League and establish the American League as a serious competitor to the then-monopoly National League. A flurry of signings occurred after Taylor telegraphed Somers on March 1: "All barriers removed. National League players free to sign with any league."[11]

Before heading to Boston to begin his duties with his new employer, Collins returned to his home in Buffalo and sent the following telegram to every Boston daily newspaper: "I have given the National League people my best efforts for several years past and often asked them for more money, knowing that I was worth it. But until now they have turned a deaf ear to all my requests, and so it is the same with many others. They tried now when it is too late with their liberal offers. I have not the least disparaging remark to make against Mr. Soden, he has always treated me nicely and paid every cent that his obligations called for, but I saw a chance to better myself and took it and I can name fifty others that will do the same thing."[12]

Very quickly, the Boston Americans, led by player-manager Jimmy Collins, overshadowed the Boston Nationals and became the fan favorite of the two baseball teams in Boston. Collins was the patron saint of twenty-first-century Red Sox Nation.

◆ 6 ◆

Changing Nature
of the Fans

Following a groundbreaking ceremony in early March 1901, the Huntington Avenue Grounds rapidly took shape over a two-month period, resulting in a grandstand that held 2,400 fans and bleachers on the first-base and third-base sides that each sat about 3,000. The total seating capacity of 9,000 people at the Huntington Avenue Grounds was comparable to the South End Grounds. However, the tracks of the New York, New Haven, and Hartford Railroad were not the only thing that separated the two ballparks. There was a lower admission price at the Huntington Avenue Grounds, 25 cents, compared to the 50 cents required at the South End Grounds.[1]

The difference in admission charge reflected the different socio-economic nature of the spectators that each baseball club sought to attract to their ballpark. This difference was portrayed in side-by-side newspaper advertisements during the spring of 1901. The American League club (the "Americans") explicitly identified its admission price of 25 cents, noting an additional charge for a reserved seat in the grandstand; tickets could be purchased at Wright & Ditson, a general sporting goods store. The National League club (the "Nationals") didn't identify the price, either for admission or for a reserved seat; tickets could be purchased at Appleton & Bassett, an upscale fishing tackle store. While the Americans presumed patrons would come to the ballpark by streetcar, the Nationals explicitly advertised "bicycles checked free."[2]

While Arthur Soden had the baseball world convinced that the Nationals had an unassailable monopoly in Boston, the Nationals in reality were a sandcastle that collapsed upon the incoming tide of the Americans. Soden had vastly overestimated the club's popularity with middle-class Boston baseball fans, believing they identified with the team, and had completely ignored the working-class ones. When the Nationals were the only ball game in Boston, baseball fans had to patronize the South End Grounds to see major-league baseball. Given a competitive option when the Americans were formed, the middle-class fans abandoned the Nationals and working-class fans eagerly leaped at the new opportunity. In addition to some latent contempt for Soden, fans identified much more with the ballplayers than to the team, and the Americans had several former Nationals.

Jimmy Collins was the leader, having been lured to switch clubs with a guaranteed personal contract for three years that would reward him handsomely if the new venture succeeded. Collins coaxed three more players from the Nationals to jump to the Americans, outfielder Chick Stahl, first baseman Buck Freeman, and pitcher Ted Lewis, who deferred his baseball retirement (and future career as a college professor).

The Irish Catholic population of Greater Boston was naturally drawn to the team playing at the Huntington Avenue Grounds for several reasons. Initially the attractions were the lower admission price and desire to see one of their own ethnicity, Collins, succeed in a managerial position. But largely the Irish Catholics felt wanted in a city dominated by an Anglo-Saxon Protestant culture, which Soden perpetuated at the South End Grounds. The Royal Rooters helped to facilitate this attraction to the Huntington Avenue Grounds, given the Irish heritage of a large percentage of that clan and their enmity for Soden. For the first time since 1891, there was a large swath of fans that were dedicated to just one team in Boston. This percentage would increase during the first few years of the decade, as the Americans played a much better brand of baseball than did the Nationals, which leveraged these underlying fan motivations.

Not afraid to overtly compete for the followers of the Nationals, the Americans in 1901 played a schedule that overlapped the one of the Nationals with numerous head-to-head games. The first head-to-head match occurred on May 8, 1901, when the first American League game was played at the Huntington Avenue Grounds. A crowd of 11,500 people packed the ballpark to watch the Americans defeat the Philadelphia Athletics. In addition to long-time Boston baseball fan Arthur Dixwell, who threw out the first ball, the spectators included "clergymen, business men, professional people, ex-ballplayers, old-time fans, and an army of fresh recruits" who came not just from Greater Boston but also "from Bangor, Maine, to Newport, Rhode Island, and many cities in between." These fans experienced not only a ball game but also the voice of a "megaphone man," a novel feature of Boston baseball, to announce the batters and otherwise inform the spectators of happenings on the field. At the Nationals game at the South End Grounds, the audience was 5,700, less than half the crowd at the Huntington Avenue Grounds.[3]

Over the course of this first overlapping homestand, the Americans easily confirmed the spectator interest in the new team, which went head-to-head with the Nationals through May 17. On Saturday, May 11, when more working-class fans could get to the ballpark, the Americans outdrew the Nationals 7,200 to 2,500. During the workweek, the audience for the games at the Huntington Avenue Grounds routinely was twice the size of the small throng at the South End Grounds, culminating on Friday, May 17, when 4,200 people watched the Americans while a mere 1,700 witnessed the Nationals.

The Americans were also not afraid to use promotions to encourage fans to come to the ballpark. The club reinstituted Ladies Day in Boston, which the Nationals had been highly resistant to since its last foray into freebies in 1890 during the battle for Boston fans with the Players' League club. On June 10, the Americans offered their first Ladies Day and continued this promotional technique at several more games during the 1901 season. Ladies Day was very popular beyond its traditional focus to attract paying male customers to escort the females who were admitted free, since "going to the ballpark gave [women] a place to enjoy fresh air and new freedoms, and they went" and became regular patrons of the grandstand.[4]

For the Bunker Hill Day holiday on June 17, the Americans added a morning game to the scheduled afternoon contest, to provide an additional opportunity for lower-income fans to attend a ball game and better compete with the single game scheduled that day at the South End Grounds. Five thousand people attended the morning game at the Huntington Avenue Grounds and another 10,000 went to the afternoon game. This attendance easily exceeded the 1,500 people who wandered into the Nationals game that afternoon at the South End Grounds. Following this box-office drubbing on the holiday, Soden lowered the admission price to 25 cents at the South End Grounds to match the fare charged at the Huntington Avenue Grounds.[5]

Sunday baseball was even considered by the Americans to generate greater appeal. Naturally, the Sunday games could not be played at the Huntington Avenue Grounds or anywhere in the Boston area. Massachusetts law provided substantial fines for those who conducted "any manner of labor, business or work" on Sunday ($50 fine) as well as for "whoever is present at a game, sport, play or public diversion, except a concert of sacred music" on the Lord's Day ($5 fine) and "the proprietor, manager or person in charge of such game, sport, play or public diversion" (fine ranged from $50 to $500). For many years to come, the "Act to Regulate the Observance of the Lord's Day" would be a powerful disincentive to stage Sunday games in Boston.[6]

Representatives from the Rocky Point amusement park in Rhode Island, where the authorities tolerated Sunday baseball in contravention of that state's equally oppressive Sunday statute, approached the Americans about playing Sunday games at their park. They promised large crowds similar to the size already being produced for the Sunday games of the minor-league Providence team. While the Americans passed on the idea, they did play an exhibition game at Rocky Point in September 1901. The following year both the Americans and Nationals regularly played exhibition games at Rocky Point; in 1903 the Nationals even played one official regular-season game there.[7]

By mid–June the Americans had a decided transportation advantage over the Nationals, because it was easier for suburban spectators to get to the Huntington Avenue Grounds than to the South End Grounds. When it opened in June 1901, the Boston Elevated Railway line supplanted the Tremont Street streetcar (which passed close by the South End Grounds) from using the existing subway tunnel under downtown Boston in order for the elevated railway to have a continuous run between its terminal at Sullivan Square in Charlestown and its Dudley Street terminal in Roxbury. For the Tremont Street streetcar, the previous occupant of the subway tunnel, a direct connection to the subway was severed. Suburban fans taking a train into North Station or South Station could get to the Huntington Avenue Grounds by taking the elevated railway (for South Station, a spur that ran along Atlantic Avenue) and changing to the Huntington Avenue streetcar. Going to the South End Grounds entailed staying on the elevated railway, exiting at the Northampton Street station, and walking a few blocks to the ballpark; alternatively, people could make the awkward connection to the Tremont Street streetcar.[8]

When it came to newspaper coverage, the Americans also had an advantage over the Nationals. Jimmy Collins was not just the manager of the Americans but also the team's public face, since the baseball club had out-of-town ownership. Collins developed great rapport with the sportswriters from the many daily newspapers in Boston, particularly Tim Murnane of the *Globe*, Fred O'Connell of the *Post*, Jake Morse of the *Herald* (also correspondent for *Sporting Life*), and Peter Kelley of the *Journal*. There was an immediate connection between Collins, the Irish Catholic from Buffalo, and the three Irish Catholic sportswriters (Murnane, O'Connell, and Kelley), which appealed to Boston's predominantly Irish-American population. Collins also had a tangible connection with Morse, who was Jewish and just as much of an outcast in the Anglo-Saxon Protestant business climate of Boston as those of the Catholic faith.

Collins changed how baseball was reported in Boston newspapers beyond the obvious need to differentiate the two baseball teams as Americans and Nationals. When the Nationals had been the only team in town during the previous nine years, baseball writers for the Boston papers had to deal with the reticence of manager Frank Selee and the condescending attitude of owner Arthur Soden. The friendly Collins was able to better connect with the newspapermen, especially as a player-manager who could better explain the happenings on the baseball diamond. Collins also made it a point to talk to the sportswriters after each game, in contrast to Selee who infrequently offered commentary and Soden who rarely attended games. Since the baseball reports now helped to sell more newspapers, companies spent more money on newspaper advertising, which drove up newspaper profits and created more editorial demand for baseball material in order to sell even more news-papers. Soon the sportswriters were actively seeking commentary from Collins.[9]

The popularity of the Americans reached its height in August when the first-place Chicago White Sox played in Boston, as a standing-room crowd of 9,500 people paid to see a two-for-one doubleheader at the Huntington Avenue Grounds. "Every seat on the grounds was taken," Murnane wrote in the *Globe*, "the [grand] stand being completely filled and with rows [of people] standing, while along the third base bleachers the walk[way] was fringed with several hundred who preferred the shade to the turf out in center field," where the overflow of people stood.[10]

Far more fans attended ball games at the Huntington Avenue Grounds in 1901 than went through the turnstiles at the South End Grounds. The total attendance for the Americans was 289,000 people, which was the second-highest one-season count in the history of professional baseball in Boston. Attendance for the Nationals was one-half that total, at 146,000 people.

Soden expected the legal system to shut down the insurgent American League following the end of the 1901 season, by ruling in favor of the reserve clause in the contracts of ballplayers in the National League, which Soden had conceived in 1879. This clause in essence bound every ballplayer to one club forever, unless the club initiated action to release the player. In addition to failing to anticipate the changing nature of baseball fans, Soden was also blinded by the inventor's obsessive belief in his creation, which led Soden to believe that each National League club owner had an indestructible monop-oly. However, the reserve clause was not as airtight as Soden and the other owners were led to believe. After the 1902 court decision in the Lajoie case provided only limited enforcement of the reserve clause, Lajoie continued to play in the American League. And the Nationals had to continue to try to compete with the Americans in Boston.

When Patrick Collins, the second Irish-American mayor of Boston, took office in January 1902, there were two men named Collins who were the toast of Boston among the city's Irish-American citizens: the mayor and the base-ball manager. This made the Americans baseball team all the more popular in Boston. Attendance at the Huntington Avenue Grounds reached 348,000 for the 1902 season, topping the previous record high of 334,000 set by the Nationals during the 1897 season.

Higher admission prices in 1902 at the Huntington Avenue Grounds didn't deter fans from buying a ticket to the Huntington Avenue Grounds. In early March, the American League club owners voted to have three levels of seating at their ballparks. While the price for an uncovered bleacher seat remained the same at 25 cents, the price for a pavilion seat (bleachers under a roof) was set at 50 cents and a grandstand seat (chair seat under a roof) was increased to 75 cents. At the Huntington Avenue Grounds, the third-base bleachers were transformed into pavilion seats to charge an additional 25 cents, while the first-base bleachers remained in the sun and still priced at a quarter. Admission to the grandstand was now an additional 50 cents beyond the 25 cents admission price, up from an extra quarter in 1901.[11]

At the season-openers in 1903, there was no question that the Americans were the favorite among the entire cadre of Boston baseball fans, not just the new Irish-American fans. In the head-to-head competition for spectators on the Patriots Day holiday, the Americans attracted nearly five times as many people for the morning and afternoon games at the Huntington Avenue Grounds (27,658 total) than attended the two games that the Nationals played at the South End Grounds (5,694 total).

Many of the general baseball fans of the 1890s had converted into dedicated fans of the Americans by 1903. Boston was now, for the most part, divided into two camps of partisan fans. While there continued to be a reasonable quorum of general baseball fans that supported both teams, many leaned toward the Americans and focused less time on the Nationals. The leaners, as well as the number of intermittent fans, dramatically increased in 1903 during the first pennant-winning season for the Americans. Saturday crowds escalated from 10,000 in the spring to 14,000 by the end of the summer, as the Americans surged into a commanding lead in the American League standings by Labor Day to finish 14 games ahead of second-place Philadelphia.

The Americans then engaged in the first modern-day World Series against the National League champion Pittsburgh Pirates. After Pittsburgh won three of the first four games in the best-of-nine match, the Americans, behind the Royal Rooters' incessant singing of the song "Tessie," forged a comeback to win the next four games. The Americans were world champions and the Rooters gained ever-lasting fame as the symbol of Boston fans. At the third game in Boston on Saturday, October 3, more than 20,000 people jammed into the Huntington Avenue Grounds, as the ballpark was overwhelmed by the demand to see the ball game.

After the fourth game, which made "Tessie" infamous as the team's theme song, Collins received the following telegram at his hotel in Pittsburgh from Charles H. Taylor, the owner and publisher of the *Boston Globe*: "The Boston Globe, believing that victory is within the grasp of you and your comrades, offers to present to each player of the Boston team of the American

The Royal Rooters, shown in this photograph with their preferential seating at the 1903 World Series, were instrumental in developing Irish-American patronage at the Huntington Avenue Grounds and enlarging seasonal attendance for the Americans to be double that of the Nationals at the South End Grounds (Boston Public Library, Print Department, McGreevey Collection).

League, if it brings to Boston the world's championship, a valuable gold medal, which can be worn as a watch charm, and be treasured as a reminder of the most notable achievement upon the diamond." With the text of the telegram printed on the front page of the next day's *Boston Globe*, Taylor created more hype to capitalize on the World Series games, setting the stage for his family to take an increased interest in the fortunes of the Boston club.[12]

According to most chroniclers of baseball history, including the authors of the four books published in 2003 to celebrate the 100th anniversary of the World Series, the upset victory by the American League over the firmly entrenched National League forever altered the landscape of major league baseball. It certainly altered the Boston baseball landscape. "It has surprised me to see the amount of interest that is being taken in this series," Collins said after the conclusion of the series. "I never thought that it would arouse so much enthusiasm."[13]

Because the National League had made peace with the American League during the 1903 season by negotiating a "national agreement" document for a common governance of both leagues, the two leagues in 1904 began to coordinate playing schedules in the two-team cities to allocate holiday dates on a rotating basis and to avoid head-to-head games for non-holiday dates.

For the five holiday dates in Boston, it was agreed to a yearly alternating of the local holidays of Patriots Day and Bunker Hill Day with an allocation to one team of two of the three national holidays (Decoration Day, Independence Day, and Labor Day) while the other team had the third national holiday. The result was that each season one team would have three holiday dates while the other team had two holiday dates. For example, in 1904, the Americans had Patriots Day as its local holiday and Decoration Day and Labor Day as its national holidays, while the Nationals had Bunker Hill Day as its local holiday and Independence Day as its national holiday.

For the non-holiday dates, conflicting games were minimized (and confined to short periods) until all the bugs were shaken out of the scheduling process to completely eliminate conflicts. In 1904 there were a few conflicting home games in Boston, in early May, late July, and mid–September. Both teams were also on the road for a brief period in mid–July. In 1905 there were no scheduling conflicts for the two Boston teams.

The integrated scheduling produced a plethora of opportunity for Boston baseball fans to watch a ball game without having to make a choice between the two teams. For each of the five holiday dates, there was a morning and afternoon twin bill at only one ballpark. For the other games, one team would always play at home while the other team was on the road. Due to the integrated scheduling, there was a ball game in Boston nearly every day of the week from Monday through Saturday. This resulted in a gradual decline in the dedicated fans that sided with the Americans and an increase in general baseball fans that supported both teams.

With the Americans winning a second consecutive pennant in 1904, there was also a rise in intermittent fans who sought an entertainment activity. The impact of the Royal Rooters upon the increase in fans was smaller than history recognizes through the perpetuation of the "Tessie" factor. Their ostentatious behavior during the 1903 and 1904 seasons, while initially palatable to Irish-Americans, became less acceptable after 1905 when Irish-Americans began their ascent to greater social prominence in Boston. As ballpark crowds became more temperate, the rowdy Rooters were tolerated less and less. A winning team, new ballpark, and excellent transportation connections made for an unbeatable combination to attract fans without the help of the Rooters. So did increased baseball coverage by the *Boston Globe*, a Democratic-leaning newspaper, which certainly inspired more Irish-American fans to follow baseball as well as other more recent immigrant groups like the Italians and Polish.

After the season-opener in 1904 at the Huntington Avenue Grounds, where the Americans raised championship pennants on the flagpole in center field, a new owner of the Americans was announced: John I. Taylor, the son of *Boston Globe* publisher Charles H. Taylor. The newspaper publisher invested around $100,000 to buy the baseball club to keep his wayward son occupied, since the younger Taylor showed little interest in the newspaper business. The younger Taylor's best qualification to be owner was his frequent appearance as a spectator at the Huntington Avenue Grounds.[14]

American League president Ban Johnson had just days earlier spurned the offer of politician John Fitzgerald to buy the Boston club, citing as his excuse that "the terms of the agreement were not lived up to by Fitzgerald." As was later revealed, though, money was not the most significant element to determine who would be the new owner, because "restoring cordial relations between the owners of the rival Boston clubs" was the top priority. In other words, under the recently concluded negotiation for a national agreement, having Boston be a viable two-team city was extremely important. Despite being a jilted prospective owner, Fitzgerald went on to have a sizeable

Middle-class businessmen filled the grandstand seats at the Huntington Avenue Grounds, as suburban businessmen attended ball games more often due to the good railroad and streetcar connections between the suburbs and the ballpark of the Americans team (Boston Public Library, Print Department, McGreevey Collection).

influence on Boston baseball when he was elected mayor of Boston in the fall of 1905.[15]

There was neck-and-neck competition in 1904 between the Americans and the New York Highlanders, which culminated with a season-ending doubleheader to decide the American League pennant. This doubleheader became the cornerstone for the storied rivalry between the Boston and New York clubs.

Originally, the American League schedule called for four games to be played in New York during the final series of the season between Boston and New York, including an innovative season-ending doubleheader on Monday, October 10. With a postponed game added into the mix, the final series soon expanded to five games, with a single game on Friday, October 7, and doubleheaders on Saturday, October 8, and Monday, October 10 sandwiched around Sunday, a day of rest, due to the Sunday law in New York. At midseason, the five-game, season-ending series in New York certainly looked to be an advantage for the Highlanders, until the owners rented the ballpark for a college football game on October 8. The upshot was that the Saturday doubleheader was transferred to Boston. Instead of five games in New York, the two teams played a Friday afternoon game in New York, jumped on a train to Boston for two games on Saturday, and then returned to New York for two games on Monday. The Americans captured the pennant in the decisive doubleheader on Monday, October 10.

By winning the opening game on October 7, the Highlanders had vaulted into first place, with a half game lead on the Americans. On Saturday, before 30,000 people at the Huntington Avenue Grounds, the Americans clobbered New York, 13–2, in the first game and edged them in the second game, 1–0. The Americans were now in first place by one and a half games; New York needed to sweep the doubleheader on Monday in order to win the pennant.

At the Saturday game in Boston, when Jimmy Collins came to bat in the second inning, he was presented with a silver loving cup by Royal Rooter Charley Lavis. The large cup on an ebony base was the result of a subscription campaign publicized in the *Boston Journal*, to honor Collins for his contribution to Boston baseball. The contributors to the loving cup, whose fund closed at $306, represented the broadening nature of Boston fans. Some baseball fans contributed a few dollars, but most fans sent in mere cents. Many, like Fred Eaton, sent in just a penny: "I am a baker but on a strike, so I can only afford one cent to Jimmy. But everything helps to make Jimmy work harder for the second pennant." Collins had certainly done his part to spark interest in newspaper sales.[16]

On Monday back in New York, the game was tied, 2–2, in the top of the ninth inning, with the go-ahead run for the Americans standing at third base. Highlanders pitcher Jack Chesbro cemented his future legacy when his spitball sailed over the head of his catcher to the backstop, which allowed Boston to score the winning run and capture the American League pennant. The 300 or so Royal Rooters who had traveled from Boston to New York, led by Lavis, commenced celebrating after the first game concluded, since the second game of the doubleheader was meaningless.

The October 10 doubleheader became legendary partially because of its impact on the 1904 pennant race, but more importantly because it was the initial major confrontation in the storied, longstanding rivalry between the American League clubs in Boston and New York. "There is no rivalry on the face of the earth that can compare with the Yankees vs. Red Sox," writer Ed Linn wrote in *The Great Rivalry: The Yankees and the Red Sox.* "It's everything a rivalry ought to be. Us Against Them. It's not only New York against Boston. It's New York against New England. The canyons of Wall Street and the caverns of Madison Avenue vs. the White Hills of New Hampshire and the Green Mountains of Vermont. We the People vs. the Barons of Entrenched Privilege. The spacious expanse of Yankee Stadium against the looming monster of Fenway Park."[17]

Over the years, the rivalry encouraged fans to flock to Fenway Park just to watch the two combatants, even if neither team was having that good of a season. There was a slight spillover to the games played by the Braves against the New York Giants in the National League, but the Braves never did develop a rivalry as intense as the one between the Red Sox and the Yankees.

Unlike 1903 when the Americans participated in the first modern-day World Series, the 1904 season had no similar culminating event since the champion of the National League, the New York Giants, refused to play a postseason series with the American League champion. The Giants ownership was still very annoyed with American League president Ban Johnson for placing a competing club in New York City in 1903. John I. Taylor issued a challenge to the Giants to play a five-game postseason series, but he never received a response. This only added more fuel to the rivalry with New York City.

On the afternoon of October 13, the Royal Rooters sponsored a testimonial for the Americans at the Boston Theatre, which was attended by a large group of baseball fans. Mike Regan, one of the leaders of the Royal Rooters, hosted the festivities. Regan was considered by *The Sporting News* to be the "undisputed champion base ball rooter of the world," since he had all the characteristics of a general baseball fan that supported not only both teams in Boston but also the sport as a whole. He was "as appreciative of the minor league as of the major league brand of his favorite sport" and had "adopted the policy of neutrality throughout the major-league war and has been strictly non-partisan during the peace period." Regan was the prototypical Boston general baseball fan for the rest of the decade. Since he was a furniture wholesaler, he had the time flexibility, and the mindset to follow both teams, to attend games at both the Huntington Avenue Grounds as well as the South End Grounds.[18]

Due to the total attendance in 1904 of 623,000 people, the seating at the Huntington Avenue Grounds had to be increased for 1905 to satisfy all the demand from an escalating number of baseball fans, especially since "it was virtually impossible last season to supply the demand for reserved seats for the big games." Since Boston had become a regional center of major-league baseball, not just a local one, "people coming to Boston from all over New England to see the games are always anxious to have their seats reserved." For 1905 a new bleacher section that spanned from left field to center field increased seating capacity by 2,500; a "ladies' retiring room," two smoking rooms for men, and new refreshment booths were also added.[19]

At spring training in 1905, John I. Taylor joined the excursion to Macon, Georgia, and brought along a trainload of people from Boston. The *Macon Telegraph* reported that sportswriters Murnane from the *Globe*, Morse from the *Herald*, O'Connell from the *Post*, Barnes from the *Journal*, and Mitchell from the *American* journeyed from Boston to Macon along with Taylor, in addition to baseball fans Fred Doe, a New England League club owner, and Regan, the ardent Royal Rooter. Suddenly, spring training for the Americans team was as much about publicity as it was about preparation.[20]

The major role of the Royal Rooters now was as a sideshow at spring training rather than vociferous fans at the ballpark. While Regan was also a congregant at spring training in 1906 and 1907, Mike McGreevey was the most visible Rooter as he participated in spring training at least through 1911. This shows that McGreevey, the owner of the now-vaunted Third Base Saloon, was great at self-promotion, but not necessarily at cheering for the Americans team.[21]

Even though their performance dipped in 1905, the Americans still attracted large crowds, with attendance totaling 468,000 people for the season. That's not counting the seven-game postseason exhibition series that October between the Americans and the Nationals, the first time the two teams ever played each other.

By 1905, the Nationals were drastically outmatched by the Americans, as the Nationals were not just a mediocre team but one that played in a dilapidated ballpark located in "one of Boston's worst slum sections." The location of the South End Grounds was a major deterrent to encouraging spectators to attend ball games. In Roxbury "along Tremont Street—that road of unrealized possibilities—the total impression is one of dismal failure, ugliness, and neglect so far as the housing of people goes," Robert Woods and Albert Kennedy wrote in *The Zone of Emergence*. By 1906 the wooden triple-decker was becoming ubiquitous in most parts of Roxbury within a mile of the South

End Grounds, to house lower middle-class residents amid the remaining factories in the rundown industrial area.[22]

In addition to these obvious disincentives for Boston baseball fans to follow the National League team, the expected transportation advantage of an elevated railway line on Tremont Street, as originally envisioned in 1894, never materialized. Legislation was approved in 1907 to extend subway lines into Cambridge and the Back Bay, nixing the once-planned extension of the elevated railway system down Tremont Street. Organized resistance by Cambridge residents surfaced in 1901 to scuttle the planned elevated railway in Cambridge in favor of a subway. By 1905 the subway plan moved forward, but the route from Cambridge once it reached downtown Boston went not to Roxbury down Tremont Street but rather into Dorchester.[23]

Improvements to the public transit system in the next few years made matters worse for the Nationals. In 1908 the Washington Street subway

Mayor John Fitzgerald, shown throwing out a ceremonial first ball at the Huntington Avenue Grounds, was the first American-born Irish Catholic mayor of Boston. With increased Irish-American influence, Fitzgerald not only changed Boston politics but also the composition of Boston baseball fans (Boston Public Library, Print Department, McGreevey Collection).

opened for the elevated railway to go under the central business district through this new tunnel, rather than use the Tremont Street subway tunnel. The new southern terminus for the elevated railway was "a most impressive terminal" at Forest Hills, which opened up the southwestern suburbs to improve commuting to downtown Boston, but the rapid-transit philosophy behind the elevated railway did little to make it easier for people seeking local transit to get to the South End Grounds.[24]

These transportation developments inhibited the Nationals in their ability to attract spectators from the suburbs of Greater Boston, whether the central and upper middle-class people sought by the club or the lower middle-class and upper working-class residents of the "great Irish belt" surrounding Boston in the rapidly growing northern suburbs of Medford, Chelsea and Everett. Many of these residents were regular attendants at Saturday games at the Huntington Avenue Grounds. Ironically, the integrated league schedules that provided a ball game in Boston on every Saturday kept the Nationals alive at the box office.[25]

Further discouraging the prospects for the Nationals was the rise of the automobile, which was inevitably tied to the potential suburban audience. Although there were only about 5,000 registered automobiles in Massachusetts in 1905, there was a five-fold increase to 30,000 vehicles by 1910, fueled by the introduction in 1908 of the low-priced Ford Model T. More and more upper-income suburban fans desired to drive their private automobile to the ballpark rather than use the streetcars and elevated railways of public transportation, which had been a crucial decision in the location of both the South End Grounds and Huntington Avenue Grounds. This was the first step toward leisure becoming a private activity rather than one conducted within a public venue.[26]

The Huntington Avenue Grounds offered more parking for automobiles than did the South End Grounds, since there was open land next to the ballpark on Rogers Avenue. However, the use of automobiles was not without incident. In 1906 Glen Mitchell of Brookline drove his automobile to the Huntington Avenue Grounds to watch the Americans play. After the game as Mitchell maneuvered his automobile through the exiting crowd, the vehicle frightened a nearby horse that "made his way down through the people, mowing them down right and left. Women screamed and men yelled, but in the surging crowd there was not one who was able to stop the horse."[27]

There would be an acceleration of population movement to the Boston suburbs during the next few years as a result of the introduction of the motorized truck around 1905. "Trucks, earlier than cars, changed the structure of the market-oriented Boston metropolitan area," Schaeffer and Sclar wrote in *Access for All: Transportation and Urban Growth*. "It was the truck's displacement of the horse-drawn dray that gave Bostonians the first inkling of the land-use changes the internal combustion engine was going to generate in the decades to come." Businesses could now more easily be located outside downtown and still be able to inexpensively move goods.[28]

Suddenly, the predominant element of baseball spectatorship—the downtown businessman in a management or sales occupation—was no longer confined to downtown. As companies relocated to the suburbs, businessmen were less likely to attend as many ball games during the workweek as they once did. If the businessman did go the ballpark, he likely would drive there in his automobile.

With the exodus of businesses from downtown to the suburbs, the ability of baseball fans to go to the ballpark to watch ball games Monday through Friday was further exacerbated by the decline in self-employed businessmen. According to *A History of Small Business in America*, the percentage of self-employed workers steadily declined from one-third of the workforce in 1900 to just one-quarter in 1920. This produced a consequent increase in salaried and wage workers, who very often had much less flexibility to leave work to go to an afternoon ball game than did self-employed people.[29]

This decline in self-employed individuals was a natural outgrowth of the industrialization of the American office that was then occurring. In his book *The Genesis of Industrial America, 1870–1920*, author Maury Klein described this change as "transforming a society of individuals into one of organizations," which possessed "hierarchical management structures and specialized departmental functions." Besides being the "harbingers of the age of bureaucracy," this transformation of employment had little "reliance on rugged individualism" that had been the foundation of self-employment. The good news was that "an enormous number of people edged their way into the middle class by serving as foot soldiers of the corporate economy in jobs that required less education and training." However, the foot soldiers could only attend ball games on Saturday, and there was a naturally shrinking corps of businessmen with the time flexibility to go to the games on Monday through Friday.[30]

In the fall of 1906 Soden finally located a willing buyer for the Nationals. The sale of the baseball club to George and John Dovey was announced that November. The new owners made some minor improvements to refurbish the South End Grounds to increase interest in the team's games, including an exclusive entrance to the grandstand with separate entrances to the first-base bleachers (50-cent admission) and third-base bleachers (25-cent admission). While that may have appeased the higher-income dedicated fans (a small number, given that only the first five rows of the grandstand were to be reserved at all times), the lower-income patrons among general baseball fans could not have been overly pleased with the entrance segregation.[31]

The Americans handled the shifting demographics better than the

Nationals did. Fans kept coming to the Huntington Avenue Grounds despite a generally poor baseball team on the field from 1906 to 1908. During these three years, the Americans never drew less than 400,000 spectators to the Huntington Avenue Grounds, while the Nationals never drew higher than 275,000 people to the South End Grounds. In 1906, even though both the Americans and the Nationals had sunk to last place, the Americans attracted nearly three times as many spectators as did the Nationals, 410,000 to 143,000. In 1907 the Americans drew 436,000 and in 1908 generated 473,000, both to watch teams that finished seventh and fifth, respectively.

Taylor christened the Americans with a formal nickname in December 1907, which was easier for fans to identify with, compared to the no-name team that the newspapers called the Americans. "Taylor has suggested red stockings to be a part of the uniforms," Murnane reported in the *Boston Globe*, "and thought the Boston 'Red Sox' might sound better to the baseball enthusiasts than the names now used by many, such as 'The Pilgrims.'" Murnane added that he thought "the 'Red Sox' will be a popular name with the Boston fans," which proved to be an understatement. Both Boston teams were late to the convention for formal team nicknames, since by 1907 most teams in both leagues had established such monikers.[32]

By 1908, a decided shift had occurred since 1904 in the overall composition of Boston baseball fans, with more general baseball fans and fewer dedicated ones. With the departure of Soden as an owner, the original enmity toward the Nationals dissipated and community support for baseball as a sport played in a two-team city congealed even further. While "championships are a great thing in baseball," New England baseball fans were "less interested in the raising of pennants than in the development of the game and the assurance of seeing hard and well-played battles," according to the analysis of Melville Webb, a sportswriter for the *Boston Globe*, in his article "Why Are You a Baseball Fan?" Webb saw this attitude not just in the good years, but also in the down years, when "interest in the sport never has wavered" because he believed the spirit of winning "always has appeared to be less than has the real interest in the game itself."[33]

Webb delved into fan motivations in his interviews with Boston businessmen who frequented the ballparks. John Haynes and Albert Pillsbury, both long-time fans, mentioned the classic reason of recreation and relaxation. "It's a business with me," said Haynes. "At a game I forget everything that has to do with my work—all my troubles—and enjoy a perfect mental rest." To Pillsbury it was a pleasure that came with "a mental relaxation that is real and which surely stimulates." For Archie Hurlbert, the ballpark was all about the athletic action. "It is not altogether the excitement, but the real sport that is going on," Hurlbert explained. "The action of baseball is exhilarating always. Even a dull game is made worth the sitting through because

More than 650,000 fans attended the ball games of the Americans in 1909. This photograph illustrates the stratified seating at the Huntington Avenue Grounds, with a covered grandstand (upper right) flanked by the roofed pavilion (middle right) and open bleachers (upper left and center), which were separate from the grandstand (Boston Public Library, Print Department, McGreevey Collection).

of some one piece of brilliant work." John Dooley concurred, saying, "It is the game itself that is the great thing that draws the crowd." The same sentiment was echoed by George Appleton, a fan for the previous 40 years.[34]

Although Webb wrote that everyday fans were not "a large proportion of the crowds," he never discussed partisanship to either the Red Sox or the National League team, likely because it was an inherent presumption that didn't need to be explicitly stated. The non-partisan nature of the Boston fan was inferred, though, through the comments from John Fitzgerald, mayor and former Royal Rooter: "It is the pride in the home team and the desire to see Boston win." While it would be expected for a politician to emphasize civic pride, the crossover to baseball was a natural one, when Webb added about Fitzgerald that "he feels that the game has a hold on the American people because of its integrity and the spirit of playing for every point that is so manifest in the players."[35]

Fostering the shift within baseball fans to being general baseball fans was the increase in suburban fans. "The crowd was largely made up of out-of-town people, many coming to see a meeting between two fast clubs, and while anxious to see the home team win out were willing to appreciate the good work of the visitors." One example was Henri Prevost, the proprietor of a drug store in Haverhill, 30 miles north of Boston, who was "one of the best known baseball fans" in that vicinity. Prevost often took the train to Boston to go to a ball game, where he "was well known to the first base fans." He smoked a pipe at the games, which was "his solace when his favorites failed to win at the Walpole St. or Huntington Av. Grounds, Fenway Park or Braves Field." Prevost was a classic general baseball fan, as he patronized the ballparks of both teams.[36]

Also contributing to the fan shift was the formation of the Winter League club, a group of upscale businessmen that basically supplanted the low-brow Rooters to become the face of the Boston fan base. The club started in a small way, "just a few of the faithful gathered together to discuss the whys and wherefores of the great national game … simply a gathering at first of a few professional men and merchants whose only affiliation with baseball was from the enthusiastic standpoint of the fan." John Dooley was the first president of the club, which held discussions at the Sunset Farm in Holliston and dinner meetings in downtown Boston. The dinner meetings always were attended by representatives from both Boston baseball clubs and a variety of other executives involved in baseball, in line with the desire of the general baseball fan to promote baseball in Boston, not one team or the other.[37]

Due to this changing nature of Boston fans, many insisted on buying only a reserved-seat ticket in the prestigious grandstand, rather than be content with a spot on the planks with the masses in the third-base pavilion or first-base bleachers. For the 1908 season the Red Sox divided the first-base bleachers into two sections, one being the area closest to the grandstand, now priced at 50 cents (and capable of being reserved), and the other being the portion farther down the line that was still priced at 25 cents (although in 1910 the price increased to 50 cents). After an immense crowd of 30,000 on August 3, 1909, the Red Sox added a new bleacher section in right-center field, which could seat an additional 3,500 people (at 25 cents per head) to increase the ballpark's total capacity to about 15,000.[38]

From 1909 to 1911, the Red Sox never drew less than 500,000 people in a season, topped by an attendance of 668,000 in 1909 with a third-place finish. While the Red Sox drew more in seasons when their performance was decent, there seems to have been a floor of 400,000 that would pass through the turnstiles at the Huntington Avenue Grounds just to watch a ball game. There was much more fluctuation in attendance numbers during the 1890s. For one thing, the neighborhood was much better than where the South End Grounds were located. By 1909 Huntington Avenue was in an up-and-coming area where many cultural institutions were located, such as Symphony Hall, the

Opera House, and the Museum of Fine Arts. Transportation connections were also vastly better than at the South End Grounds.

Aimed at upscale audiences such as the resurgent general baseball fans who sat in the grandstand at the Boston ballparks, *Baseball Magazine* began publishing in 1908, under the editorial leadership of Jake Morse, who had been forced out of the sports editor position at the *Boston Herald*. One of the editorial topics that Morse pushed in *Baseball Magazine* was Sunday baseball, as exemplified by this article disclaimer: "*Baseball Magazine* wishes to make clear its firm stand in favor of Sunday baseball." This was a subject that clearly was "deep at the root of all future prosperity in the National Game" as it related to Boston.[39]

Although the legal ability to conduct Sunday games by professional ballplayers was a long way from reality in Massachusetts, legislation to permit Sunday baseball played by amateurs was narrowly defeated in the Massachusetts legislature in April 1911. Proponents, to no avail, tried to appease opponents in the conservative legislature by presenting a new condition at the last minute to prohibit Sunday ball games within 1000 feet of a church. This church-proximity restriction had been a provision contained in the 1909 Indiana Sunday baseball law, which that state's highest court had recently upheld as being constitutional.[40]

A Saturday game during the summer of 1911 demonstrated that the Huntington Avenue Grounds were inadequate to meet the fan demand. "The crowds showed the absolute necessity for new grounds ... [as] fully 5,000 went to the grounds and walked away again when they found they could not get a seat" and refused to sit in the open bleachers exposed to "lower-paying riffraff." In September 1911 Taylor announced that a new ballpark would be built in the Back Bay, replacing the Huntington Avenue Grounds. Taylor also announced the sale of the Red Sox baseball club to new owners, who would rent the new ballpark from the Taylor family for its ball games.[41]

Fenway Park was the first of two new ballparks to be built in Boston in the next four years to handle the huge demand by Boston baseball fans to watch major-league baseball. However, the Taylors undoubtedly were completely unaware of the significance of the land for the new ballpark being within 1000 feet of a place of worship, the Church of the Disciples on Peterborough Street, which 17 years later would have an immense impact on the future of the Red Sox in Boston.

◆ 7 ◆

New Ballparks
for Big Crowds

Both ballparks in Boston were quite scruffy by 1911, as the wooden structures had seriously deteriorated from the exposure to snowy winters and rainy springs. Although the Huntington Avenue Grounds was seven years younger than the 1894-rebuilt South End Grounds, the Red Sox in 1912 were the first of the city's two baseball clubs to replace its ballpark to keep fans flowing through the turnstiles.

Rather than rebuild on Huntington Avenue, the Red Sox initially considered moving the playing venue to Forest Hills in Dorchester, the new southern terminus of the elevated railway line, but decided on a parcel in the Back Bay between the Boston & Albany Railroad and the Fens parkland. The land for the new ballpark was near Governor Square, at the intersection of Commonwealth Avenue and Beacon Street, which 20 years later would be renamed Kenmore Square. The Governor Square location had a distinct transportation advantage over Forest Hills, since the city had decided in 1911 to locate the new subway extension under the existing Boylston Street streetcar line rather than pursue the original riverbank plan for the subway run under the Charles River embankment. The subway extension from Boston to Cambridge also opened in March 1912.[1]

The new ballpark was christened as Fenway Park, ostensibly due to its location within Boston geography in the Fenway neighborhood, but also to promote the Fenway Realty Company, operated by Red Sox ownership to market other real estate holdings in the area. Arguably, the latter was a more important consideration, as the name of the ballpark helped to foster the name for the Fenway neighborhood rather than merely adopt an existing widely recognized name.[2]

Architecturally, Fenway Park was a palace for baseball fans compared to the Huntington Avenue Grounds. The new ballpark was the first steel-and-concrete baseball facility in Boston, providing spectators with more expansive, fire-resistant, seating areas. The construction technique was modeled after the new ballparks built the previous three years in Philadelphia (Shibe Park, 1909), Chicago (Comiskey Park, 1910), and New York (new Polo Grounds, 1911).

There were 10,000 more seats at Fenway Park than at the Huntington Avenue Grounds (24,000 to 15,000), with nearly half of the seating at Fenway dedicated to the grandstand, which was five times the size of the Huntington Avenue grandstand (11,400 to 2,400). However, grandstand seats at Fenway, at $1.25 for reserved and 75 cents for unreserved, were no longer the best seats in the house. The Red Sox unveiled a new premium seating arrangement—box seats—which were seats in private piped-off areas for a small group of people, priced at $1.50 per seat. The closest seats to the playing field were 47 boxes that provided exclusive seating. A walkway separated these boxes from the grandstand seating, where an additional 45 boxes were positioned in front of the grandstand seats.[3]

The box seats and expanded grandstand seating signaled a change in the spectator composition, as more people sought prestigious seating in 1912 than had back in 1901, as the Irish-American middle class expanded significantly during this period of Irish-American control of the Boston mayor and other city offices.

To have the ballpark ready for the 1912 season-opener, the remainder of the original seating at Fenway Park contained only pavilion and outfield bleachers. From the end of the grandstand on the first-base line to the right-field fence, Fenway Park had a pavilion section to provide bench seating for 8,000 people under a roof. There was a bleacher section for 5,000 people in center field. However, unlike at the Huntington Avenue Grounds, Fenway Park did not have an uncovered bench seating section along the third-base line. Beyond the end of the grandstand along the third-base line and beyond the pavilion in right field, there was just empty space. New features at Fenway Park included a tall left-field wall, to provide for increased advertising than was possible on the low walls at Huntington, and an automobile parking lot in the empty space between the first-base pavilion and the center-field bleachers. There was an exclusive entrance at Fenway Park on Jersey Street for grandstand and box-seat ticket holders; pavilion and bleacher entrances were on Ipswich Street near the streetcar line.[4]

Fenway Park was elegant in contrast to the shabby South End Grounds used by the city's National League team. Under new ownership in 1912 for the third time in six years, the Nationals immediately announced plans to renovate the South End Grounds as well as a new name for the team, the Braves. The name came from the term for common members of the Tammany

Fenway Park, two years old in this 1914 photograph, continued to have stratified seating for spectators. There were chair seats in the grandstand section, with plank seating in the first-base pavilion (foreground) and third-base stand (far right). Note the corridor separating the grandstand from the first-base and third-base stands (Library of Congress, Prints and Photographs Division, LC-USZ62–103059).

Society in New York City, where new owner James Gaffney was a prominent leader. The irony of the Braves name was that it was diametrically opposite to the original audience of upscale businessmen for the pre–1901 club. The Red Sox had co-opted that heritage with their nickname that was linked to the Red Stockings of the 1870s.[5]

Fans packed Fenway Park as the Red Sox won the American League pennant in 1912. Attendance for the season totaled 597,000, attracted by a new ballpark, star players in pitcher Joe Wood and outfielder Tris Speaker, and a winning team. Many were general baseball fans, but there were also intermittent fans that jumped on the championship bandwagon. Even with the increased number of reserved-seat tickets at Fenway Park available for pre-sale, there was still a crush of humanity at many games for the unreserved seats that were sold only on the day of a game. For a few big games, this practice erupted into a safety problem when disappointed fans that couldn't purchase tickets milled around outside the ballpark.

To boost seating capacity for the World Series with the New York Giants, the Red Sox added wood-plank seating sections to fill in the open spaces behind third base (to seat 5,000) and in right-field (to seat 4,500), as well as bleachers in front of the left-field and right-field walls (each to seat 1,200). Two additional rows of box seats added another 900 seats, to bring the total increase to 12,800 seats and an overall capacity of 36,000. Much of this new seating became permanent following the World Series.[6]

The Red Sox's plan for World Series tickets was to sell reserved tickets for the first three games in Boston of the best-four-of-seven-games World Series to "genuine fans," who could submit a ticket application with stubs from regular-season games as "indisputable evidence that they are genuine fans and regular attendants at the games." Reserved seats were set aside in the boxes, grandstand, and the new third-base stand. Selected applicants received a card in the mail to be redeemed at the Fenway Park ticket office, where cash was exchanged for a three-game block of tickets. Another 20,000 tickets for the first-base pavilion, outfield bleachers, and the new right-field stand went on sale the day of each home game in the series, as "rush seats" sold on a first-come-first-served basis.[7]

For the 1912 World Series, the games were scheduled to alternate between Boston and New York for the first six games; the first game was played in New York City, since the Giants won the coin flip to decide where the first game would be played. If a deciding seventh game were needed, a coin flip would determine where the final game would be played.

For those who couldn't obtain tickets to watch the games in person, Boston fans could follow the World Series, particularly the games in New York, through a variety of ways. Telegraphic re-creations were still popular, with the Boston Theatre advertising "games reproduced exactly as played" for seats priced from 50 to 15 cents. Fans seeking free results could stand among the multitudes on Newspaper Row to hear a man with a megaphone shout details received from the telegraph wire. The telephone was put to use as well. The Boston Electric Show advertised 90 loud-speaking telephones providing World Series information "in clear, distinguishable tones." Fans could access the scores of the games by calling Fort Hill 4500, where a special service was staffed by ten telephone operators to answer calls on 40 telephone lines. The service reportedly received 150 per minute during the games.[8]

By 1912 the Royal Rooters had become a quaint custom given the more sedate audiences that suburban grandstand fans brought to at Fenway Park, since the Rooters were more reflective of the boisterous dedicated Red Sox fans of 1903 vintage. What kept the Rooters in the mix for World Series tickets was one of the group's founders, John Fitzgerald, who was now in his second term as mayor of Boston. The Red Sox obtained some political goodwill by taking care of the Rooters with a few hundred tickets.

A tie in the second game of the World Series (the first game at Fenway Park) caused some ticket confusion, since the third game, planned for New York City, was to be played in Boston because the tie was treated as a rainout as far as the alternating pattern was considered. The second ticket in the three-game block was good for the third game, making the third ticket good for the fifth game (assuming no more tied games). Eventually, the disruption in the ticket pattern erupted into a huge problem when a fourth game was played at Fenway Park.

With the Red Sox ahead in the Series after six games, three games to two with one tie, the Series returned to Fenway Park for the seventh game. Although the Red Sox had publicized the ticket policy for this fourth game in Boston—showing the ticket stub from the fifth game by noon to receive a seventh-game ticket—there was some confusion over whether the Royal Rooters had made arrangements with Red Sox management to pick up their tickets later in the early afternoon. When their tickets were put on sale a few minutes past noon, their entrance into the ballpark caused a near-riot when there was no place for the Rooters to sit. Police on horseback quelled the disturbance between the ticketed patrons and the Rooters who expected those seats. Standing room for the Rooters was eventually found scattered around the ballpark. The apparent snubbing of the fan group resulted in a political firestorm, when Mayor Fitzgerald issued a statement calling for the replacement of the team secretary, who was responsible for ticket sales, with "a Boston man who understands conditions here."[9]

When New York won the seventh game to set up a deciding eighth and final game, the Red Sox won the coin flip for the game to be played in Boston. More ticket confusion ensued, even though the Red Sox used the same stub system as for the seventh game, which resulted in a small crowd (boycotted by the Royal Rooters) to see the Red Sox win the 1912 World Series title. There was a parade the next day, which culminated in a rally at Faneuil Hall. Mayor Fitzgerald took the opportunity at the rally to not only praise the team and the Royal Rooters, but also made a pitch for the many lower-income fans in the city. "I hope the management of baseball in Boston this year will give us a better show in the 50-cent seats next year," Fitzgerald shouted with political verve to the crowd, many of whom were Boston voters. "There is no excuse, not withstanding the splendid management of baseball in Boston, why the people who occupy 50-cent seats should not be better provided for." By using the term "baseball in Boston," Fitzgerald showed his recognition of the many general baseball fans in the city, who were not dedicated to either of the two teams in Boston.[10]

Success in the World Series in the new Fenway Park did not result in an increase in dedicated Red Sox fans, but rather converted many Sox-centric fans to increase the preponderance of general baseball fans. The Boston baseball public was a term used by newspapers quite a lot, rather than "Red Sox fans." The baseball public had transitioned from an Irish-American community to a Boston community, supporting baseball in general in Boston, much like the attitude of the Boston fans in the 1870s and 1880s. At a Winter League dinner in 1913, Hughie Jennings, the manager of the Detroit Tigers, "said some pretty nice things of the Boston baseball public, which he described as one of the fairest, the most sympathetic and the most loyal in the country."[11]

Many frequent spectators at Fenway Park, now cast by history as dedicated Red Sox fans, were, in reality, general baseball fans. John Dooley is a prime example. In a memoir of her father, Elizabeth Dooley wrote that "my father rooted for both Boston teams." Her first baseball memories were "of being taken to both Fenway Park and Braves Field by my father, who enjoyed the status of one who could place his daughter in the secure confines of the press box while making the rounds of friends and players prior to the games." The elder Dooley was typical of the many general baseball fans in Greater Boston at the time.[12]

In 1913 the Red Sox and the Braves initiated an informal cooperative arrangement, basically an unwritten mutual-assistance pact. For the first dozen years of two-team competition in Boston during the twentieth century, there had been an adversarial relationship between the owners of the Nationals and the Americans. This perspective softened a bit after Soden sold the Nationals in 1906, weakened further with two more Braves ownership changes, and then eroded when Taylor sold the Red Sox in 1911.

Cooperative is a good description of this arrangement, which in essence was an industry association for major-league baseball in Boston, albeit consisting of just two companies. The cooperative arrangement involved mutual assistance in working toward a common goal rather than price-fixing or other consumer negatives that are involved in a consortium or cartel. The common goal was a good experience for the baseball public (i.e., general baseball fans that followed both teams) to watch a quality ball game whether it was played at Fenway Park or the South End Grounds. This goal was publicly demonstrated through the side-by-side New Year's Day greetings in 1914 from the two clubs that were published in the newspapers, which addressed the "baseball-loving public of Boston" and "baseball fans of Greater Boston" rather than using competitive prose directing the greeting to their own dedicated fans.[13]

The Winter League club, which had expanded from a small group of fans in 1908 to several hundred by 1913, helped to foster both the cooperative arrangement and the development of general baseball fans. Since the mission of the Winter League was to promote baseball in Boston, there were always a variety of baseball executives at the Winter League dinners. At the dinner in January 1913 were James McAleer (president of the Red Sox) and Herman

The Winter League fan group helped to foster general baseball fans in Boston, who supported both the Red Sox and the Braves. Seated in the front row of this photograph from the January 1913 Winter League dinner are Mike McGreevey (far left, with mustache) and John Dooley (with cigar in hand) seated to his right (Boston Public Library, Print Department, McGreevey Collection).

Nickerson (secretary of the Braves) along with owners of clubs in the New England League and International League, baseball writers from a variety of newspapers, and "100 dyed-in-the-wool fans." Mike McGreevey was the only Royal Rooter listed among the dinner guests, signifying a change in the complexion of Boston baseball fans.[14]

The first manifestation of the informal cooperative arrangement surfaced in February 1913 when the Red Sox agreed to allow the Braves to borrow Fenway Park for their holiday twin bills on Patriots Day and Memorial Day that season to maximize attendance beyond the much smaller capacity of the South End Grounds. According to the *Boston Globe*, the deal "shows the cordial relations existing between the two Boston clubs."[15]

Although the Braves decided not to borrow Fenway Park in 1914 for their holiday games, by August the Braves were playing all their games at Fenway. After being in last place for most of the first half of the 1914 season, the Braves suddenly rose in the National League standings during a very successful road trip in July. In their first game back in Boston on July 25, a swarm of 16,000 members of the "baseball-loving public" surged into the South End Grounds, as "the crowd was the largest seen at the Walpole St. grounds in years." Clearly, the Braves ballpark was not capable of holding all the fans that wanted to watch the Braves chase the pennant. An experiment with the

Saturday, August 1, game played at Fenway Park attracted 20,000 people, the largest crowd to see a National League game in Boston up to that point.

In early August the Red Sox again exercised the cooperative arrangement by offering the Braves the use of Fenway Park, free of charge, for their remaining games of the 1914 season. The new nature of the Boston baseball public was seen at the Labor Day holiday twin bill, which drew a combined 73,000 people to the morning and afternoon games, a record one-day turnout for Boston baseball fans. The turnout exceeded the seating capacity of Fenway Park, as thousands of fans watched the games from behind ropes in the outfield. The Braves established a new seasonal attendance record with 382,000 patrons between their stints in 1914 at the South End Grounds and Fenway Park.[16]

The Braves soon clinched first place in the National League and headed to the World Series to play the Philadelphia Athletics, with the games in Boston to be played at Fenway Park, under a continuation of the informal cooperative arrangement. Coincident with the fervor for cheering both Boston teams, the Royal Rooters showed their stripes as general baseball fans when John Keenan arranged a trip for 300 Rooters (including former mayor John Fitzgerald) to go to Philadelphia for the opening two games of the World Series.

To follow the World Series games in Philadelphia, fans back in Boston had many options in this pre-radio era. There were the same methods as available two years earlier for the 1912 World Series, a mob of people at the bulletin boards on Newspaper Row, the *Boston Globe* telephone line, and telegraphic reproductions at places such as the Boston Arena and Tremont Theatre. In 1914 there was a new option for a live reproduction at the South End Grounds, where 1,000 people watched 18 young men, representing stand-ins for the Braves and Athletics, physically re-create the action in Philadelphia.[17]

After the Braves won the first two games in Philadelphia, more than 35,000 people squeezed into Fenway Park for each game played in Boston. Fans headed to the World Series games at Fenway by using the newly opened subway extension that ended near Governor Square, by getting off at the first above-ground stop at the intersection of Commonwealth Avenue and Beacon Street, and then walking the short distance to Fenway Park. The Hotel Kenmore was built a few years later, which provided additional cachet to the Kenmore term that was increasingly being used to describe the rapidly developing area of Governor Square. The Braves won the third and fourth games to win the World Series in a sweep, as fans celebrated the second championship in three years won by a Boston team.[18]

Braves owner James Gaffney, though, never considered renting Fenway Park permanently. Instead, Gaffney proceeded to build a new ballpark for the Braves, which was conveniently located, for the growing number of general baseball fans, a mile from Fenway Park on the above-ground streetcar line on Commonwealth Avenue that connected to the end of the Boylston Street subway in Governor Square.[19]

Even though the Braves had won the pennant, the Red Sox outdrew the Braves for the 1914 season, as the first term of Mayor James Michael Curley encouraged many Irish-American fans to get out to Fenway Park. However, the World Series victory by the Braves helped to convert many Sox-leaning general baseball fans into more bipartisan general baseball fans (and a few Braves-leaning general fans) as well as increase the number of intermittent fans interested in the Braves. Therefore, Gaffney anticipated an uptick in attendance for Braves games at the new ballpark, which he named Braves Field.

Gaffney designed Braves Field to maximize attendance on Saturday and holidays, which were the best times for suburban fans to get to the ballpark as well as virtually the only times that lower middle-class and working-class fans could attend. For the predominant businessman audience for weekday games, there would be more than enough room for all interested spectators. Seating capacity at Braves Field was around 44,000 people, which was "the largest ballpark ever fitted up" at the time. There were 1,400 box seats, 16,500 seats in the grandstand, 10,000 seats in the first-base pavilion, 9,000 in the third-base pavilion, and 5,000 in the outfield bleachers.[20]

The new ballpark was built into a lot of land that was a natural amphitheater overlooking the Boston & Albany Railroad tracks that hugged the nearby Charles River, with the seating embedded into the hillside and the field laid out in a valley that was 20 feet below Commonwealth Avenue. "As the observer stands on the diamond and gazes up into the vast ocean of seats that swarm around him, he is lost in the immensity of the scene," F.C. Lane described Braves Field in a 1915 *Baseball Magazine* article. "In the grandstand, forty-six rows of seats rise tier on tier, above the triple row of boxes, in the first base section this soars in the farther corner to seventy-six rows. The bewildered fan who undertook to walk from one end of the wide sweeping stand to the other would traverse along the outer edge of the crescent a full quarter of a mile before he reached the last seat on the other side."[21]

The playing field was as immense as the seating area. "Braves Field is certainly a baseball park of magnificent distances," Lane wrote. "No more excuse for the criticism of short right field fences which produce pop home runs, or constituting barriers that prevent a hit from traveling its allotted distance, before rebounding into the pursuing fielder's hands." With a distance of 375 feet from home plate to the right-field and left-field fences along the foul lines, and more than 500 feet to center field, there was little concern about the hitting of home runs. Actually, it was considered a positive in 1915 that Braves Field was a place "on which you can play an absolutely fair game

The Braves won the 1914 World Series, following the Red Sox championship in 1912, to solidify the base of general baseball fans who followed both Boston teams. In the foreground, catcher Hank Gowdy (left) sits with pitcher Lefty Tyler (middle) and outfielder Joe Connolly behind the batting-practice cage (Library of Congress, Prints and Photographs Division, LC-DIG-ggbain-17527).

of ball without interference of fences." The love of "inside baseball" soon changed among Boston baseball fans, as the result of an occurrence at Fenway Park in June 1915, two months before the opening of Braves Field.[22]

In the second inning of a game on June 25 at Fenway Park, Red Sox rookie pitcher Babe Ruth hit a home run over the fence fronting the bleachers in right-center field, a distance of more than 400 feet. Ruth's homer stunned the crowd, since it was only the second time that a batted ball had ever cleared that fence at Fenway. It was the Babe's third homer of the 1915 season (the other two were hit in road games), but more importantly the blast signaled the beginning of a new era in how baseball would be played, what motivated fans to follow baseball, and which of the two teams in Boston would most interest fans. Since the skill of playing baseball still ruled the day in 1915, Ruth remained a pitcher for the time being, and a dominating pitcher at that. One footnote to this game was that it was doubleheader that started at 1:30 "to give the out-of-town people plenty of time to return for their evening meals."[23]

As Braves Field was being built, both teams played at Fenway Park during the 1915 season. This helped to perpetuate the concept of general baseball fans in Boston, which was reinforced by the increasing number of suburban fans, who represented as much as two-thirds of the audience at the ballpark in 1915, especially at a Saturday game. At one game late in 1914, "besides the local fans, there were a couple of thousand from Springfield and Windsor Locks Conn. on hand."[24]

To encourage attendance at Braves Field by suburban fans arriving by train at North Station or South Station, Gaffney worked with the Boston Elevated Railway Company to build a spur line off the main streetcar line on Commonwealth Avenue to go into a fenced-in area of the ballpark, for easier entrance and exit by fans to streetcar transportation. He also planned to work with the Boston & Albany Railroad to build a station behind the outfield fences, which would be an easier approach for fans from the western suburbs than the nearby Cottage Farm train station. Gaffney also reserved the vacant land abutting Commonwealth Avenue in front of the ballpark for automobile parking, which had enough room for 400 vehicles.

The great irony about the streetcar and railroad connections was that Braves Field was located on a stretch of Commonwealth Avenue known as Automobile Row. Numerous automobile dealerships spanned from the Peerless dealer in Governor Square (intersection of Commonwealth and Beacon Street) to the Packard dealer at Packard's Corner (intersection of Commonwealth and Brighton Avenue). Soon, there was a Ford dealer, Burnett & Sherman, across the street from Braves Field.[25]

Automobile ownership in Massachusetts had tripled since 1910, growing from 30,000 registered vehicles to 90,000 by 1915, the result of the assembly-line production technique. The automobile was fast becoming the preferred mode of suburban transportation to the ballpark. However, the 400-vehicle parking lot at Braves Field was woefully inadequate to handle the influx of suburban drivers, which was compounded by the meager on-street parking along the residential streets of suburban Brookline on the other side of Commonwealth Avenue.[26]

With 3,000 automobiles reportedly descending upon Braves Field for the first game played there in mid–August 1915, there was a "wonderful horde of 46,000 baseball fans" at the opening game, most arriving via streetcar. Mel Webb of the *Boston Globe* wrote that "it was a crowd that stands as a thrilling tribute to the popularity of baseball and to the loyalty of Boston and New England," or with greater hyperbole, a "crowd of crowds, and, indeed, it fittingly dedicated the park of parks." If not for the 14,000 guests (only 32,000 paid their way in), the additional 6,000 fans milling outside the ballpark, who were shut out at the ticket window, would not have caused the massive congestion of mayors arriving from cities all over Massachusetts and thousands of suburban fans arriving by train and automobile from their homes and offices dozens of miles from Braves Field.[27]

While the Red Sox won American League pennant in 1915, the Braves also challenged for the National League pennant. The twin pennant contenders encouraged general baseball fans to attend ball games at both of the city's ballparks late in the season. Nearly one million fans (915,000) watched both teams in 1915, which established a new high for the combined attendance of both Boston teams. Casual observers often wondered how thousands of men "find it possible to get away from their daily work" and "manage afternoon after afternoon to rush for the [street]car lines to go out to see their ball club." Attending a game was more than just the interest of the general baseball fan, as it was also a way to support the Boston business community.[28]

The excitement over a possible streetcar World Series changed the general temperament of the crowds. "Boston crowds have always been very polite and seemed as anxious to applaud good plays by the visitors as much as if made by the home players," Albert Mitchell of the *Boston American* wrote in September 1915. However, when Detroit played the Red Sox that month, the crowd booed Ty Cobb at each at-bat. Mitchell blamed the impropriety on the Royal Rooters, who made a rare in-season appearance with their boisterous, irreverent rooting in an exception to their having "always reserved their energies for the World Series."[29]

Under the informal cooperative arrangement between the two baseball clubs, the World Series was played at Braves Field in 1915, against the National League champion Philadelphia Phillies. In addition to the grandstand as reserved seats, the Red Sox also used the first-base pavilion for reserved seating, increasing the ticket pre-sale to 24,500 seats for each game; another 14,000 tickets were available on the day of the game for the third-base pavilion and outfield bleachers. In addition to the vast number of fans seeking tickets on the day of the game, the number of automobiles being driven to the game contributed to a massive traffic jam in front of Braves Field, which had only one entrance into the ballpark. After the available parking lots in the vicinity were filled, "the motorists simply parked along the curbs and the [street]car tracks for a mile down Commonwealth Avenue." Even though the thoroughfare was turned into a one-way road after the end of the game, the parked automobiles inhibited an easy exit for most patrons at the game, whether they came by automobile or trolley.[30]

Fans could follow the World Series games played in Philadelphia in 1915 through the usual ways of the time, electric scoreboards indoors at the Boston Arena and Tremont Theatre, outdoor bulletin boards at both Fenway Park and Braves Field, or milling around for free on Newspaper Row to hear score updates. For fans aboard ships in the Atlantic Ocean, there were now wireless reports, in the first vestige of radio broadcasts of baseball games.[31]

After the Red Sox won the 1915 World Series for the city's third cham-

Early arriving baseball fans, wearing straw hats in the warm weather, sit in the expensive seats and watch Red Sox catcher–manager Bill Carrigan (front) observe the pre-game activity on the field. Carrigan managed the Red Sox to World Series titles in 1915 and 1916 (Library of Congress, Prints and Photographs Division, LC-DIG-ggbain-22679).

pionship in four years, the continuing war in Europe (to be dubbed World War I) weighed heavily on Boston businessmen in 1916. Attendance at Saturday games in 1916 remained robust, but for the ball games played on Monday through Friday the two new ballparks in Boston began to be relatively empty much of the time. Additional Ladies Day promotions were conducted at Fenway Park, but were prohibited at Braves Field by National League rule.[32]

Doubleheaders proliferated in 1916 due to a very wet spring, "the deadliest rain baseball ever experienced," since the precipitation "fell in continuous blocks, knocking out games in a heap, thus necessitating a swarm of doubleheaders later on and completely killing the attendance." In addition, on days when games were actually played, all too often "the dark gray sky and low-hanging clouds kept away the people." While the Red Sox played ten doubleheaders at Fenway Park during the 1916 season (representing one-quarter of their home games), the Braves staged 17 doubleheaders, or nearly 45 percent of their home-game schedule.[33]

On September 4, 1916, both the Braves and the Red Sox were in first place in their respective leagues, setting up another potential streetcar World Series. However, the Braves faded down the stretch, while the Red Sox forged ahead to snag their second consecutive pennant and went on to win the team's third World Series title in five years and the city of Boston's fourth World Series title in five years. It was a great time to be a general baseball fan in Boston, with two highly competitive teams to follow.

Fan interest in Boston was bolstered by the winning teams, interesting ballplayers (if not star quality), and new ballparks. The Red Sox had just won consecutive World Series with strong pitching, speed, and defense. What more could a discerning general baseball fan in Boston want? That answer came to fruition in the very near future as power hitting supplanted small-ball as a prime motivator for baseball fans.

◆ 8 ◆

Home Runs Convert Fans

After the Red Sox fell short of a third consecutive pennant in 1917, the entry of the United States into World War I began to depopulate the roster of both the Red Sox and the Braves. In particular, the Red Sox lost half a dozen ballplayers when they enlisted in the military service and began serving their duty (including on the baseball team) at local bases such as the Charlestown Navy Yard.

There was also a reduction in the population of baseball fans in Boston, as many young men entered the service, either voluntarily or via the draft, and were no longer in the Boston area to attend ball games or even read the scores in the local newspapers. The war altered the baseball landscape in Boston, since many baseball followers were preoccupied with the war and had less time to devote to the fortunes of the two local baseball teams.

Influenced by the war being waged in Europe, the Massachusetts legislature passed a law in April 1918 to permit men serving in the Army and Navy to play baseball on Sunday. This first Sunday baseball law in Massachusetts restricted ball games to the five hours between 1:00 and 6:00 in the afternoon, in order to not disrupt church services in the morning or evening, and expressly prohibited an admission charge.[1]

Sunday baseball as played by servicemen at Braves Field was wildly popular among Boston baseball fans. In the first game played on April 28, the 302d Regiment of the Army infantry defeated Commonwealth Pier, representing the Navy, before an audience of 25,000 people. Jim O'Leary of the *Boston Globe* remarked that "the size of the crowd was significant of the interest in baseball and the popularity of Sunday games." The second game played on May 5 between the Charlestown Navy Yard and Camp Devens attracted 40,000 spectators, a larger crowd since five former Red Sox players and two previously with the Braves played for the Navy Yard. Subsequent Sunday games were viewed by audiences of 25,000 to 30,000 people.[2]

Red Sox owner Harry Frazee, in what he must have felt was the spirit of the law, scheduled a Red Cross benefit game for Sunday, May 26, by moving up the game with the White Sox scheduled for Monday, May 27. Frazee believed playing the game on Sunday would attract $50,000 more for the Red Cross. The state police and the Boston Public Safety Committee gave the Red Sox licenses to play the game that Sunday. However, when the Boston police commissioner voiced the opinion that the game would be in open violation of the Sunday law, Frazee backed off and restored the Monday game.[3]

More people went to Braves Field in 1918 for the free Sunday games played by servicemen than paid to watch the Braves play there on Monday through Saturday. The paltry 82,000 total attendance for the Braves during the 1918 season was the lowest level for either Boston baseball club during the twentieth century. Part of the reason for the five-figure attendance, though, was that the Braves lost their September homestand when the season was prematurely halted on Labor Day due to the war.

In May the federal government had proclaimed that baseball was a non-essential industry and proceeded to issue a "work or fight" order that by July ballplayers must either join the military or work in a defense-industry job. Major-league baseball managed to convince the government to extend the baseball season to mid–September before its shutdown, about a month earlier than planned. The 1918 season concluded on Labor Day and the World Series began a few days later.

With such uncertainty in the completion of the season, fan interest waned in Boston. To put some fans in the stands, the Braves gave free admission on Mondays to soldiers and sailors in uniform; on and after July 24, servicemen were admitted free for any game. The Braves also took the unprecedented step of playing a two-for-one doubleheader on the Labor Day holiday, rather than play the traditional morning and afternoon separate-admission games.[4]

Since the country observed War Time in 1918 to maximize the use of daylight, by setting clocks forward one hour, ball games could be played later into the evening during the summer months. The Braves experimented with a twilight game on July 1, hoping to attract workers who couldn't make it to a 3:00 game, but attracted only 1,500 spectators (including servicemen) to the 6:00 game. O'Leary at the Boston Globe observed that "everybody concerned was anxious to get to the dinner table," and aptly concluded that "twilight games are not likely to become a fixture."[5]

Even as the Red Sox charged ahead in 1918 to a third pennant in four years, attendance was flat at Fenway Park, even with the emergence of Babe Ruth as a formidable pitcher–hitter combination. Ruth took a regular turn on the mound as pitcher and played in the field at first base or left field on the other days. But it was not just normal singles and doubles that Ruth produced with his bat that made him a gate attraction; rather it was his prodigious swing that sent the ball over the fence for a home run that intrigued baseball fans in Boston. "Babe Ruth will outshine all stars of baseball as an attraction if he keeps up this home run habit," one sportswriter remarked. "When a man hits three in successive games and comes back and makes it four [games] in a row another time, he has accomplished an unheard-of stunt."[6]

Ruth hit 11 home runs during the 1918 season to lead the league, but none were hit at Fenway Park. Actually, Ruth did hit one ball over the right-field fence at Fenway, in the bottom of the tenth inning on July 8. "The crowd yelled loudly and long for a home run," the *Boston Herald* reported. "Babe took his stance, made his bid on the very first pitch, a curve ball, and zowee how it traveled ... up into the realm of eagles, high and higher, far and farther." However, under the rules of the day, it was scored only as a triple, since the game was considered ended when the baserunner on first base crossed home plate, leaving Ruth at third base.[7]

Due to wartime travel restrictions, the World Series was scheduled to be played with the first three games in Chicago, with the remaining games as necessary in Boston. There was no frenzy to buy tickets for the wartime World Series. The Royal Rooters, under the leadership of John Keenan, tried to mobilize an excursion to Chicago, and failing at that, attempted to arrange a group outing at Fenway. The little newspaper publicity afforded the Rooters signified their dwindling influence on Boston baseball. Only 15,000 spectators were at Fenway Park to watch the Red Sox win the sixth game to capture their fourth World Series championship in seven years. No one had the slightest inkling that the next championship would not occur for another 86 years.[8]

After Armistice Day in November 1918, the Red Sox and Braves prepared for the postwar 1919 season. Sunday baseball could now be played in six of the eight American League cities—all except Boston and Philadelphia—after the New York legislature passed a Sunday baseball law in April 1919. In the National League, Sunday baseball was legal in five of the eight cities, the same two exceptions as in the American League plus Pittsburgh.

"Does any sane man mean to tell me that the people of Chicago, St. Louis, and Cincinnati are any worse than those of ... Boston and Philadelphia because they sanction Sunday baseball?" Charles Murphy wrote that spring in *Baseball Magazine*. "Is any moral question involved? No. I say the citizens of Chicago, St. Louis, and Cincinnati are simply a great many steps ahead of their eastern brethren in regard to the doctrine of human rights. No wonder there is a feeling of unrest among the workers of this country. The poor fellow who works hard all week to support his family is denied the most innocent forms of amusement on Sunday."[9]

Without the ability to play Sunday baseball in Boston, Saturday continued to be the best-drawing day on the baseball calendar at Fenway Park. This was the day when many intermittent fans within the lower middle class had a respite from work and could travel to the ballpark to watch Ruth, rather than merely read about him in the newspaper. For example, on Saturday, August 2, the *Boston Globe* called the 31,000 people (5,000 above seating capacity) who watched the Red Sox battle the pennant-bound White Sox "a crowd of World Series dimensions." Police ordered the entrance gates locked when "the grandstand became filled to every inch of available standing room," the pavilion and bleachers were packed, and "right and center fields were roped off, so that thousands found comfortable seats on the turf."[10]

Ruth hit 29 home runs for the Red Sox in 1919 to establish a new major-league record. While only nine of his homers occurred at Fenway, Ruth's pursuit of the home-run record drew fans to Fenway for the chance to see him chase that record by hitting another home run. "For perhaps the first time in baseball history, fans, en masse, were not so much rooting for a team, and following the score, but rooting for an individual player," Glenn Stout observed in his book *The Selling of the Babe: The Deal That Changed Baseball and Created a Legend.* Newspapers described "damn near every swing in excruciating detail." This created a new fan motivation in Boston. It was not just following a star player, but following that player's pursuit of an important milestone in baseball history.[11]

The Babe was particularly rewarding to the droves of Ruth-watching spectators at Fenway Park on Saturdays in 1919. For example, on Saturday, July 5, Ruth hit two home runs (his eighth and ninth of the season) against the Philadelphia Athletics, the first being "a line drive into the right field bleachers," while for the second blast, "just to show his versatility, he bumped one over the scoreboard in left field." Over the next two months, fans followed Ruth as he broke the American League record of 14 homers and the modern major-league record of 24 homers. When sportswriters dug up the mark of 27 homers hit by Ed Williamson in 1884 (most over a right-field fence in Chicago that was not very distant from home plate), Ruth took aim at that record too. He delivered for Boston fans by tying that record at Fenway Park on Saturday, September 20 at Babe Ruth Day, when "every one of the 31,000 fans came out there to see the big fellow add to his record string of home runs."[12]

"He was the talk of baseball. He had a home run in every park in the American League, including the longest home runs ever seen in New York, Detroit, St. Louis, and Boston," Leigh Montville wrote in his book *The Big Bam: The Life and Times of Babe Ruth.* "Fan mail arrived in such piles that he now asked teammates and the Red Sox front office to handle it. He had opened the window to the future of the game while playing for a sad sixth-place team." However, while attendance doubled in most American League

Babe Ruth, with his prodigious home runs, changed the dynamics of Boston baseball fans, since many fans soon favored the power-hitting American League style of play over the less exciting small-ball style of the National League (Library of Congress, Prints and Photographs Division, LC-DIG-npcc-00316).

ballparks due to the postwar euphoria for baseball, attendance was disappointing at Fenway Park. "Despite his home run record, Ruth wasn't worth as much at the gate in Boston as [was] a winning team."[13]

The traditional baseball public in Boston, the general baseball fan that followed both teams with relatively equal fervor, was not impressed with home runs. They stopped going to Fenway Park in 1919. In their place were the new general baseball fans, many of whom leaned to the Red Sox and were less enthusiastic about the Braves. Dedicated fans were also minted in larger numbers during the 1919 season, who only rooted for the Red Sox. They liked the American League style of play.

Ruth's home-run barrage in 1919 established another new Boston baseball fan motivation, the league style of play. The American League became known for power hitting and the long ball (i.e., home runs), which led to high scores, while the National League became synonymous with superb pitching and small-ball production of runs, which led to low scores.

Small ball at its best was a pitcher's duel, ending 1–0, in which the one run was scored via a walk, stolen base, ground out that advanced the runner, and a squeeze bunt. Batting average was considered the best measure of a ballplayer's talent; a home run was almost a mistake. During the Deadball Era from 1901 to 1919, "Small-ball strategies were at their apex," according to author James Szalontai, author of *Small Ball in the Big Leagues*, and "were ubiquitous throughout the major leagues as a quick, intelligent style of play was showcased." The inside baseball displayed through small ball was intelligent, but it could be quite boring to watch.[14]

Boston had the perfect dichotomy, the antithesis of excitement in a 26-inning 0–0 tie that was played at Braves Field in 1920, compared with the hitting of Ruth who excited fans with his home runs in 1919.

In a world that was moving faster, the long ball was the perfect answer. "Baseball was keeping up with the times and evolving from a game in which victory was wrung out like a snake coiled around a rat, a slow squeeze of defeat, to a sudden strike," Stout wrote in *The Selling of the Babe*. "It wasn't trench warfare anymore; it was a revolution. The air force had been called in and Ruth, the deadliest of the aces, was leading the way by showing the awesome power contained in the home run, dropping bombs into the crowd."[15]

When they hear the crack of the bat and see the ball arch toward the outfield, "Fans often jump to their feet en masse when a slugger crushes a ball," David Vincent wrote in *Home Run: The Definitive History of Baseball's Ultimate Weapon*. "Sometimes it seems as if all the air is sucked out of the ballpark by the collective intake of thousands of breaths as animated people watch the flight of the ball. This is followed by an immediate expelling of all the air accompanied by amazed shouts that are either joyous or sad, depending on the rooting preference of the person." Fans may have appreciated, but were not awestruck, by the hit-and-run plays and squeeze bunts of small ball. But fans were enamored by fly balls that approached the outfield fences.[16]

In deciding to sell Ruth, Frazee had accurately analyzed the past, but did not adequately see the future. "What the Boston fans want, I take it, and I want because they want it, is a winning team, rather than a one-man team which finishes in sixth place," he told sportswriters when the sale of Ruth was announced in January 1920. Frazee wanted to stay with the past, giving his audience small ball through a winning team. However, the future was the long ball, since Ruth was transforming the game of baseball.[17]

Boys playing baseball on the sandlot "didn't imagine themselves to be Ty Cobb or Joe Jackson, slashing out singles and committing acts of daring on the bases. They were Babe Ruth, grabbing the bat at the end and swinging for all it was worth." The impact to the sport would be dramatic. "Transformative is simply not a strong enough word," Stout wrote. "Ruth didn't transform the sport; he remade itself in his image." The home run soon became a metaphor for success in business, entertainment, and life.[18]

Frazee's thought process was that the Babe didn't produced sufficient attendance, wanted more money (by renegotiating his existing three-year contract), and had turned "petulant," a nice way to say he was difficult to deal with. Perhaps worst of all, he led a less than ideal middle-class lifestyle. "Ruth liked his food, his booze, and his women," Michael Lynch wrote in his book *Harry Frazee, Ban Johnson and the Feud That Nearly Destroyed the American League.* "He was a philanderer of the highest order, picking up prostitutes on a regular basis and maintaining an apartment in Boston where he could entertain his lady 'friends.' Meanwhile, his wife lived on their Sudbury, Massachusetts, farm." From Frazee's perspective, the downside greatly exceeded the upside. Ruth had to go.[19]

Frazee found a ready taker in Jacob Ruppert, who owned the New York Yankees. The sale was announced on January 6, 1920, Ruth to New York for $100,000 ($25,000 in cash, with three notes for $25,000 payable over the next three years). Ten months later came a $300,000 loan in exchange for a mortgage on Fenway Park. Lynch in *Harry Frazee* called the transaction "the most misunderstood deal of the century," since it had absolutely nothing to do with funding the play *No, No, Nanette,* which Frazee didn't produce until 1923. The Yankees were willing to pay a great deal to obtain Ruth because he was a far more valuable ballplayer to produce attendance in New York than in Boston, since the Yankees could play Sunday baseball under the legislation passed in New York in 1919. Frazee remained shackled by the prohibition on Sunday baseball under Massachusetts law.[20]

For Boston fans, there was some progress on the Sunday baseball front in April 1920, when the Massachusetts legislature finally consented to allow amateurs to play Sunday sports. The ball games needed to take place between 2:00 and 6:00 in the afternoon, with no charge for admission, and with participants "that are not promised and do not receive, directly or indirectly, any pecuniary reward." Permitted sports and games could not take place within 1000 feet of a church. Perhaps most importantly, the law was subject to local option, where each community could decide for itself whether to allow the permitted sports and games on Sunday. Both provisions helped the measure finally break through the Puritan wall of Sunday sports prohibition. In 1920, baseball could finally be played on Sunday in Boston—by unpaid players at least.[21]

The bill's proponents had ensured that religious backing of the bill attended the hearing. The Rev. E.D. Robinson of Holyoke told the Senate hearing, "I'd like to know if it is holier to stand on the street corner Sunday afternoon, criticize the people who are passing and spit tobacco juice, than to take part in a good healthy game of baseball." Opposition also spoke at the hearing. The Rev. Martin Kneeland of the Lord's Day League "protested that Sunday baseball would lower the Sunday ideals of the community."[22]

The Boston fans did not forget Babe Ruth, who, now in a New York Yankees uniform, hit 54 home runs during the 1920 season. Twenty thousand fans packed Fenway Park for the games the Yankees played in Boston in April and May, while, on September 4 for another Babe Ruth Day, 33,000 overfilled Fenway Park.

However, the exportation of Ruth to New York eventually alienated Boston baseball fans, who abandoned Fenway Park after the 1920 season. They returned for the most part only when the Yankees were in town, especially on a Saturday, to see Ruth swing for the fences. The trade of Ruth to the Yankees changed the Boston baseball landscape to enable the Braves to better compete with the Red Sox for baseball fans. Over the next ten years, though, fans had to endure two bad baseball teams.

◆ *9* ◆

Radio Broadcasts
and the Vote
on Sunday Baseball

During the early 1920s both the Red Sox and the Braves were perpetually at or near the bottom of their league's standings. After another change in ownership in both clubs during 1923, the Braves finally mustered a sustained period where the Braves had an edge over the Red Sox among Boston baseball fans after two decades as second banana in the two-team city. While this edge was often in developments off the field, the Braves did have a substantial box-office superiority for several years.

In 1921 the Braves outdrew the Red Sox for the first time since the two teams began sharing the Boston baseball public in 1901, when 318,000 spectators went to Braves Field in contrast to the 279,000 tabulated at Fenway Park. With the Braves in third place in the National League standings for much of the summer, large crowds went to Braves Field to watch the pennant contender, highlighted by the 40,000 who witnessed the July 23 doubleheader against Pittsburgh. At the time this was the largest regular-season crowd for a baseball game in Boston.

The fourth-place finish by the Braves in 1921 was the beginning of a 13-year stretch where the Braves, for the only time in the twentieth century, had an edge over the Red Sox. If not for the Babe Ruth effect that put fans in the seats at Fenway Park to watch the Yankees slugger, the Braves' edge would have been more dominant. When the Braves reverted to their losing ways in 1922, the 1921 attendance advantage might have been simply a blip on the radar screen had both clubs not changed ownership in 1923. The Braves were acquired in February 1923 by Emil Fuchs, a New York lawyer known in Boston as Judge Fuchs, while the Red Sox were bought in July 1923 by a group headed by Bob Quinn, former business manager of the St. Louis Browns.

By 1923, there were lots of empty seats at both Braves Field and Fenway Park during weekday afternoons, as many of the general baseball fans had lost interest in major-league baseball in Boston. Interest waned since both teams were not all that good on the field, but also because of the changing nature of the potential audience.

Business had changed in the Greater Boston area. While the middle class had grown in numbers, they now worked less as self-employed owners of small businesses and more as salaried workers in chain-store and corporate facilities. Many companies had also relocated from Boston to the inner suburbs, due to the advent of motorized trucks, which "was dispersing the residential patterns beyond the area of economic activity," i.e., downtown Boston. This resulted in fewer people that had the means and time flexibility to attend an afternoon baseball game in the city.[1]

Among ballpark spectators in general, there were fewer Bostonians and more suburbanites, as the population growth in the city had stagnated while the growth of the suburbs was exploding. The first ring of suburbs grew at close to a 25 percent rate during the 1920s (particularly the towns of Medford and Everett) and nearly 40 percent in the second ring (notably Arlington and Belmont), as "emerging middle class families sought to display their status by purchasing an attractive single-family home."[2]

Compounding these suburban trends was the continuing popularity of the automobile, which was quickly supplanting public transportation (streetcar and rail) as the primary means for baseball fans to get to Braves Field and Fenway Park. Automobile ownership in Massachusetts doubled between 1919 and 1923 to reach 400,000 cars, and would nearly double again between 1923 and 1930 to 750,000 vehicles. Not only did the automobile stifle demand for public transportation, but public road construction to adequately handle vehicular traffic did not move forward at nearly the same pace as the number of cars on the inadequate roads.[3]

Traveling by automobile from the suburbs to either Boston ballpark was no easy task, since drivers needed to negotiate traffic-filled narrow streets because traffic-friendly highways into Boston were many years into the future. Suburban drivers could use the new numbered routes leading into Boston, which the state first implemented in 1922, such as Route 28, although these roads were no more than just wide streets. To provide for speedier travel by automobile into the city, a few suburban thoroughfares were constructed by 1927, the Northern Artery from Medford to Cambridge and the Southern Artery from Quincy to Dorchester. However, drivers still needed to negotiate congested city streets within Boston proper to reach either Braves Field or Fenway Park. Once drivers reached the ballpark, though, parking was extremely limited.

The rapid growth of automobile ownership in Massachusetts quickly supplanted public transportation (streetcar and rail) as the primary means for baseball fans to get to Braves Field and Fenway Park, which had been built for public streetcar access (Library of Congress, Prints and Photographs Division, LC-USZ62–46286).

Perhaps more important than the obstacles posed by Greater Boston roadways was the changing nature of how amusements were consumed by residents of Massachusetts. The automobile was a private approach to personal amusement, as exemplified by the classic Sunday drive as a leisure activity for relaxation. Before World War I, adult amusement activities were all staged in public venues such as ballparks, theaters, amusement parks, and the beach, but by the 1920s "more and more Americans were beginning to entertain themselves at home, with radio and phonograph." The automobile accelerated the movement of leisure away from public venues to private ones. As Cotton Seiler observed in *Republic of Drivers: A Cultural History of Automobility in America*, the automobile was not merely a tangible vehicle for transportation but also an metaphorical intangible vehicle for "the affirmation of self" that fostered a renewed sense of the "sovereign self of the republican past," i.e., the independence of the open road.[4]

The rise of the middle class in the suburbs, in conjunction with the consequent middle-class decline in the Boston neighborhoods, increased demand for Saturday games, and the shift from self-employment to corporate jobs lessened demand for games Monday through Friday. With the legal inability to conduct Sunday games using professional ballplayers in Massachusetts, major-league baseball in Boston during the 1920s was mostly a Saturday-only affair. Saturday games generated, by far, the largest attendance. Two-for-one doubleheaders during the week were the next-best draw. Signaling the waning interest among general baseball fans, the once-hallowed holiday twin bill of separate-admission morning and afternoon games became obsolete in Boston. By 1924, both teams conducted single-admission doubleheaders on the Memorial Day, Bunker Hill Day, Independence Day, and Labor Day holidays. Only the Patriots Day twin bill on April 19 remained a separate-admission staple on the Boston baseball calendar, since the Boston Marathon passed nearby during the intermission between the morning and afternoon games.[5]

Braves president Fuchs attacked this dependence on Saturdays, holidays, and doubleheaders by offering a number of promotions to entice baseball fans to the ballpark for a single game staged on Monday through Friday. Although his team couldn't play baseball at Braves Field on Sunday, he could open the ballpark for free movie nights on Sunday evening to indirectly develop interest in baseball. He rededicated the club to having regular Ladies Day promotions, and extended that to fraternal-group days (like Elks Day), to prop up flagging weekday attendance. His most famous promotion was the Knot Hole Gang, which populated the often empty third-base pavilion seats with boys who would grow up to be men that were likely to be dedicated Braves fans. This program was hatched in 1925 in conjunction with a number of area youth organizations to allow free admission to boys aged ten to 16 who were card-carrying members of organizations like the Boy Scouts and Roxbury Boys Club and who took a pledge to not skip school for a ball game, use clean language, and be a fair sportsman at the ballpark by not calling an umpire "a bonehead, blind man, robber, or thief."[6]

Fuchs also tackled the Sunday baseball issue head on. He had seen the success of Sunday baseball in New York City. Sunday baseball was the reason why the Yankees were willing to pay so much to acquire Babe Ruth from the Red Sox in 1920 and then build Yankee Stadium in 1923. Before purchasing the Braves, Fuchs, an astute lawyer, likely examined the 1920 law passed by the Massachusetts legislature that not only restricted Sunday baseball to amateur players but also limited games to a four-hour window (2:00 to 6:00 in the afternoon), provided for adoption by local option, and precluded ball games with 1000 feet of a church. By duplicating the terms of the 1920 law to apply to a new law for professional baseball, Fuchs knew the Braves would have a monopoly on Sunday baseball in Boston, since there were no churches within 1,000 feet of Braves Field but there was one church within that distance of Fenway Park. The Church of the Disciples was located 800 feet from Fenway Park.

Rather than go the normal legislative route, which appeared to be a fruitless venture, Fuchs sought another legal route. Amendments to the state constitution in 1918 permitted initiative petitions. With enough voter signatures on a petition, Fuchs could get a proposed law on the ballot for a voter referendum even if the legislature disapproved of the matter. In October 1923, a petition was filed with the Attorney General of Massachusetts to start the ball rolling to put the matter of professional Sunday baseball to the voters. Stephen Littleton filed the petition, on behalf of the Braves, in an attempt to keep the Braves out of the public eye on the issue. Once the Attorney General approved the petition as to form, 20,000 signatures had to be filed with the Secretary of State. When enough signatures were obtained, the legislature was required to consider the issue. If the legislature failed to enact the proposed law, another 5,000 signatures on petitions would then place the issue on the state ballot.[7]

When enough signatures couldn't be obtained in the fall of 1923, the Braves enlisted Fred Doe, an icon among local baseball followers for his work with young players and a long-time player and manager in the local minor leagues, to take up the banner for the professional Sunday baseball cause. Doe symbolized the benefit that young people would get by attending professional and semi-pro baseball games on Sunday. Proponents also hoped that Doe's leadership would minimize the focus on the reality that the Braves might make a few dollars from expected large crowds at Sunday games in Braves Field. In September 1924 Doe delivered petitions containing 20,000 signatures to satisfy the first requirement to get a voter referendum on the state ballot.[8]

In February 1925, the Massachusetts legislature held hearings on the proposed Sunday baseball bill. Even though it had been nearly five years since the amateur Sunday sports bill had become law, its opponents hadn't forgotten how that bill come to be. The Rev. A.Z. Conrad spoke for the opposition: "I have been at hearings on amateur Sunday sports and heard these same men lift their hands and swear to Heaven they never would desecrate the Sabbath by charging admissions to a ball game. How they have the gall to come now and ask for admissions is beyond me." Arguments from the proponents that the bill would benefit workers who labored six days a week fell on deaf legislative ears.[9]

After the conservative Republican-dominated legislature overwhelmingly voted against the Sunday sports bill, the Braves focused on the 1926 state election to get the issue of professional Sunday baseball before Massachusetts voters. In August 1925, Doe filed petitions with 17,000 signatures with the Secretary of State, far more than the 5,000 required to put the issue on the November 1926 ballot. "The question of whether professional baseball games may be played on Sundays in Massachusetts will be on the ballot for approval or rejection by voters at the 1926 election," the *Boston Post* reported.[10]

In addition to bankrolling the effort to change the Sunday baseball law, the Braves also initiated an annual preseason city series with the Red Sox. The preseason games helped to generate enthusiasm among general baseball fans to attend games during the regular season. Before a crowd of 15,000 fans at Braves Field on Saturday, April 11, 1925, the Braves and Red Sox played each other in Boston for the first time in more than a decade.

The most forward-thinking promotion introduced by Fuchs was the radio broadcast of Braves games. During the summer of 1925, radio accounts of ball games from Braves Field were periodically broadcast by the WNAC radio station, which was owned by department-store executive John Shepard III. Except for the Chicago Cubs, most major-league clubs were fundamentally opposed to radio broadcasts, since they believed radio would dissuade people from going to the ballpark and thus damage the business model that was virtually completely dependent on ballpark attendance. Rather than giving away the game for free, Cubs president William Wrigley (of chewing gum fame) understood the power of advertising, and thus saw how radio broadcasts could attract new baseball fans. Fuchs was convinced that such a strategy could also work in Boston.

The radio broadcasts served a dual purpose for Fuchs. They helped to expand interest in the Braves within the growing suburbs of Greater Boston, particularly among women and children, to reach a new segment of potential baseball fans. More importantly, the broadcasts created interest in the Sunday baseball issue expected to be on the ballot in 1926. Because women now could vote in elections in Massachusetts (due to the Nineteenth Amendment to the U.S. Constitution in 1920), female listeners to the radio were an important component to the passage of the Sunday baseball voter referendum.

The very first live radio broadcast of a Braves game occurred on April 14, 1925, when WBZ broadcast the season-opener from Braves Field. However, not many people heard that first broadcast of a major-league game in Boston. At the time WBZ was located in Springfield, Massachusetts, 100 miles west of Boston, before the station moved to Boston a few years later.[11]

By July 1925, Fuchs had teamed up with Shepard to have five games broadcast from Braves Field on WNAC. The station at the time was housed on the fourth floor of the Shepard Department Store in downtown Boston, which Shepard had established in 1922 as a way to draw shoppers into the store. It was the beginning of two-decade partnership with WNAC to engage radio listeners with baseball. The first WNAC broadcast was the July 8 game against the St. Louis Cardinals, with Ben Alexander, of the Boston Chamber

Radio broadcasts of baseball games, initiated by the Braves in 1925 and 1926, expanded interest in the Braves among women and children living in the suburbs of Greater Boston. Radio sets were then rudimentary, as shown in this photograph, but female listeners were important to the passage of the Sunday baseball voter referendum in 1928 (Library of Congress, Prints and Photographs Division, LC-USZ62–35068).

of Commerce, at the microphone. Charles Donelan, a local cartoonist who drew sports cartoons for several Boston newspapers, did the July 20 and later broadcasts that year.[12]

The Braves had an advantage over the Red Sox when it came to radio broadcasts in 1925 and 1926, since the National League permitted them during those years while the American League prohibited them (except for season-opening games). In 1926 the Red Sox did allow WNAC to broadcast the first game at Fenway Park on April 13, with Gus Rooney, a Boston sportswriter, at the microphone. But that was it for radio broadcasts from Fenway Park that year. The Braves accelerated the radio experiment by allowing WNAC to broadcast a larger number of games in 1926 than the original five in 1925. Shepard probably used a variety of local writers and radio hosts to man the microphone at Braves Field for these periodic broadcasts, as no broadcasters were named in the radio listings published in the newspaper.[13]

Radio moved entertainment further away from public venues, as people during the 1920s increasingly began to "consume a significant portion of their entertainment within the household rather than in public spaces," according to Richard Butsch, author of *The Making of American Audiences: From Stage to Television, 1750–1990*. Not many people heard the broadcasts of the Braves games in 1925 and 1926, as only one-tenth of American households owned a radio at the time. However, ownership quickly increased when "by 1926, there were substantial alterations in receiver design. Technical controls had been simplified down to two knobs (tuning and volume) so that practical know-how was no longer needed, and the cumbersome headphones were replaced with a central loudspeaker that permitted the entire family to enjoy the radio together." By 1927 one-quarter of American households owned a radio, which significantly increased the audience for baseball broadcasts in Boston.[14]

Quinn and the Red Sox had a much lower impact than Fuchs and the Braves had with the Boston baseball public. Quinn did try to broach the Sunday baseball barrier in June 1925 by arranging a Sunday exhibition game against the North Cambridge team of the Boston Twilight League, a semi-pro team that was notorious for skirting the 1920 Sunday baseball law that prohibited charging an admission fee to amateur games. When that game was deemed as too big of a legal risk, the Red Sox instead played a twilight game in North Cambridge that began at 6:00 in the evening, which attracted 6,000 spectators. Although Massachusetts opted to observe daylight saving time, neither the Red Sox nor the Braves ever attempted to play twilight games at Fenway Park or Braves Field, given the stiff competition from the popularity of local twilight leagues.[15]

The Boston Twilight League in 1925 was representative of the composition of Boston major-league baseball fans in 1925, having a foundation in urban Boston but mostly residing in the suburbs. There was only one team from a Boston neighborhood (South Boston) in the Boston Twilight League in 1925, with all the other teams organized in various suburbs ranging from Somerville and Malden in the inner suburbs, to Lawrence and Westford in the Merrimack Valley 20 miles outside the city, to as far north as Manchester, New Hampshire.

The environment for Boston baseball fans attending Red Sox games took a significant downturn on May 8, 1926, when a fire destroyed the third-base pavilion at Fenway Park. The financially-strapped Red Sox pocketed the insurance check rather than use the money to rebuild the seating area, which became a "cinder-strewn vacant lot" that was an expansive foul territory where batted balls remained in play. Quinn declined the Braves' offer to use Braves Field for Red Sox games. Quinn never recovered from the wreckage inflicted by the blaze. In 1926, Quinn's chief investor, Palmer Winslow, a glass magnate in Columbus, Ohio, became seriously ill, which hampered Quinn's effort to improve the product on the field and to fill the seats in Fenway Park.

When Winslow died in 1927, his widow became a passive investor in the Red Sox, which resulted in a gradual deterioration in the quality of the Fenway Park facility.[16]

With the Red Sox ownership reeling and the Braves presumptively on their way to a Sunday baseball monopoly following the November 1926 election, the Braves were on the verge of dominating the Boston market for general baseball fans and for the first time creating a modest body of dedicated Braves fans. The Red Sox were never involved in the movement during the 1920s to legalize Sunday baseball in Massachusetts. It is unclear when Quinn first discovered the wording in the Sunday baseball voter referendum that prohibited ball games within 1000 feet of a church, which would impede his ability to play Sunday baseball at Fenway Park.

There was a snag, however, which derailed the Sunday baseball voter referendum. The nearly 15 months between gathering enough signatures and the next state election gave the opponents of Sunday baseball ample time to find a way to defeat the referendum. Indeed, in May 1926, it was discovered that the description of the proposed law differed in the two sets of petitions, with the first set containing 20,000 signatures referencing "Sunday sports" and the second set with at least 5,000 signatures referencing "Sunday baseball." Although the Secretary of State admitted that the use of different terms was a clerical error made in his office, the matter was taken up by the Massachusetts Supreme Court. In September 1926 the Supreme Court ruled that the issue needed to be removed from the November ballot due to "the substantial differences between the proposed law and the descriptions of it" contained in the two sets of petitions. It didn't matter that the state, not the petitioners, created the clerical error, nor was there any consideration of whether that clerical error was intentional or not.[17]

Opponents of Sunday baseball would have been better off allowing the voter referendum to go forward in 1926. With Republicans sweeping the 1926 state elections, there was a very good chance that the referendum question would have gone down to defeat and perhaps quelled its proponents for a few more years. As it turned out, the political climate in Massachusetts changed markedly two years later for the 1928 election, which enabled the passage of the voter referendum at that time.

The nixing of the Sunday baseball voter referendum from the 1926 ballot dealt a severe blow to the opportunity for the Braves to create a dominant position among Boston baseball fans. In 1926, for a second consecutive year, the Braves outdrew the Red Sox (303,000 at Braves Field, with 285,000 at Fenway Park). While the margin was slim, the difference indicated the power of radio broadcasts to mint new Boston baseball fans, since both teams were at the bottom of their league standings. The Braves finished next to last in the National League and the Red Sox were dead last in the American League.

This was typical of the period 1922 to 1931, where both the Braves and Red Sox finished either last or next-to-last every year, with just marginal exceptions of the 1925 Braves (fifth place) and 1931 Red Sox (sixth place).

Without a winning team and the inability to play Sunday baseball, it was very difficult to attract gobs of spectators to the ballpark. That is, from the traditional workers in the central business district in downtown Boston and others who lived in the nearby neighborhoods and inner suburbs within five to six miles of downtown. Radio helped to extend that reach to the outer suburbs of Greater Boston, which in 1927 for the first time included the broadcast of Red Sox games. In 1927 and 1928, the combined attendance of both teams was roughly 600,000, which was the same volume as in 1925 and 1926, but the Red Sox topped the Braves in both these two seasons that led up to the 1928 federal election.

WNAC broadcast all the home games of both the Braves and Red Sox in 1927. Quinn could now buy into Fuchs' belief that radio would bring new fans to the ballpark, since the American League had relented on its previous prohibition of radio broadcasts. "Weekday daylight games could reach women, children, and some men, while weekend contests could add most of the rest of the male population to baseball's radio audience," James Walker wrote in *Crack of the Bat: A History of Baseball on the Radio*. "Added to increasingly engaged local fans were hundreds of thousands of listeners in outlying regions, who could use increasingly available automobiles and paved roads to come to the ballpark on weekends." This radio policy was good for both Quinn and Fuchs, as the escalation from an occasional game from Braves Field to all games at both ballparks helped to create more general baseball fans.[18]

Shepard also benefited greatly from this total immersion of baseball on WNAC because he could easily and cheaply fill the airwaves. "In an era before night games, baseball provided relatively inexpensive programming during daytime hours when the national networks offered relatively little sponsored programming," Alexander Russo observed in his book *Points on the Dial: Golden Age Radio Beyond the Networks*. "The chief production costs were low, consisting of telephone line rentals and the salaries of an announcer and an engineering team." Note how Russo wrote "announcer" in the singular.[19]

Shepard had a long-lasting influence on Boston baseball fans because the radio broadcaster worked for the radio station, not the baseball club. As part of the "inexpensive programming," Shepard used just one man as broadcaster to do the games of both Boston teams. Employing a single radio station to broadcast games, with a single announcer at the microphone, reinforced the general principle of consistently providing a baseball product to Boston fans, rather than a more specialized Braves product or Red Sox product. This solidified the base of general baseball fans in the Greater Boston area, while minimizing the level of dedicated fans for either team. It also optimized the ability to attract new fans that would start out with an intermittent commitment, and then progress to becoming a general fan that followed both teams.

While the single broadcaster helped both the Braves and the Red Sox, the approach also helped Shepard beyond merely saving a few dollars in production costs. The common broadcaster for all baseball games appealed to advertisers, giving them a broader radio audience to reach for their products and eliminating the risk of alienating a portion of the target audience that was dedicated to one team or the other.

Eventually these decisions regarding one single radio station and a common broadcaster evolved into a coordinated radio broadcasting policy used by both the Braves and Red Sox. This re-engaged the old informal cooperative arrangement between the two clubs from the 1910s, and would later expand to coordinated policy for other aspects of ballpark operations.

In the spring of 1927 Shepard continued to try out a variety of announcers on WNAC, using Gerry Harrison for the season-opener at Braves Field and Dan Barry at the microphone in early May. By mid–May, though, Shepard had settled on Fred Hoey to be the only voice heard on the radio from Braves Field and Fenway Park, as Hoey began a 12-year reign as the "Voice of Boston Baseball."[20]

Curt Smith, in his acclaimed book *Voices of the Game*, described the impact of Hoey as "having (largely) made New England (arguably) the most rabid baseball region in America." According to Ken Coleman, a future Red Sox announcer who grew up listening to Hoey on the radio in Quincy, Massachusetts: "He wasn't polished. He wasn't professional. But there was an electricity to him. Not in how he used the language, particularly, but in the feeling he gave that this mattered, that baseball counted, that it meant something special in our lives."[21]

Hoey made fans out of thousands of radio listeners with a curt, staccato pace that combined informality with detail "to describe exactly what he saw, without embellishment." Hoey established a New England style that future generations of Boston baseball announcers used to win over baseball fans, which Smith described as "respect and understatement over schlock, kitsch, and shtick." When Hoey died in 1949, the *Boston Globe* summarized his impact in one sentence: "Hoey was generally credited with building up baseball broadcasting to the lofty spot it holds in the American sports scene today." Hoey arguably built a larger following among Boston fans than did any ballplayer on the field from the late 1920s through the mid–1930s.[22]

As the consistent radio voice in 1927 and 1928, Hoey helped to increase the possibility of the passage of the Sunday baseball voter referendum on the November 1928 ballot, as listeners became accustomed to dialing in to WNAC at 3:00 in the afternoon to hear Hoey call the games. As the radio coverage increased, so did the increased interest in having the ball games played on Sunday among the majority of Massachusetts residents. With Hoey spreading the popularity of the exciting power-hitting American League style of play, the Braves tried to replicate that fan interest by moving in the fences at Braves Field to encourage more home runs.

During the spring of 1928, Fuchs doubled down on the radio coverage of the Braves games to expand the baseball exposure prior to the Sunday baseball voter referendum that fall. WBET was the second radio station to broadcast games from Braves Field in 1928, employing Richard Grant as the announcer, who jostled for space in the press box with Hoey, the WNAC announcer. However, once the Braves homestand ended in late June, WBET ended the experiment and left baseball broadcasting solely in the hands of WNAC.[23]

Proponents of Sunday baseball worked even harder to put the voter referendum on the 1928 ballot, after being outfoxed on a technicality that removed the referendum from the 1926 ballot. Assisting matters was a change in the attitude of state residents toward Sunday, shifting from a belief that it was a "day of rest" to one of a "day of leisure." Also helpful was that the referendum's opponents became more polarized.

As expected, the Massachusetts legislature once again voted down the measure, but this time by a narrower margin, which indicated a warming of the legislature toward the issue. The Braves had no trouble obtaining the required number of signatures to put the matter on the 1928 ballot as a voter referendum. This time, proponents ensured that the bureaucracy didn't do them in, when they formed the Outdoor Recreation League, led by Claude Davidson, who had recently revived the venerable local minor league, the New England League, which desperately needed Sunday baseball to remain economically viable. Organized opposition not surprisingly emerged, led by the Reverend Conrad and the Lord's Day League. However, they could not repel the changing attitudes of the majority of the Massachusetts electorate. The Outdoor Recreation League organized efforts to counter the obstacles. As *The Sporting News* noted, "The state has been placarded and covered with letters and workers." Sample ballots were also a big item, to avert the necessity of voters having to actually attempt to read the awkwardly worded ballot question and just have them mark the "yes" box.[24]

With Al Smith as the Democratic nominee for President, many voters with Irish or Italian heritage went to the polls for that November 1928 election to cast a vote for Smith, who was the first Catholic to run for President. The Catholic voters also voted overwhelmingly for the Sunday sports referendum, which passed with 63 percent "yes" and 37 percent "no." The state's largest county, Suffolk County, where Boston is located, voted 76 percent in the "yes" column to lead the way. "No longer will office boys, with tears in their eyes, be induced to tell piteous tales to their employers of the sudden demise of aged relatives, in order to spend the afternoon in bleacher seats at the ball parks," Ford Sawyer mused in the *Boston Globe*. "They can see their diamond heroes on Sundays now."[25]

The 1928 voter referendum that legalized professional Sunday baseball mirrored many aspects of the amateur 1920 Sunday law, including the four-hour window to play ball games from 2:00 to 6:00 in the afternoon, the 1000-foot church-proximity restriction, and the local-option clause that required every city and town in the state to decide on its own whether or not to issue a permit for Sunday baseball.[26]

The Braves seemed to be on the way to having a monopoly on Sunday baseball. However, Massachusetts voter approval was just the first step toward the playing of Sunday baseball at Braves Field, since the Braves needed to obtain approval from the Boston City Council under the local-option provision of the law. While the count of Boston voters had been substantially in favor of the Sunday sports referendum, those results did not mean that the Boston City Council would be necessarily quick to issue a permit for Sunday baseball at Braves Field.

◆ 10 ◆

Sunday Games Permitted
Only at Braves Field

After the passage of the Sunday baseball voter referendum in 1928, the Braves would not easily obtain a permit to play Sunday baseball at Braves Field in 1929. The baseball club was forced to navigate its way through an acrimonious public debate with charges and counter-charges of illegal activities allegedly used to gain approval from the Boston City Council.

Two months after Massachusetts voters approved the Sunday baseball referendum in November 1928, the following headline appeared on January 2, 1929, in the evening edition of the *Boston Globe*: "Fuchs Names City Councilor W.G. Lynch as Bribe Solicitor." Braves president Judge Fuchs contended that he had been solicited by a city councilor for a bribe two weeks after the election, which if not paid would result in the council not taking action on a permit for Sunday baseball. Lynch allegedly represented a group of a dozen city councilors who sought $5,000 each to approve the Sunday baseball permit.[1]

Three weeks of public hearings were conducted about the bribery scandal, which resulted in confusing testimony about a meeting conducted in the early morning hours where liquor was consumed. However, the hearings quickly changed course from suspected illegalities of public officials to the potential improprieties of Fuchs and the Braves organization.

Ed Cunningham, the Braves secretary, exposed the dark side to the Sunday baseball ballot issue during his cross-examination about how the voter referendum campaign had been financed. Cunningham's testimony led to the investigation of "a violation of the corrupt practices act on the part of Braves officials through their connection with the Outdoor Recreation League, which is alleged to have spent $30,000 in a campaign for passage of the Sunday sports referendum," one newspaper summarized the day's hearing on January

116

4, 1929, since evidently "the Braves and the Outdoor Recreation League were one, and that the substantial part of the funds of the league, which were used to further the cause of Sunday baseball, were contributed by the Braves."[2]

Cunningham said that he had contributed $200 in cash to the Outdoor Recreation League. When asked why he contributed cash so his name wouldn't be on record, Cunningham replied, "I didn't want any connection with the Braves shown in these contributions." Following Cunningham's statement, "a hush fell over the room." Cunningham went on to say, "The Lord's Day League was probing everything connected with Sunday baseball just at that time and I didn't want them to trace any contributions that I had got." Cunningham acknowledged that many contributors were either Braves employees or connected to operations at Braves Field.[3]

These public hearings, which had transitioned from alleged bribes by the city council to potential falsification of campaign contributors by the Braves, opened the door for the Red Sox to thwart the monopoly that the Braves could have had on Sunday baseball in Boston. Even though Burt Whitman of the *Boston Herald* had declared in mid–November 1928 that "the Braves and Red Sox will play Sunday baseball the coming season," there was never any certainty that the Red Sox would play home games on Sunday in 1929. Patently, the Red Sox couldn't play at Fenway Park on Sunday because the new law specified that ball games were not permitted within 1000 feet of a church. The Church of the Disciples, a Unitarian church located on Peterborough Street at the corner of Jersey Street, was clearly within 1000 feet of Fenway Park, according to city engineers.[4]

Red Sox president Bob Quinn was decidedly quiet on the topic of Sunday baseball, beyond telling the newspapers the day after the election that he was pleased with the vote result. The American League was also silent on the issue. While National League president John Heydler issued a lengthy statement about the virtues of the Sunday baseball vote in Massachusetts, there was no public word from American League president Ernest Barnard. Boston sportswriters surely expected the informal cooperative arrangement that had emerged from the détente of 1913 between the two Boston baseball clubs to lead to an agreement for the Red Sox to use Braves Field on Sundays. Sportswriters in New York City and other major-league cities naturally assumed that both Boston teams would engage in Sunday baseball. Quinn apparently worked behind the scenes to rent Braves Field on Sundays, a solution to Quinn's dilemma that was proposed by one newspaper: "It was suggested by many that, even though Fenway Park were barred from Sunday licenses, both teams could use Braves Field." When the bribery scandal involving the Braves went public in early January, Quinn had serious leverage to consummate that rental negotiation for Braves Field to not be left out in the cold on Sunday baseball.[5]

In mid–January the Red Sox filed a petition with the Boston City Council for a permit for Sunday games, in anticipation of the Braves being granted a Sunday permit for Braves Field and consequent discussions with the Braves about renting that facility. Several days later, the mayor of the nearby city of Revere extended an invitation to officials of both the Red Sox and Braves to consider an alternative to Boston politics for Sunday baseball, by establishing baseball parks in Revere. The mayor said "he would personally guarantee them a permit for Sunday baseball" and pointed out "a wonderful site for a baseball park," the former amusement park at Revere Beach where there was ample parking space for the automobiles driven by suburban baseball fans. Quinn used the Revere overture as leverage to bring Fuchs to the negotiation table regarding the rental of Braves Field for Sunday games.[6]

As the public hearings on the bribery scandal lingered on pending the commission's final report, the Boston City Council passed the Sunday sports ordinance on January 28. With the ordinance in place, the Braves applied for a permit on February 2, but the council deferred action until the committee report was finalized. On February 7, the report was released and punted the situation to the Suffolk County district attorney. "While the report of the finance commission of its investigation into the Sunday baseball scandal, made public last night, found an 'array of very suspicious characters' it was virtually a whitewash of all accused parties to the controversy by reason of inconclusive findings as to responsibility," the *Boston Herald* reported. "The commission passed the question of future action, if any, to District Attorney William J. Foley."[7]

With no egregious findings made against Fuchs in the report, the Braves were on target to receive a Sunday baseball permit. However, Commissioner Landis commanded that Sunday games be included on both the National League and American League schedules for 1929, with the details for a rental of Braves Field to be worked out in a meeting in his office. Landis, unlike the Boston City Council, was concerned with meeting the desire of Boston baseball fans by having a universal policy for Sunday baseball applicable to both teams. The existence of this Landis decision is revealed by comments at the permit-approval meeting of the city council and, immediately thereafter, the dissemination of the league schedules.

The Braves got their Sunday baseball permit for Braves Field approved at the February 11 meeting of the Boston City Council. One city councilor expressed concern "that the Sunday sports law will benefit no one but the Boston Braves" since the Red Sox were prohibited from using Fenway Park by the church-proximity restriction in the law, and "the rental that will be asked the Red Sox by the Braves management for the use of Braves Field will be highly profitable to the Braves." Two days later the National League schedule was released on February 13, providing 12 Sunday dates to the Braves, while the American League schedule was released on February 14, with 13 Sunday dates for the Red Sox. Interestingly, the Red Sox still had yet to secure an official location to play Sunday games, although officials from Revere had blueprints for a ballpark ready to move on while Quinn unrealistically hoped the City Council "would waive the technicality" of the church-proximity restriction in the law and leave him with "the constant danger that an injunction might be sought during the season" by Sunday baseball opponents.[8]

At the meeting in New York City to discuss the Sunday rental of Braves Field to the Red Sox were Commissioner Landis, Quinn, Fuchs, and the presidents of each league. With Fuchs already backed into a corner on the matter of the Red Sox playing on Sunday, Landis "suggested" that Quinn draft the rental agreement. Quinn offered to pay rent to use Braves Field, not just on Sunday, but also on holidays, to make the deal more amenable to Fuchs, who readily agreed to the terms without change. Through some heavy-handed tactics by Commissioner Landis, the Braves would not have a monopoly on Sunday baseball in Boston.[9]

Sunday games became one more operational item embedded into the informal cooperative arrangement between the two Boston baseball clubs, which at the time encompassed radio broadcasts, Ladies Day promotions, and the preseason city series.

Due to the interlocking nature of the league schedules, there always would be a Sunday ball game scheduled in Boston every week of the baseball season. This further engendered the grooming of general baseball fans in Boston, especially those who lived outside of Greater Boston, who attended whatever game was at Braves Field when they could travel to Boston. WNAC contributed to the development of more general baseball fans through the radio broadcasts of Sunday games, as males listened to whichever game was on the radio on Sunday afternoon, on the man's only day off from the conventional six-day work week.

While Fuchs escaped damage at the public hearings, except to his reputation, the saga was not yet over. Two days after the City Council granted a permit for Sunday baseball at Braves Field, the Suffolk County district attorney issued complaints against the Braves regarding the funding of the Outdoor Recreation League that violated the corrupt practices act. Unlike the politically charged public hearings that had precipitated extensive newspaper coverage, the actual court proceedings associated with the resulting legal charges against the Braves barely made a ripple in the news. The case was concluded on May 12, when a $1,000 fine was imposed on the Braves after a plea of no contest.[10]

To be able to play Sunday baseball at Braves Field, Fuchs spent nearly a quarter of million dollars to influence voters to approve Sunday baseball in Massachusetts. According to Harold Kaese, author of *The Boston Braves,*

"Fuchs admits he spent close to $200,000 out of his own pocket. A million booklets were printed and four million sample ballots were printed. Placards were placed in every streetcar." When Fuchs died in 1961, he was remembered as being "instrumental in bringing Sunday baseball to Massachusetts." But the aftermath continued to follow him as well, as his obituary in the *Boston Herald* noted, "In his campaign, which led to a referendum approving Sunday baseball, the judge once charged that 13 Boston City Councilmen tried to hold him up for $5,000 each."[11]

Since Fuchs had led the fight for acceptance of Sunday baseball in Boston, the Braves were accorded the distinction of hosting the initial Sunday game in Boston, which was slated for April 21. However, an all-day rain canceled the planned festivities. Thus, the Red Sox had the honor of playing the first Sunday baseball game in Boston the following week on April 28.

"Major league Sunday baseball became a reality in Boston yesterday afternoon," the *Boston Globe* reported, "when upwards of 22,000 fans defied discouraging weather conditions to see the Athletics defeat the Red Sox 7 to 3 at Braves Field in the first scheduled Sunday game between two major league teams ever played in this city." Baseball fans showed their appreciation with admirable decorum at the ballpark. "The attitude and behavior of the crowd was a practical demonstration of the fact that a baseball field is a far healthier spot than a street corner or a back room, even if you have to pay Bob Quinn or Emil Fuchs to get there," *Boston Globe* sportswriter Dave Egan wrote about that initial Sunday game. In a satirical column, Egan went on to write about the sin of pocketing a foul ball and how disappointed the Anti-Enjoyment of Anything League must have been.[12]

The weather was better for the Braves' Sunday opener on May 5, although the Pittsburgh Pirates defeated the Braves before a crowd of 35,000. After playing Cincinnati the next Sunday, May 12, before 25,000 fans, it rained again on May 19 to cancel the game with the Phillies. Two of the first four Sunday games on the Braves' schedule were rained out; a third rainout occurred two months later on July 14.

The Braves were able to make up two of the Sunday rainouts by scheduling Sunday doubleheaders on June 23 and July 21. But with just a four-hour window in the Sunday baseball law (games could only be played between 2:00 and 6:00), finishing the second game could be problematic. For example, at the June 23 doubleheader, the second game was stopped to comply with the law when 6:00 neared, after the Phillies had batted in the top of the seventh inning. The Braves had staged a late rally to score seven runs in the bottom of the sixth inning to pull ahead of the Phillies 7–5, which was how the game ended. This was the first instance of the Sunday curfew impacting the fans' baseball experience in Boston.

Sunday doubleheaders exposed one negative about the WNAC radio

This aerial photograph of a Sunday game at Braves Field in the early 1930s shows not only the substantial number of fans watching a ball game on Sunday, which had been legally prohibited just a few years earlier, but also the limited parking space for automobiles in the vicinity of the ballpark (courtesy Boston Public Library, Leslie Jones Collection).

broadcasts, which was the station's insistence to cut to its 6:00 news programming. "There could be a tie score, ninth inning, bases loaded, three-and-two count, the crowd going berserk—and if the clock struck six, the carriage became a pumpkin. Boom! You went to the news." It was a small price for Boston baseball fans to pay for the existence of Sunday baseball.[13]

Despite their lackluster playing success, as both teams finished in last place in 1929, Sunday crowds accounted for a significant proportion of the season-long attendance for both teams. Of the Braves season attendance of 373,300, four Sunday games drew 28 percent of it, if newspaper accounts can be believed. The Red Sox drew 394,600 in 1929, with four Sunday crowds (three against the Yankees) representing 26 percent of the total number of fans that paid to see the Red Sox that year. Sunday games easily represented at least one-third of total attendance for each team and possibly up to one-half.

The Red Sox outdrew the Braves in 1929 because they had the advantage of booking the New York Yankees and slugger Babe Ruth for three Sunday games in 1929. Ruth didn't disappoint the Boston fans with his home-run hitting. On May 26, Ruth hit a home run in a 15–4 rout of the Red Sox. On June 30, Ruth hit a two-run homer, which turned out to be the decisive blow in a 6–4 victory. Then on September 1, Ruth hit his 40th home run of the season in another 6–4 win over the Red Sox. Ruth's home runs at Braves Field created more followers of the American League power-hitting style of play, many of whom became solid Sox-leaning general baseball fans and a few became dedicated Sox fans.

One of the Babe's most famous home runs at Braves Field occurred on May 18, 1930, when his homer popularized a nickname for the right-field bleachers. "The big fellow sent the ball on a bee-line to the back of the 'jury box' in right field," the *Boston Globe* reported. "But for the obstruction the ball would have gone on a line to the Armory on the other side of Gaffney St." The "jury box" at Braves Field was reportedly coined by an earlier baseball writer who had once observed just a dozen spectators in the right-field bleachers during one sparsely attended game.[14]

Fred Hoey, the baseball broadcaster for WNAC, described these home runs by the Babe, as well as those by Braves power-hitter Wally Berger who poked 38 homers during the 1930 season. Hoey helped to elevate fan interest through his description of "word pictures" that reached "countless thousands of baseball fans all over New England," which resulted in "thousands of letters of commendation from men and women in every walk of life." Attesting to his popularity, and ability to indirectly draw people to the ballpark, was the tribute to him at Fred Hoey Day in June 1931 when 30,000 fans at Braves Field "wished to show their appreciation of his efforts to entertain them."[15]

Hoey's appeal to radio listeners expanded beyond Greater Boston in July 1930 when John Shepard made WNAC the flagship station of the newly created Yankee Network, which greatly extended the reach of Hoey's voice to listeners beyond Massachusetts into other New England states. By 1930, nearly 50 percent of American households owned a radio, which provided a healthy audience for radio advertisers. John Shepard of WNAC was not bashful about exploiting this business opportunity, to the delight of lovers of baseball located far from Greater Boston, many of whom began making weekend excursions to Boston to watch a ball game (or increasingly often a doubleheader) at Braves Field on Sunday afternoon.[16]

The Yankee Network started out modestly, branching out from Boston to the Massachusetts cities of Worcester (WORC) and New Bedford (WNBH) as well as the out-of-state affiliate stations of WEAN in Providence, Rhode Island, and WLBZ in Bangor, Maine. Within a year, Shepard had expanded into Connecticut, at WDRC in Hartford and WICC in Bridgeport, and was soon in New Hampshire at WFEA in Manchester.

With more doubleheaders played on Sunday in 1930, the Sunday baseball law continued to be problematical regarding the completion of the two games of doubleheader. Concern elevated when the skullduggery of managers and ballplayers seemed to make a mockery of fairness when it came to the artificial 6:00 ending time specified in the law.

On July 13, the Braves, leading 3–0 in the eighth inning of the second game, stalled considerably trying to delay the start of the ninth inning, which included Rabbit Maranville fouling off numerous pitches with check swings to kill time. When the ninth inning did begin at 5:38, the Cubs managed to score four runs to go ahead 4–3 and then executed a hurry-up strategy to minimize time. Knowing that time was running out, a baserunner allowed himself to be thrown out half-heartedly trying to steal third base and a batter purposely struck out to end the half inning. At 5:55 the Braves went to bat and began to stall again, since if the ninth inning was not completed, the score would revert to that at the end of the eighth inning. After a Braves batter fouled off a half dozen balls before finally striking out, the clock struck 6:00 and a Boston policeman entered the field and warned the umpires about the Sunday law. The game was halted and the Braves declared the winner, since the Braves were ahead at the end of the last complete inning. The Cubs were not happy about the verdict.[17]

These shenanigans precipitated changes in the Sunday baseball law that were passed by the Massachusetts legislature in April 1931 to extend the time frame for doubleheaders to be five hours, from 1:30 to 6:30 in the afternoon. However, even with this extended length of time, the second game of the Red Sox's doubleheader on September 13 had to be shortened due to the new Sunday curfew. Further skullduggery would occur in future Sunday doubleheaders in Boston.[18]

By 1931 the Sunday doubleheader had become a virtual staple of the baseball calendar at Braves Field, although none of them appeared on the preseason schedule released by the two leagues. Pre-scheduling doubleheaders would have encouraged fans to wait for the 2-for-1 promotion days and thus reduce attendance for single games on Sunday. However, the weather often failed to cooperate with the original schedule, causing rainouts that needed to be made up through a second game on Sunday before the visiting team left Boston.

Both Boston clubs found that even when doubleheaders materialized on the fly the attendance increased significantly, since during these economic hard times of the Great Depression many people sought a bargain for entertainment. In 1931 the Braves, in particular, engaged in arranging "synthetic doubleheaders," which had been popularized by the St. Louis Cardinals.

Rather than wait for erratic Mother Nature to cancel a game, the Cardinals would just move a weekday game (where a small audience was expected) to another date to be part of a doubleheader. Three known synthetic double-headers arranged by the Braves in 1931 were the May 10 Sunday doubleheader, by moving up the Monday game, and Wednesday doubleheaders on June 24 and August 12, by putting off the an earlier Monday or Tuesday game.[19]

Over the next few years, while the synthetic doubleheader was a great boon for baseball fans, the extensive use of the technique troubled many in the major-league baseball community. "Fear is voiced in some quarters that baseball is going to become a weekend sport, instead of a daily affair," *The Sporting News* editorialized. "Its possibility does counsel serious consideration of the probable effects of the arbitrary shifting around of week-day games to make possible double-headers on Sunday." It wasn't so much the decline of weekday games that troubled the owners, but rather the changing nature of the fans who attended the Sunday doubleheaders. Middle-class businessmen, once the chief audience at games during the work week, were being sup-planted by people in lower socio-economic classes, who comprised a large portion of the audience on Sunday.[20]

There was a change in the nature of business organization that funda-mentally reduced the number of businessmen who could attend an afternoon ball game during the workweek. The rapid expansion of the "chain store" concept, which involved "retailing merchandise through store units owned and controlled by a corporation," forced many independent businessmen to shut down in the 1930s and arguably "produced a nation of clerks as a result of their policy of centralizing control at the home office" as a replacement for local owners. Grocery stores, gas stations, and variety stores were the largest segments of the economy affected by chain stores. "That chain stores in many instances have forced independent retailers out of business cannot be denied," James Palmer observed in his journal article "Economic and Social Aspects of Chain Stores" in 1929. "To the extent that these retailers are desir-able citizens and a valuable part of the social life of the community, the com-munity suffers." The decline in independently-owned businesses in Greater Boston significantly impacted attendance on weekdays, since these men had the time flexibility to attend an afternoon ball game, in stark contrast to the chain-store employee.[21]

The Braves played half a dozen Sunday doubleheaders at Braves Field in 1931, which were highly popular with fans, particularly suburban ones, despite the significant number of people who were unemployed during the Great Depression. Ironically, the greater number of leisure hours due to unemployment in the 1930s actually resulted in increased spending on recre-ation, not less spending, which spawned a 10 percent federal amusement tax in 1932 that applied to tickets for movies and ball games. "Despite economic hardship, leisure time had continued to grow, and an increasing share of the national income was spent on recreation ... revolutionizing the way Americans spent their nonworking hours," Susan Currell wrote in her book *The March of Spare Time: The Problem and Promise of Leisure in the Great Depression*. According to Currell, "Attending the movies was the third most popular leisure activity, only topped by the cheaper pursuits of radio listening and reading newspapers." Movie promoters offered giveaway nights and double features "to lure the Depression-hit public into spending their last few dollars." Braves Field offered its own double feature in the Sunday doubleheader.[22]

The geographical reach of suburban fans for Sunday games was shown in the owners of the nine automobiles that were damaged in a fire in the crowded parking lot on the other side of Commonwealth Avenue from Braves Field during the Sunday game on May 17, 1931. As reported in the article entitled "Fire Threatens 400 Autos While Owners Watch Game," two cars that were owned by baseball fans from nearby Medford and Dorchester were severely damaged, while the other seven damaged vehicles were owned by fans from Gardner, Worcester, Lynn, Townsend, and Wellesley in Massachusetts and from Providence, Rhode Island, and Manchester, New Hampshire.[23]

This parking-lot fire highlighted a huge flaw in the location of Braves Field, since there were not nearly enough parking spaces for the automobiles at a ballpark built in 1915 specifically to accommodate streetcar transportation of fans. Although the original 1928 plans for the extension of the Boylston Street subway had it going under Commonwealth Avenue all the way to Braves Field before converting to above-ground service, the revised 1930 plan provided for the subway extension to go under Governor Square but emerge above-ground on Commonwealth Avenue near its intersection with Blandford Street, which was far short of Braves Field. The new subway stop in 1932 near Fenway Park helped the Red Sox, and the inability to improve public transit to Braves Field hurt the Braves.[24]

The Braves attracted 515,000 spectators to their ball games at Braves Field in 1931 to dramatically outdraw the Red Sox, which had an attendance of 350,000, the bulk of which occurred at Braves Field during their Sunday and holiday games there. Another 20,000 fans went to Braves Field to watch the unemployment benefit game between the Braves and Red Sox in late September. The Red Sox seemed destined for uncomfortable times as a tenant at Braves Field, with few people interested in watching the weekday games at Fenway Park.

♦ 11 ♦

New Law Allows
Sunday Games
at Fenway Park

In the midst of the Great Depression in 1932, the Red Sox were mired in last place in the American League for the entire season, while the Braves were near the top of the National League standings for most of the season to contend for the pennant. Although the Braves faded to fifth place by the end of the season, the Braves attracted 507,000 spectators to Braves Field, nearly triple the 182,000 people that attended Red Sox games. Thousands more throughout New England listened to the broadcasts of the ball games on the radio. Clearly, the Braves were one knockout punch away from a dominant position with Boston baseball fans.

However, in May 1932, the Massachusetts legislature gave the Red Sox a reprieve from a very bleak future when it passed a law permitting Sunday baseball to be played at Fenway Park. Bob Quinn could now sell the nearly bankrupt Red Sox to a new owner, who could infuse money to resuscitate interest in the team and improve a decrepit Fenway Park. Without control of its Sunday destiny, by playing all of its holiday and Sunday games at Braves Field, no one would pay much to buy the Red Sox. Although there is much reverence for Tom Yawkey for his rescue of the Red Sox after he purchased the club in February 1933, the role that the 1932 Sunday baseball law played in that transaction has never been recognized.

The 1932 revised Sunday baseball law provided a specific exemption for "the present American League baseball park in the city of Boston, commonly known as Fenway Park" from the provision in the Sunday baseball law that prohibited ball games within 1000 feet from a church. This law was needed because the Church of the Disciples was located 800 feet from Fenway Park.[1]

How did the Red Sox manage to convince the Massachusetts legislature to amend the Sunday law in 1932, when the legislature had been so intransigent on the church-proximity provision for so many years? Explanations by the participants are now lost to history, and contemporary newspaper accounts provide little insight concerning the rationale. One exception is the *Boston Globe* headline published on May 17, 1932, during the legislative hearings on the proposed bill, which was entitled "Church Withdraws Its Objection." But the article itself provided no elaboration on the reason why.

Two Republican legislators did play key roles in the passage of the 1932 Sunday baseball law. Arthur Burgess of Quincy, the sponsor of the bill, and Leverett Saltonstall, the Speaker of the House, quietly marshaled the bill through the conservative Republican-dominated legislature, without much debate or controversy. Burgess was a well-known baseball fan, involved in amateur baseball in Quincy; Saltonstall was a Unitarian, the same religion preached by the Church of the Disciples. The bill was quickly signed by the sitting Democratic governor, Robert Ely, who was the first Democrat elected to that office in 15 years.[2]

In addition to the religious connection, Saltonstall was also a moderate Republican, being conservative on economic issues (pro-business) and more moderate on social issues (e.g., people attending a Sunday sports event). One hint of his support for the 1932 Sunday baseball law was contained in his autobiography: "If I were asked to single out the type of legislation most carefully considered during that period [as Speaker of the House], I would answer: laws protecting the individual."[3]

While it is unclear exactly how the Red Sox enlisted the aid of Abraham Rihbany, the 62-year-old minister at the Church of the Disciples, to support the proposed revision to the Sunday baseball law, Saltonstall appears to be an important link. Ardent Boston baseball fan John Dooley claimed to have a role in the matter, using his connections to set up a meeting between the two Unitarians, Saltonstall and Rihbany. Chuckling as he retold the story years later, Dooley recalled: "Saltonstall went to see the minister and everyone was delighted when the good man said he had no objection to baseball being played on Sunday. There was no conflict between his morning service and the afternoon ball game, the minister said." Saltonstall, if Dooley's story is true, or whoever did talk to Rihbany, would have appealed to Rihbany's ecclesiastical mission at the Unitarian church, which espoused one of the most liberal philosophies among Protestant sects. Among the defining characteristics of Unitarianism in the early twentieth century were "its openness, tolerance, love of freedom and its optimistic view of human nature and progress." The freedom to attend a Sunday ball game meshed perfectly with this line of thinking.[4]

Rihbany had an intriguing background. He grew up poor in Syria, where

The Church of the Disciples was within 1000 feet of Fenway Park, which prohibited the playing of Sunday baseball there under the terms of the voter referendum approved by Massachusetts voters in the 1928 election. A revised law in 1932 permitted Sunday games at Fenway Park, which paved the way for the sale of the Red Sox in 1933 (Boston Public Library, Print Department).

he practiced the Greek Orthodox faith. After his father sent the restless Abraham to a school run by American missionaries of Presbyterian faith, he left Syria for America at age 21 in October 1891 with no money in his pockets and a $40 debt for his steerage ticket on the ship. One twenty-first-century commentator characterized Rihbany as "the immigrant who comes to the United States, rises from poverty to achieve the American Dream, and confirms his adopted country's self-image as the land of freedom and opportunity." He published numerous books and articles related to freedom. In his autobiography *A Far Journey*, Rihbany wrote that his experience coming to America taught him "to contemplate the dwellers of tenement houses with a greater measure of respect than I could otherwise do. Not a few of the noble possibilities of future America lie hidden in those dark, musty, shabby dwellings, awaiting the call of this country's wondrous opportunities to resurrect them to the newness and glory of a free and useful life."[5]

With his background, Rihbany would have been receptive to the argument that people should be allowed to watch a baseball game on Sunday unconstrained by an artificial distance between church and ballpark. Additionally, Rihbany could have been swayed by the logic that the existing 1000-foot restriction in the law had little practical negative impact to religious services at the Church of the Disciples, because the church was closed for three months during the summer months. Records of the church's business meetings, held by the Andover–Harvard Theological Library at the Harvard Divinity School, indicate that the church shut down from mid–June to mid–September every year during the early 1930s. For instance at a meeting in April 1930, church records contain the following resolution: "Voted, that the church be closed Sunday June 15 to Sunday September 14 inclusive, reopening Sunday September 21, 1930." Therefore, church services were effectively only impacted by Sunday ball games at Fenway Park during one-half of the baseball season, in April, May, early June, and late September.[6]

Part of Rihbany's acquiescence may have involved some assistance (by a friend of the Red Sox club) to store up the church's deteriorating financial condition to keep the church functioning in the face of dwindling membership during the bleak economic times of the Great Depression. The business meeting records of the church show an intriguing entry in January 1932 when a special meeting was called to reconsider an earlier decision to suspend the printing of the annual Year Book: "to vote to rescind previous vote [and] to print the annual Year Book; so voted." Since the Year Book was printed and distributed to church members, some unidentified person suddenly came up with the $300 to cover the printing cost, since the church did not have enough money to pay for it.[7]

However, Rihbany would not have given his blessing to the change in the Sunday baseball law without concurrence by the Lord's Day League, which had not weakened its position following the 1928 voter referendum. Dr. Arcturus Zodiac Conrad, a fundamentalist minister in Boston, was an ultraconservative, not willing to compromise on doctrine, and unafraid to publicly voice his opinion in a "pugnacious tone," Margaret Bendroth wrote in her book *Fundamentalists in the City: Conflict and Division in Boston's Churches, 1885–1950.* Since there was surprisingly no organized religious objection to the revised law, Quinn apparently quelled the local religious concerns through the new radio policy for 1932 to discontinue radio broadcasts of all Sunday ball games, both at Fenway Park as well as at Braves Field. The Lord's Day League was likely appeased by the principle that fewer people would be exposed to the perceived evil of Sunday baseball if there were no radio broadcasts of those games to listen to.[8]

After three years of having Fred Hoey describe all the Sunday action from Braves Field on WNAC, the Red Sox, Braves, and WNAC owner John

Shepard all agreed to abruptly, and very quietly, drop Sunday games from radio coverage for the 1932 season. There was no public announcement in 1932, although a careful perusal of the Lloyd Greene's "Radio Broadcasts" programming listings published in the *Boston Globe* shows the ball games "reported by Fred Hoey" listed for Monday through Saturday, but other shows being broadcast on Sunday afternoons.

Radio broadcasts of baseball games continued to be a touchy subject in 1932 among major-league baseball owners, since many of them continued to feel that radio reduced attendance at the ballpark. Sixty percent of American households now owned a radio, up from the one-third ratio in 1929. Boston was the only eastern city in either major league that permitted radio broadcasts, supporting the position strongly expressed by Chicago Cubs president William Veeck, Sr., that radio advertised the game and thus enticed people to the ballpark. In December 1931, the owners had barely voted to continue the radio experiment for the 1932 season, on a "local option" basis rather than ban the practice entirely. Most clubs that permitted radio broadcasts banned them on Sunday, so Boston was just following suit. Of course, except on Sunday and holidays, both Braves Field and Fenway Park were populated only by a small coterie of dedicated fans and general baseball fans. Radio could only improve the attendance situation in Boston.[9]

The decision to discontinue Sunday radio broadcasts was beneficial to all constituencies, except those baseball fans who could travel to Boston to see a game only on Sunday.

For Shepard, the policy removed an impediment to growing the Yankee Network, since non-baseball Sunday programming was a big profit maker and selling point to radio stations to join the network, since most people still worked a 48-hour week, eight hours per day for six days, and had only Sunday off. Cutting off the ball game broadcast at 6:00 for the news was also a persistent issue. Sunday doubleheaders that consumed five hours of air time were a problem not only for Shepard but also announcer Hoey, since the long day in the radio booth contributed to his drinking problem.[10]

For Judge Fuchs, the policy enabled him to maximize attendance for Sunday games at Braves Field. Quinn received the same benefit, but more importantly he secured the necessary ingredient to enable him to sell the Red Sox. Without the ability to attract spectators on the most popular day of the week to watch a game at Fenway Park, even the most ardent wealthy sportsman like Tom Yawkey would not have been interested in taking on the moribund team and hefty mortgage on the ballpark. Just a few days following the passage of the revised Sunday baseball law, the Boston newspapers were publishing rumors that Quinn planned to sell the Red Sox.[11]

Yawkey met with Quinn "sometime in the summer" of 1932 to discuss the sale of the ballclub, according to the recollection of Eddie Collins,

Yawkey's partner as general manager of the Red Sox. This timing coincides with the implementation of the new Sunday baseball law. Collins, then a coach with the Philadelphia Athletics, would have been very cognizant of the Sunday law impact to the operation of a ballclub, since Pennsylvania law still prohibited Sunday games in 1932, which eventually forced Connie Mack to sell off his star players to meet expenses. The actual sale of the Red Sox had to wait until late February 1933, when Yawkey turned age 30, when his trust fund could be tapped for the $1.0 million purchase price.[12]

The Red Sox waited for the Church of the Disciples to shut down for the summer before playing the first Sunday game at Fenway Park. On July 3, 1932, the first-place Yankees defeated the last-place Red Sox, as 10,000 people viewed the first Sunday game ever played at Fenway Park. The Sox conducted five more Sunday games during July and August of 1932, all doubleheaders, which each drew between 7,500 and 10,000 spectators.

Huge crowds continued to pour into Braves Field for the Sunday games played by the Braves. For the first time during the radio era, one of the two Boston teams was furiously engaged in a pennant race, as the Braves challenged for first place until mid–August of the 1932 season. The Sunday crowds were even larger than in 1931 due to the new radio policy with WNAC that eliminated broadcasts of Sunday games. If fans wanted to follow the game played on Sunday, they needed to be at the ballpark.

A record crowd of 51,331 filled Braves Field on Sunday, May 22, 1932, to watch the second-place Braves split a doubleheader with the New York Giants. "Pennant starved New Englanders piled up a new Boston big league baseball attendance of 51,331 by storming and overflowing Braves Field yesterday afternoon," Whitman described the crowd in the *Boston Herald*. "Every seat of the 45,000 was taken and more than 6,000 watched either from behind the ropes hurriedly thrown up around the outfield or from standing positions in the grandstand, pavilions, and bleachers." Automobiles had begun arriving at Braves Field at 10:00 in the morning, causing intolerable congestion on the city streets. "Because so many fans motored from afar—from Maine, New Hampshire, Vermont, and Rhode Island—streets for many blocks were lined with parked automobiles all afternoon and there were big jams after the game."[13]

The huge Sunday crowds for Braves games in 1932 exacerbated the parking problem at Braves Field, since more people were driving automobiles not only from the suburbs of Greater Boston but also from far-flung areas of New England to see Sunday baseball. Far fewer people were using the elevated railway and streetcar systems to get to Braves Field, whose trolley-line heritage was now a liability, not a benefit.

More than half of the 500,000 total attendance of the Braves in 1932 came from Sunday games; by adding holiday games, the percentage might reach as high as two-thirds. Few people attended the ball games played Monday to Saturday. However, despite the lackluster crowds for weekday ball games, neither the Braves nor the Red Sox considered night baseball, which many minor-league clubs had successfully adopted to reverse declining attendance. Night games were considered baseball for the masses, though, which wasn't upscale enough for most major-league club owners to showcase the sport as the national pastime.

National League president John Heydler spoke for the owners: "I find there is no demand in the major leagues to get away from baseball and all that it means as a great sport through tradition and development and get it into the show business, which after all is all that night ball is or can be." However, as F.C. Lane pointed out in a *Baseball Magazine* article, there was no denying one huge positive attribute of night baseball. "The main advantage is, of course, the fact that many more patrons can attend night baseball than can possibly attend day baseball. In short, night baseball multiplies the prospective customers greatly, perhaps, as William Veeck suggested, even twenty-fold," Lane wrote. "Baseball does not belong to the owners nor to the players. It belongs to the public. And if the public want[s] night baseball, you may rest assured they will get night baseball."[14]

The Braves did experiment with one night game in early August 1932 at Braves Field, using the portable lighting system of the barnstorming House of David team. Only a sparse crowd of 2,500 people showed up that evening to watch the nocturnal spectacle. "Six floodlights, set at sporting distances like cuspidors in an old-fashioned hotel, illuminated the field, and made the ball visible to a certain degree," the *Boston Globe* reported. "But when all is said and done, baseball is a national pastime only when the sun is hot and high, and the clouds scud off the Charles." The *Globe* further editorialized: "It is hard to believe that the big leagues will ever abandon the sunlight for the arc light. As a novelty, night baseball is all right. As a permanent diet, its value is at least doubtful."[15]

If the Braves had won the National League pennant in 1932, Boston baseball history likely would have been vastly different. The Red Sox might not have been able to survive the competition from a strong Braves team; indeed, Quinn might never have been able to sell the club. But when both leagues finally came to agreement that radio broadcasts were here to stay, the Red Sox still had a potential future in two-team Boston.

The codification of "local option" for radio broadcasts was the only roadblock remaining for Quinn to finalize the sale of the Red Sox. Prior to the December 1932 owners meeting, Fuchs had staunchly said that he was "strong for radio," while Quinn demurred that "the value of radio is open to debate" even though he supported it. When the owners approved continuation of radio for 1933, the two Boston clubs used the informal cooperative arrangement to have radio broadcasts for games on Monday through Saturday, but never on Sunday, for 14 more years until the policy was changed for the 1947 season.[16]

With the danger of a complete prohibition of radio broadcasts now eliminated, the Boston radio policy slowly became more publicly clear, not just privately understood. "Weekday games" was the terminology used by *The Sporting News* in 1933 and 1934 to communicate the fan-negative of no Sunday broadcasts, which evolved in 1936 to the less oblique use of "128 games to be broadcast," which, if readers did the math, was 26 games fewer than the 154 games played in a season and coincided with the number of Sundays during the season.[17]

When Quinn had first negotiated his rental of Braves Field in 1929, Whitman wrote an article entitled "Bob Quinn Thinking of Closing Fenway." Whitman forecast the demise of Fenway Park since "it is only a question of a few years when the Red Sox and Braves will be using one major league park jointly" for all ball games, not just Sundays and holidays. Due to the rundown nature of Fenway Park, fewer spectators now saw the distinct benefit of watching a game there, which was the "chummy nature of Fenway Park" compared to the more distant seating at Braves Field. "At Fenway Park you can look right into the eyes of the athletes. It was one of the charms of the yard enjoyed most by casual visitors to the American League park," Whitman wrote. "If you were in the grandstand, or in almost any of the pavilions or bleachers, you were near enough to see every fatal characteristic of the players."[18]

With the advent in 1932 of Sunday baseball at Fenway Park and no radio broadcasts of the Sunday games, Quinn had the perfect recipe to coax someone to buy the Red Sox and rejuvenate Fenway Park, to take advantage of that "chummy nature" not available at Braves Field. Quinn announced the sale of the Red Sox in February 1933.

◆ 12 ◆

Braves Continue
to Outdraw Red Sox

The announcement in late February 1933 that Bob Quinn had sold the Red Sox to Tom Yawkey signaled the end of the only time that the Braves ever had an extended period of fan preference in the 52-history of Boston as a two-team city.

During the depth of the nation's Great Depression, the 1933 season was the last chance for the Braves to solidify that fan preference into the future before Yawkey began to re-engineer the Red Sox. "The new owners propose to start at once in strengthening the club in every way possible, and hope eventually to build a winner," the *Boston Globe* reported on the purchase of the Red Sox by Yawkey. "They realize that this will take time and money, but they have plenty of both." The strengthening "in every way possible" included not just an improvement of the team on the field but also a renovation to upgrade Fenway Park.[1]

At the opening of the 1933 season, the Braves might have been able to cement the team's favorable position among Boston baseball fans had its concession vendor, the Harry Stevens Company, been able to acquire a license to sell beer at Braves Field. Although it would have been only "non-intoxicating" brew, so-called 3.2 beer, the beverage would have been legal beer under the new federal law signed in March by President Roosevelt, which took effect on April 7. It was too quick a turnaround as the Massachusetts legislature grappled with new rules for beer sales in the state, which had been non-existent since the institution of Prohibition in 1920, as the country marched forward to completely repeal Prohibition in December 1933. No beer would be sold in either Boston ballpark in 1933, since Stevens could, at best, obtain a license for only one facility.[2]

By the season-opener at Fenway Park on April 21, not much had changed with the Red Sox, since the sale of the club needed the approval of the other American League owners before Yawkey and his general manager Eddie Collins could officially take over. The one visible change at the ballpark was that spectators could now exit the subway from downtown at the recently opened Kenmore subway station, which was part of the traffic improvement project for Governor Square (renamed Kenmore Square in December 1932) to substitute below-ground rapid transit for above-ground streetcars to improve automobile flow through the heavily traveled intersection.[3]

Yawkey did negate a decision made before the sale by Quinn to move Ladies Day to Saturday, to have a common policy between the Red Sox and Braves, since the Braves wanted Ladies Day to be held on Saturday during the 1933 season. The Braves also wanted an earlier 2:15 start for Saturday games "to allow women working in offices and department stores who have a half-holiday on Saturday to attend and be home by early Saturday evening." In a precursor to the decline in the informal cooperative arrangement between the two baseball clubs, Yawkey mandated that Ladies Day remain on Friday at Fenway Park and Collins talked to the management of the Braves "as a courtesy" before making the announcement.[4]

The policy for Ladies Day was important in 1933, because baseball in Boston had contracted into a Sunday-only proposition (with the exception of holidays). The volume of spectators at games played Monday through Saturday had dropped to a trickle while the audiences on Sunday had dramatically expanded. Ladies Day and two-for-one doubleheaders were the dominant ways to get fans into the stands during the work week. In addition to free admission for women on Ladies Day, the Braves also extended half-price tickets for women at games played Monday through Wednesday.[5]

Saturday as Ladies Day at Braves Field was not terribly successful, though, because many fans waited for the games on Sunday, since that day usually also featured a two-for-one doubleheader (to eliminate one unprofitable weekday game) and there was no radio broadcast of the game to listen to outside the ballpark (due to the agreement to prohibit Sunday broadcasts). For instance, at the game on Saturday, May 13, "There were a large number of Ladies Day guests, and a big crowd of boys in the third-base pavilion" who were part of the Knot Hole Gang program," the *Boston Globe* reported, while "the attendance of cash customers was rather meager," estimated to be 3,000 people. At the Sunday doubleheader on May 14, paid attendance was more than six times higher at 20,000 people.[6]

Fans enjoyed watching 16 Sunday doubleheaders in Boston during the 1933 season, 11 at Braves Field and five at Fenway Park, even though the original schedules released during the winter showed just a single game on every Sunday. With the rampant shifting of a weekday game to become the second game of a Sunday doubleheader, not just in Boston but also in most major-league cities, there was a national outcry for more sanity in scheduling. "If Sunday doubleheaders are to become a regular thing, they should be so incorporated in the schedules," *The Sporting News* editorialized that spring. "We know nothing more meaningless than the present schedules, with games charted for as late as September being moved up at the whim of a club owner to create a Sunday doubleheader in May." As a result of these synthetic doubleheaders, the original schedules became mere scraps of paper once the season started. "There is such a thing as carrying the practice so far that the fans through habit will expect double bills as a regular diet," *The Sporting News* continued. "It's a known fact that some people deliberately stay away from the week-day games where it is a known fact that twin bills will be held on Sunday."[7]

This pattern existed not only at Braves Field but also at Fenway Park, with a surge of spectators on Sunday and minimal crowds during the rest of the week. For example, a five-game series with the New York Yankees began on Sunday, June 11, with a doubleheader that attracted 30,000 people. There was no game on Monday, since that game had been pushed up to be the second game of the Sunday doubleheader. The single games on Tuesday and Wednesday drew only 2,000 to 3,000 people. On Thursday, billed as Ladies Day, the paid attendance was 5,000 with another 3,500 women admitted free.[8]

Maximizing attendance on Sunday with synthetic doubleheaders was also augmented by doubleheaders during the work week, as the Braves played seven such twin bills in 1933 while the Red Sox engaged in four. Combined with the 11 Sunday doubleheaders and the Independence Day holiday doubleheaders, the Braves played one-half of their home games in 1933 as part of a doubleheader (38 of 77 games). The Braves had one of the highest percentages of doubleheaders played during 1933, a year that saw a record ratio of doubleheaders across both leagues, when nearly two-fifths of all games were played during doubleheaders. The great fear of club owners—giving away the product as part of a two-for-one doubleheader—had intensified in 1933.[9]

The Braves never did solve the mostly-on-Sunday dilemma at Braves Field. Beyond the promotional techniques of the doubleheader and Ladies Day, there was little that Braves owner Judge Fuchs could do to encourage patrons to go to the ballpark other than on Sunday. Potential customers during the week either had no money, because they weren't working in the middle of the Great Depression, or they used what spare money they had to legally buy a beer or travel up to Salem, New Hampshire, to legally gamble on horse racing at newly opened Rockingham Park. Even a decent Braves team in 1933 failed to draw fans to the ballpark during the week.[10]

On the other hand, Red Sox owner Yawkey, a more astute businessman than Fuchs, did achieve some success during the next few seasons at attracting more spectators to weekday games at Fenway Park. After the sale of the Red Sox to Yawkey was approved by the American League in early May 1933, Yawkey told sportswriters: "Boston is a good baseball town and deserves a winning team. I am in the market for good players and will buy any that are available. I do not intend to stop until the Red Sox are strong enough to compete with any other club in the league on even terms." Yawkey immediately opened his checkbook to acquire two ballplayers from the St. Louis Browns and another pair from the Yankees. This was the first step toward bringing fans to the ballpark during the week, not just on Sunday.[11]

Neither the Red Sox nor the Braves overwhelmed the competition during the first half of the 1933 season. After winning four of the five games in that June series with the Yankees, the Red Sox moved up from the cellar of the American League to seventh place, where they remained for the rest of the season. The Braves lost more than they won and were in the lower middle

This full house at Braves Field for a Sunday game circa 1933 shows typical fans that sat in the less-expensive seating of the third-base pavilion (foreground). Although the audience was primarily men in white shirts and straw hats, there were some women and children, indicating that families were in attendance (courtesy Boston Public Library, Leslie Jones Collection).

of the pack in the National League standings in late July. However, the Braves then proceeded to win 20 of 24 games between July 30 and August 26 to move into second place.

Fans flocked to three Sunday doubleheaders at Braves Field during that winning streak, with steadily increasing crowds: 30,000 on August 6; 35,000 on August 20; and 40,000 on August 27. "Staid, conservative Boston has the pennant fever," Ford Sawyer wrote in *The Sporting News*. "In the short space of a couple of weeks, the Braves, marching steadily onward and upward into a challenging position, have fairly carried the fans off their feet by their sensational playing." The *Boston Globe* observed: "Pennant fever has stung Boston fans this year as it hasn't done in many, many seasons and all on the account of the Battling Braves. The outpouring of 35,000 fans yesterday proved anew that Boston is one of the best baseball towns on the map."[12]

On the eve of the six-game series with the first-place New York Giants that began on August 31, the Braves were six games behind the Giants. If the Braves could have swept the Giants, they would have been tied for first place; winning four or five of the games would have kept them in the running for the pennant. There was even talk that the Sunday doubleheader would be broadcast on the radio, since "Sunday games have not been broadcast for some time, but as a sellout is practically assured for Sunday and the interest so keen."[13]

Although the Braves won the opener, they proceeded to lose the next four games (and tie the last game, which was stopped by the Sunday curfew) to dash the pennant hopes of Boston fans. For a brief four-day stretch in that series with the Giants, the Braves were the toast of Boston, rekindling memories of the Miracle Braves of 1914. Following the Giants series, the Braves went on a season-ending road trip and soon plunged to fifth place, but eked out a fourth-place finish with a victory on the last day of the season.

The doubleheader on Friday, September 1, was billed as "Boston's biggest crowd" ever, when an on-field crowd that was "a serpentine ribbon of humanity, ten rows deep, lay upon the turf," separated from the ballplayers not just by ropes but also by policemen on horseback. "Last night the Braves management was not yet prepared to announce official figures on the subject, but more than 50,000 were in the park and 15,000 cursing customers were driven out of Gaffney St. by mounted police after the gates had been shut half an hour before the first game started," the *Boston Globe* reported. "If this was not Boston's largest baseball crowd in history, it came within a few hundred of that mark and easily beat every existing record for a week-day crowd."[14]

For the six games with the Giants at Braves Field, the total attendance was 150,000 people. Friday's crowd of 50,000-plus was the largest of the four days, easily topping Thursday's 35,000 crowd at Ladies Day and Saturday's 20,000 weak crowd. The audience for the Sunday doubleheader approached Friday's tally, but it fell a bit short at 45,000 people.

The Braves outdrew the Red Sox in attendance during the 1933 season, as 517,000 spectators visited Braves Field while 268,000 (up significantly from 182,000 the previous year) went to Fenway Park. While it was the third straight year that Braves attendance had been above half a million, 1933 was the last year that more people visited Braves Field than went to Fenway Park, while the Braves played in Boston.

Unfortunately, most of the spectators at Braves Field in 1933 were intermittent fans, rather than Braves-leaning general baseball fans or even just garden-variety Boston general baseball fans. This is seen through the combined attendance of 250,000 for seven dates, four in the Giants series in September (150,000) and three Sunday doubleheaders in August (100,000), which represented one-half the team's total attendance for the entire 1933 season.

One such intermittent fan was interviewed at the Saturday, September 2, game. "My first victim was a fan who had not been out to the park for a decade. The old urge had caught up with him once more," the *Globe* wrote. The man responded: "I'm still a family man and have to support them. But I've made it my business to find the time to hike out to Braves Field and watch the Braves repeat their performance of 1914. The old spirit is still with me and the team."[15]

This pattern did not bode well for the future of the Braves. Once the team's competitiveness dissipated, so did the crowds at Braves Field, a decline that accelerated with the increasing preference for private entertainment venues, such as radio and the automobile, and viable alternative entertainment at a public venue like the horse-racing track. Attendance at Braves Field would not exceed the level of 1933 until night baseball debuted there in 1946, when the Braves discovered the elixir of combination public-private entertainment.

After reading the newspaper coverage about the attendance surge at Braves Field for the series with the Giants, Yawkey was convinced that he not only had to have a winning team but one that was also power-hitting and had some name stars. This was the second step toward competing with the Braves. The third step was to renovate Fenway Park, a plan that was announced in mid–September 1933.[16]

Yawkey inherited a small band of dedicated Red Sox fans and a quorum of Sox-leaning general baseball fans, who both loved the power-hitting American League style of play. Otherwise, there was still a strong community of followers of both teams, the "Boston fans" as the newspapers referred to them, or general baseball fans, as well as the whims of intermittent fans. Swaying these groups was a tough proposition in 1933 when the Braves had a chase at the pennant. By refurbishing Fenway Park and retooling the team, Yawkey quickly converted general baseball fans into Sox-leaning general fans, a group that soon morphed into dedicated Red Sox fans.

◆ 13 ◆

Renovated Red Sox

Tom Yawkey refurbished the Red Sox for the 1934 season, when he secured better ballplayers to produce a winning team and overhauled Fenway Park to provide an improved atmosphere for spectators. Crowd sizes that just two years earlier would only occur for Braves games at Braves Field now materialized at Fenway Park.

In December 1933, Yawkey made good on his promise to spend money to improve the team on the field. He and Collins negotiated a trade with the Philadelphia Athletics to obtain star pitcher Lefty Grove along with pitcher Rube Walberg and second baseman Max Bishop for $125,000 in cash and two ballplayers. One year later, Yawkey spent another $250,000 to purchase shortstop Joe Cronin from the Washington Senators for the 1935 season. There were also numerous smaller trades that took place during the 1934 and 1935 seasons to bring in new ballplayers to recast the fortunes of the team, now often referred to as the Gold Sox due to the expensive acquisitions of Grove and Cronin.

The renovation of Fenway Park took place over the winter of 1934, since major construction had to wait until the Boston Redskins, tenants that fall in the ballpark, to complete their National Football League schedule. What started out as a moderate rehab quickly expanded into a full-blown rebuilding of the ballpark.

Most visible to Boston baseball fans were the erection of additional grandstand seating along the left-field line to replace the vacant lot and the replacement of the wooden right-field pavilion with a concrete base and a roof. The right-field bleachers were also replaced and expanded into center field. Overall, the renovation of Fenway Park increased the seating capacity from 26,000 to 38,000 people. There were now 1,600 box seats ($1.65 per ticket) 16,400 grandstand seats ($1.10), 8,900 pavilion seats (85 cents), and 11,200 bleacher seats (55 cents).[1]

There was also a new left-field wall. The old wooden wall was razed, as was its fronting incline known as Duffy's Cliff, and replaced with a wall made of concrete and tin. Embedded in the renovated left-field wall was a new scoreboard. "The electrically-operated scoreboard at the foot of the left field fence, and operated from the press box by Eddie Cummings, is the last word. The system of balls, strikes, outs and batters is somewhat similar to a traffic system. The green lights represent balls, the red lights strikes and the batters' figures are illuminated in yellow."[2]

Unfazed by a fire in January that destroyed much of the new bleacher construction, Yawkey and Collins had the improved Fenway Park ready for the season-opener on April 17, 1934. Since Yawkey and Collins "know full well that the fans want a game and not a lot of forensics," there was little cere-monial fanfare and the only speech-making was said to be "the umpire's stentorian 'Play Bawl.'" As the 30,336 spectators entered the refurbished ballpark for the first game of the 1934 season, "their eyes opened with amazement at the magnificent structure which the Yawkey for-tunes erected," and to many "it hardly seemed possible that only last November it was an entirely different park."[3]

Less than a week later, the capacity of Fenway Park was truly put to the test for the Sunday, April 22, game against the Yankees. The first of several

Red Sox owner Tom Yawkey, shown in this photograph with his first wife, Elise, spent millions of dollars to ren-ovate Fenway Park and create a winning baseball team. Yawkey changed the nature of Boston baseball fans, which shifted from general baseball fans that supported both teams to become dedicated Red Sox fans (Library of Congress, Prints and Photographs Division, LC-USZ62-119405).

newspaper headlines over the course of 1934 and 1935 heralded a record for "the largest local American League crowd," as 44,361 people paid to watch the single game that Sunday. At least another 8,000 were reportedly denied purchase of standing-room tickets in the outfield. Attendance for the first five playing dates of the 1934 season at Fenway Park was close to 150,000 people, nearly the total for the entire 1932 season just two years earlier. The five playing dates included the season-opener, the Patriots Day morning-and-afternoon twin bill, and Saturday and Sunday games with the Yankees. "Should the Sox be within reach of the pennant in mid or late season," the *Boston Globe* speculated, "the above figures may look insignificant, so enthused is New England's baseball famished populace."[4]

Two Sunday doubleheaders in August 1934 broke the attendance record at Fenway Park. For what was anticipated to be Babe Ruth's last game in Boston, a crowd of 46,766 jammed the ballpark on August 12 to pay tribute to the Bambino. Many of the spectators remembered Ruth when he began his baseball career in Boston with the 1915–1919 Red Sox. One week later, 46,995 paid to watch the Detroit Tigers, under the leadership of Mickey Cochrane, who grew up 30 miles south of Boston in the little town of Bridgewater, as the Tigers headed for the American League pennant.[5]

At both Sunday doubleheaders in August, it was estimated that 15,000 to 20,000 people had sought tickets but could not get into the ballpark. This was a function of the club selling only 10,000 to 12,000 reserved grandstand seats in the days leading up to the game, resulting in more than 20,000 tickets becoming available for purchase only on the day of the game. This taxed the capacity not only of the ballpark, but also the Boston subway system (which put on extra cars to handle the volume), the roadways around the ballpark (to handle the suburban drivers), and the Boston police department (which required additional staffing for crowd control).

Two more 47,000+ crowds occurred in 1935, at the Independence Day doubleheader against the Yankees on July 4 and at a Sunday doubleheader on September 22, also against the Yankees. Given the unknown number of complimentary tickets used ("Annie Oakleys" in the parlance of the day), it is unclear which game created the largest number of people actually within the ballpark. What is important was the rabid interest in the Red Sox, with their highest attendance figures in more than 20 years, as 610,000 people went to Fenway Park in 1934 and 558,000 in 1935. However, there was not enough room for all of them to comfortably watch a ball game.

An incident at the packed September 22, 1935, game put an end to the enormous 45,000+ crowds at Fenway Park. Charles Droggitis of Biddeford, Maine, a standing-room patron in the outfield, was struck in the face by a broken bottle "thrown during one of the barrages which some of the inhabitants of the bleachers unleashed on the overflow patrons standing on the field, as a protest to the latter's obstructing the bleacherites' views." The Red Sox club physician closed the wound with two stitches and treated his scalp for lacerations. Because this incident highlighted the lack of safety at the ballpark, the sale of standing-room tickets was substantially reduced beginning in the 1936 season.[6]

Suburban fans and others from outside Greater Boston comprised a large portion of the record Sunday crowds, as the newspapers often noted that "a great part of whom are made up of residents of Maine, New Hampshire, Rhode Island, and the distant Massachusetts spots." Two trends in the 1930s caused the influx of suburban fans to watch baseball in Boston.[7]

People had more free time as the Great Depression trudged into the mid–1930s, as employers, in general, reduced the hours of their employees to minimize the impact of unemployment rather than lay off large portions of the workforce. The "weekend" was becoming the norm for many people, with both Saturday and Sunday as days of rest; at worst, the workweek had slimmed down to five and a half days, with just a half-day of work on the sixth non-full day (often Saturday morning). Therefore, suburban residents, whether white-collar or blue-collar, had more time to devote to amusement activities.[8]

The second trend was the city of Boston suffering a one percent decline in population during the 1930s, while the population of its suburbs in Greater Boston experienced a four percent increase in population. The city of Boston now represented just one-third of the population of the Greater Boston area, whereas 50 years earlier the city had comprised one-half of the area's population. The largest suburban growth was in the towns ten or more miles from downtown Boston, including Winchester to the north, Lexington to the west, and Weymouth to the south.[9]

For suburban fans, driving into Boston was not much better in 1935 than it had been ten years earlier in 1925. Improvements included Route 9 (the Worcester Turnpike) now being a divided highway, although not a limited-access road, and the Sumner Tunnel opening to automobile travel from East Boston. Towns in the western outlying areas of Greater Boston within the Route 9 corridor, such as Framingham, began to see population growth.

The Massachusetts Department of Public Works issued a futuristic plan in 1937 for its roadway building, which included a "freeway" to run northeast across the state from Douglas, near the Connecticut border, to Tyngsboro, near the New Hampshire border, to permit drivers to travel at high speeds to make their way from New York to Maine. They called it "a magnificent super-super-highway, to dwarf even such a thoroughfare as the Worcester Turnpike." Also on the drawing board was a spur off this freeway to go 40 miles east to Boston, "to absorb practically all of the New York to Boston traffic and take a great burden off the Worcester Turnpike." Almost an afterthought was the upgrading of Route 128 for drivers to more easily travel around the outskirts of Boston.[10]

The freeway and its spur to Boston would have ensured the livelihood of both the Red Sox and the Braves, by enabling suburban residents and those in more outlying areas to efficiently drive into Boston. Unfortunately, the freeway extension into Boston would not be completed for another three decades. This delay completely changed the dynamics of encouraging suburban fans to travel to Boston, and, consequently, whether Boston could remain as a two-team city.

During 1934 and 1935, the term "Boston baseball fans," which signified followers of both teams, began to crumble into a distinct bifurcation of "Red Sox fans" and (less often) "Braves fans," as both these terms now entered the standard lexicon of Boston sports. Many general baseball fans quickly gravitated from being Sox-leaning fans to dedicated fans exclusively devoted to the Red Sox. While the fast demise of the Braves, both financially and playing-wise, helped to constrain the number of general baseball fans, as well as their growth prospects, general baseball fans (a.k.a. Boston baseball fans) continued to be an influential component of overall fandom in Boston for another dozen years.

The creation of "Red Sox fans" was seen in the larger crowds at Saturday and Sunday games at Fenway Park than at Braves Field, largely populated by intermittent fans. The renovated ballpark, enhanced team on the field, and the American League power-hitting style of play quickly transformed these intermittent fans into Sox-leaning fans who then converted to dedicated Sox fans. However, it was the patrons for games conducted Monday through Friday that set the Red Sox apart from the Braves as the fan favorite in Boston during the waning years of purely day baseball in the major leagues. Weekday audiences of a respectable volume returned to Fenway Park, with renewed interest by businessmen, both those working in downtown Boston as well as those from the suburbs. This precipitated the perspective that Red Sox fans were generally white-collar workers while Braves fans were blue-collar workers.

There was not much of a natural base for weekday games left over from the 1920s, since the Great Depression had fundamentally altered the economic landscape in Boston. "The number of day-by-day fans is surprisingly small," Henry Harris wrote in a 1938 analysis of baseball fans in Boston. "Outside of the gamblers, there are probably not more than a couple of hundred men who come out to see every game." Therefore, it was a constant struggle to entice people who held everyday jobs to go to the ballpark during the work week and not listen to the games broadcast on the radio. "Most of those at the ball game are those who find themselves with an unexpected afternoon off, or feel themselves due to see one. There is a party which comes down from Maine once a month to see a game. A Boston business executive says that he gets the urge every so often and sneaks off to see a game."[11]

There were several reasons why fans populated weekday games at Fenway Park more than those held at Braves Field, beyond the aesthetics of the ballpark, the competitiveness of the Red Sox team, and the American League power-hitting style of play. One reason was the easier effort to get to Fenway Park from downtown Boston or either train station (North Station or South Station), since it was a shorter trip on the Boylston Street subway to Kenmore Square to get off for Fenway Park; to go to Braves Field required continuing on an above-ground streetcar. For fans that drove an automobile to the game, there was better parking near Fenway Park along Boylston Street and Brookline Avenue. Another reason was that businessmen, the bulk of the weekday audience, had a kindred spirit with Yawkey, who ran a lumber business in addition to the Red Sox club, and confidence in Collins, who was a former ballplayer making most of the baseball decisions. This combination was in stark contrast to Braves president Fuchs, a lawyer who had mangled both the financial and personnel sides of the Braves. Decent crowds at weekday games gave the Red Sox a big edge over the Braves in sustaining the economic viability.

Ballpark spectators were just one part of the triad of Boston fans, though, so Yawkey also took action to improve matters for radio listeners and newspaper readers.

To appeal to radio listeners, a new broadcasting booth was built as part of the refurbishing of Fenway Park, a "goldfish bowl made of shatter-proof glass." This provided a more comfortable setting for WNAC announcer Fred Hoey to describe the ball games over the airwaves of the Yankee Network and develop radio listeners all over New England into Red Sox fans.[12]

Hoey was by now an institution with Boston baseball fans. "Hoey owned New England. He had a dry, rough voice, and he barked balls and strikes without elaboration," Red Barber wrote in his book *The Broadcasters*. "New England was conservative in the matter of words, so, by and large, Fred was a most satisfactory announcer for that close-knit part of the world." Hoey added supplemental information to his straightforward play-by-play, with out-of-town scores passed down from the press box and knowledge that he compiled himself about the ballplayers. "On this chart we list the name of the player, his age, height, weight, home, his record for the previous season, including all the batting features, together with the pertinent facts of his career that might be of interest to fans," Hoey told *The Sporting News*. "Nothing that we announce is trusted to memory."[13]

WNAC liked Hoey because he was skillful in pitching commercials that integrated easily into his baseball broadcasts, or, more bluntly, "how to shill for sponsors." In the early 1930s John Shepard, the owner of WNAC, had moved beyond advertising by local businesses to national advertisers, by

Radio became a common fixture in most living rooms in New England by the mid–1930s, where fans listened to broadcasts of Braves and Red Sox home games. The radio broadcasts helped to develop dedicated Red Sox fans, since the power-hitting style of play in the American League games at Fenway Park excited listeners (Library of Congress, Prints and Photographs Division, LC-USZ62–54356).

creating "a mythical New England, one that held value for advertisers and that could only be accessed using Shepard's facilities," where they could reach "hometown audiences." Kentucky Club (tobacco) and Mobil (oil and gasoline) were early sponsors of the baseball broadcasts on the Yankee Network.[14]

General Mills sponsored the broadcasts in 1936, which proved to be the undoing of Hoey. General Mills had a significant footprint in sponsoring radio broadcasts of baseball in a number of cities, in an aggressive marketing effort to promote its Wheaties breakfast cereal. While Hoey's austere approach to broadcasts sold Kentucky Club tobacco products to men, it didn't work nearly as well with women who were the primary buyers of Wheaties. When General Mills wanted a more sophisticated approach to pitching its cereal during baseball games, Hoey was fired in December 1936. However, when considerable outrage was expressed by Boston baseball fans to WNAC, General Mills relented and Hoey was reinstated.[15]

With radio now in two-thirds of American households, Hoey was instrumental in developing Red Sox fans, since many radio listeners were more receptive to the hard-hitting ballplayers at Fenway Park. The Red Sox games were more exciting to listen to than those of the National League team in Boston. As one future dedicated Red Sox fan recalled of his formative years listening to Hoey: "Fred also announced the Boston Braves games, but it would be the Red Sox games you would be more apt to remember. There just seemed to be more excitement when you heard Hoey expound on such heroes as Jimmy Foxx, Joe Cronin, Pinky Higgins, and Joe Vosmik than when he would talk about the Braves."[16]

The 1934 and 1935 seasons provided the foundation for Boston to be known as an American League city, due to the emphasis on home-run hitters at cozy Fenway Park versus the focus on pitching, and small-ball offense, at expansive Braves Field. While Red Sox power-hitters Carl Reynolds and Julius Solters did not hit a barrage of home runs, visiting-team sluggers such as Hank Greenberg of the Tigers, Jimmie Foxx of the Athletics, and Lou Gehrig of the Yankees provided enough power-hitting to entertain the fans at Fenway. This helped to develop a larger interest in the Red Sox among intermittent fans, who attended games on Sunday, many of whom then converted into being Sox-leaning general baseball fans.

To enhance newspaper coverage of the ball games, a new press box was built and a press room was added as part of the Fenway Park renovation. The press room provided free food and drink (alcoholic and otherwise) to the sportswriters. In 1935, to further encourage positive coverage of the Red Sox to newspaper readers, Yawkey began to pay travel expenses of the sportswriters to report directly on the team's road games, rather than have the Boston newspapers run out-of-town "special dispatch" stories that added no insight into the Red Sox. This provided newspaper readers with more detailed coverage of the Red Sox road games while the Braves played at home, which gave a subtle advantage to the Red Sox in their quest to mint more dedicated and Sox-leaning general baseball fans.[17]

In just two seasons, the Red Sox had developed a formidable edge among Boston baseball fans with many general baseball fans now following the Braves to a lesser degree and many new fans wholeheartedly following the Red Sox without much interest, if any, in the Braves.

◆ 14 ◆

Braves Change
Name to Bees

By the end of the 1934 season, it was very clear that the Braves would not be able to compete with the free-spending Red Sox, which now sported a reconstituted team fortified with talented ballplayers that played in a handsomely refurbished Fenway Park. While both teams had finished in fourth place, and the Braves had a better won-lost record, twice as many people went to Fenway Park than to Braves Field in 1934.

It wasn't just the Red Sox that were tough competition, however. The Braves were hit hard by the advent of legalized horse racing with pari-mutuel wagering in 1934 at Rockingham Park in New Hampshire and Narragansett Park in Rhode Island. Things looked even worse in 1935 with legalized betting in Massachusetts at Suffolk Downs in East Boston, where the ponies ran, and at Wonderland Park in nearby Revere where dog racing was conducted. "If you were into sports, fashion, and a fast crowd during the late 1930s and 1940s, then Suffolk Downs was the place to see and be seen in Boston," one horse-racing chronicler wrote. "The horses at the East Boston oval became the dominant local pastime."[1]

While not immune to the horse-racing competition, the Red Sox were impacted less than the Braves because they now displayed a solid product on the field and played their games in a new, more spectator-friendly, ballpark. These new elements motivated general baseball fans, created a healthy swath of dedicated fans, and encourage more intermittent fans to sample the new atmosphere at Fenway Park. "Major league baseball's answer to the local challenge of horse racing with pari-mutuel betting was given at Fenway Park yesterday when 14,000 persons paid to watch the rampaging Red Sox divide a double-header with the Chicago White Sox." The Braves, on the other hand, had a mediocre product on the field and played in an aging 20-year-old ball-

149

park, with few dedicated or Braves-leaning general baseball fans. For non-leaning general baseball fans and intermittent fans seeking entertainment when the Red Sox were on the road, it was an easy decision to skip the Braves game and head to the rack track.[2]

In the fall of 1934, to compound the situation, Boston baseball fans were left in the lurch by Judge Fuchs when he announced plans to convert Braves Field into a dog-racing park. This announcement raised the ire of Commissioner Landis, who was staunchly opposed to a major-league owner being involved with gambling, with still-fresh memories of the 1919 Black Sox scandal. Fuchs also never bothered to obtain permission from the owners of Braves Field (which the Braves rented, not owned), Commonwealth Realty, which was less than enamored with the idea of dog racing and proceeded to evict the Braves for breaking their lease. Fuchs then floated the idea of playing the Braves games at Fenway Park, counting on the largesse he had supplied (involuntarily) under the informal cooperative arrangement between the two clubs, for the Red Sox to use Braves Field for Sunday games under Quinn's previous ownership. Yawkey despised the idea of dog racing in addition to having a deep-seated aversion to sharing Fenway Park. Red Sox general manager Eddie Collins issued a statement strongly indicating the Red Sox were not interested in renting Fenway Park to the Braves: "No arrangement has been made for the Braves to play their home games at Fenway Park the coming season, and, so far as I know, no such an arrangement is pending."[3]

Amid headlines like "Boston Baseball Fans Await Solution of Braves Field Situation," the National League, at a January 1935 league meeting, bailed out the homeless, and nearly bankrupt, Braves by guaranteeing the rent at Braves Field and warranting that the ballpark would not be used for dog racing. This meeting is best remembered for authorizing the Cincinnati Reds to experiment with night baseball during the 1935 season, with a strict limitation of just seven night games (one against each other team in the league) to be played only Monday through Friday and never on Saturday, Sunday, and holidays. Day games also could not be completed under the lights, effectively mandating the start of night games to be after dusk. Fuchs announced that the Braves, given their dismal financial situation, would not install lights at Braves Field, but were willing to play night games on the road.[4]

This was a huge missed opportunity for the Braves to compete against the Red Sox. If the struggling Braves had begun staging night games at Braves Field during the 1930s, they likely would have had a more formidable presence with Boston baseball fans. The use of temporary lights at Braves Field for boxing and other evening events clearly indicated that many people were interested in watching night-time outdoor entertainment, although they were often not the ilk of the preferred middle-class, general baseball fan. This was a lesson learned with the 1932 exhibition night game against the House of

David, which was later reinforced in the 1940s after lights had been erected at Braves Field.

Desperate for an inexpensive way to attract spectators to Braves Field during the 1935 season, Fuchs hatched the stunt to bring Babe Ruth back to Boston to play for the Braves to capitalize on Ruth's renown as a home-run hitter. Because the Babe had continually drawn people to Fenway Park as a member of the visiting New York Yankees, Fuchs hoped he would have the same impact at Braves Field. It wasn't the position as manager that Ruth wanted, but Fuchs portrayed the job as an "executive" position with the title of vice president and assistant manager in addition to "occasional" duty as an active ballplayer. Unfortunately, the titles were merely a ruse; the primary role for Ruth was to be an active ballplayer so that people would buy tickets to the ball games.

The signing was announced in New York City in late February. The Yankees, looking to dump the aging star, were happy to grant Ruth's release so that he could join the Braves. Ruth's ignorance of the situation was unveiled the next day when he announced that he would be the Braves manager in 1936. "The deal had a stench to it from the beginning," Leigh Montville wrote in his biography of Ruth. "The Babe was the only pure heart in the entire proceeding. He had said he wanted to be a manager. Period. That was his goal. The other parties in the transaction took that desire and bent it to fit their needs. The Babe never knew what hit him."[5]

Ruth did spark some ticket sales in Boston, based on the enthusiastic reports from spring training published in the Boston newspapers. At the season-opener at

Babe Ruth played for the Braves in 1935, after his spectacular career with the New York Yankees, illustrated by this 1933 Goudey Gum Co. baseball card. Ruth, though, lasted only a few weeks with the Braves, once he realized he had been hired only for promotional purposes to attract fans to Braves Field (Library of Congress, Prints and Photographs Division, LC-DIG-ppmsca-38379).

Braves Field on April 16, the stands were only half filled with 20,000 fans; at the Patriots Day holiday twin bill, attendance was a bit better, with 23,000 at the afternoon game but just 6,000 at the morning game. While Ruth hit a home run in that first game, he limped off the field a few days later. Then he caught a cold, had knee problems, and locked horns with Fuchs about making personal appearances for the Braves outside the ballpark. Reality hit home with Ruth during a May road trip where fans in St. Louis, Pittsburgh, and Cincinnati treated him as a carnival act on a farewell tour. After the Braves returned to Boston, Ruth resigned in early June after days of friction with Fuchs.

Fuchs soon joined Ruth as a former employee of the Braves himself, being forced out on August 1 as the Braves became a ward of the National League. On Saturday afternoon, July 27, while discussions abounded about what to do about the ownership of the Braves, 45,000 people watched horse racing at Suffolk Downs. Only 1,100 people wandered into Braves Field that afternoon to watch the Braves play the Philadelphia Phillies. Later that Saturday evening, 13,000 people watched dog racing at Wonderland Park.

It was a moribund 1935 season, in which the Braves finished in last place and lost 115 games. Attendance at Braves Field dropped to 232,000. One of the 115 games lost by the Braves was on July 24 at Cincinnati in a night game watched by 23,000 fans, about ten times the normal attendance for a weekday afternoon game. People did like night baseball, even if the major-league owners continued to believe it was just a cheap trick, passing fad, or desperation move to cater to the unwashed masses who labored all day for work.

George Marshall, the owner of the Boston Redskins football club in the National Football League, looked into purchasing the Braves during the summer of 1935. Marshall, though, was deemed a bit too progressive, since he advocated beer and night baseball at Braves Field, among other low-brow enhancements he would make if he owned the Braves. Marshall became more famous as the man who moved the Redskins to Washington, D.C., after the 1936 season.[6]

In November 1935, there was talk of the possibility of the first franchise shift in major-league baseball since 1902, but new National League president Ford Frick vowed to keep the Braves in Boston. Bob Quinn, the former owner of the Red Sox, put together a consortium of men to acquire ownership of the Braves. Quinn was a traditional baseball man, who believed that a good product on the field would encourage people to come to the ball games. Quinn was not a proponent of installing lights at Braves Field to play night baseball, since "he had some doubt as to whether it would be worth the money," estimated at $75,000 to play just seven games a season. He thought "night baseball was at best a necessary evil."[7]

The owners of the Red Sox felt even stronger about the prospects for night baseball in Boston. "I am now, and always have been, opposed to playing baseball in artificial light. Baseball is a daylight game," general manager Eddie Collins said. "We want no part of it, nor do I think the fans want it." Owner Tom Yawkey was even more adamant: "I certainly hope I will never live to see the time when I shall see a major league night baseball game at Fenway Park."[8]

These feelings were not out of line in light with the early results of night baseball in the local minor league, the Northeastern League, which used a portable lighting system that rotated around ballparks in the league in 1934. These night baseball experiments in New England did not inspire optimism at the major-league level. The first night game in Lowell, Massachusetts, was played on a cold night on June 8, starting at 8:30 and not ending until just before midnight. According to the sportswriter for the *Lowell Sun*: "Suffering from a lack of red flannels and ear muffs, some 1200 fans shivered and shook last night at Laurier Park in an atmosphere better suited for a trial practice of Admiral Byrd and his Antarctic crew than a game of baseball." The night before at Springfield, Massachusetts, a batter was knocked unconscious when he couldn't see the pitched ball in the dim lighting, which produced "shadows in many spots and the outfield was so dark that balls that got away from outfielders were limited to two bases."[9]

While the Braves and Red Sox both swore off night baseball, another professional team sport played night games at Braves Field in the fall of 1936 using a temporary lighting system, when the Boston Shamrocks football team of the upstart American Football League played three night games. If Quinn noticed the attendance at the Shamrocks' first night game on Wednesday, September 30, and compared that to the Braves' dismal attendance for baseball on a Wednesday afternoon, he didn't publicly comment.[10]

Quinn changed the name of the baseball team, hoping to give Boston fans a fresh start and perhaps attract a few new ones as well. In a contest to rename the Braves, there were 1,327 different names suggested by fans. Quinn asked 25 baseball writers to choose among those submissions. Bees was the overwhelming favorite (14 votes), with Blue Birds second (four votes), Beacons third (three votes), Colonials fourth (two votes), and Blues and Bulls tied for fifth (one vote each). Since 15 fans had submitted the Bees name, the contest winner was drawn at random from the names placed in a hat. Arthur Rockwood of East Weymouth was the winner, receiving two season tickets as his prize. "As a new name for your club, I submit 'The Boston Bees,'" Rockwood wrote in his contest letter. "The B is significant of many things, Boston, Beans, Baseball, etc., and not too hard to learn, being similar to Braves. And if your club develops the bees' characteristics, you should have honey this fall." The other 14 fans received a consolation prize of two tickets to a Bees game.[11]

What gave the Bees a glimmer of hope at succeeding in Boston was the lack of minor-league baseball in New England. The closest minor-league team was 150 miles away in Albany, New York. The Great Depression had wiped out minor-league ball in the New England states, with the Hartford, Connecticut, club folding in 1932 and the latest resurrection of the New England League disbanding in 1934 after two seasons. With WNAC using its Yankee Network to broadcast the Bees home games from radio stations in a dozen cities throughout New England, reportedly reaching five million listeners, there was ample opportunity to use the voice of Fred Hoey to build a fan base outside Greater Boston that could be convinced to travel to Boston to attend Sunday ball games.[12]

In 1936, even with an improved team and a new name, the Bees did not gain much ground in the ballpark attendance battle with the Red Sox. The club even had to suffer through the indignity of having its renamed National League Park called the Bee Hive as the new nickname to replace the Wigwam that sportswriters had so often called Braves Field in previous years. In 1936 the Bees moved up two slots in the National League standings and attracted 100,000 more customers than did the last-place Braves in 1935; however, even though the Red Sox moved down two slots in the American League standings, they managed to attract 70,000 more customers than the fourth-place Red Sox in 1935.

Interestingly, on the same day that Quinn was announced as the new president of the Braves, the Red Sox announced a trade with the Philadelphia Athletics in which the Red Sox acquired slugger Jimmie Foxx. As seen by the above attendance numbers, the appearance of Foxx in a Red Sox uniform at Fenway Park in 1936 immediately changed the dynamics of competition for Boston baseball fans to greatly favor the Red Sox over the Braves-cum-Bees.

◆ 15 ◆

Power Hitting
at Fenway Park

With the arrival of right-handed slugger Jimmie Foxx, the Red Sox solidified the allegiance of a wide swath of general baseball fans in New England and converted many former Braves-leaning fans into dedicated Red Sox fans because of the team's power-hitting style of play.

"During the World Series I said that I was not interested in Foxx," Yawkey told the editor of *The Sporting News* before the 1936 season. "I felt that he had lost his incentive, and that it would be a mistake to bring him to Boston. Then I met Foxx. I got to know him intimately. I appreciated that we could rebuild his ambition and his incentive, and that Boston offered a tremendous opportunity to him. So I went after him."[1]

Not only did Yawkey get the slugging Foxx in a trade with the Philadelphia Athletics, but he also obtained outfielder Doc Cramer and several other athletes in exchange for a large amount of cash and a couple of surplus ballplayers. This trade furthered the reputation of the Sox as the "Millionaires" of the American League, which made it nearly impossible for the Bees to compete for the cheers of Boston fans.

"I want to give Boston the kind of ball team it deserves," Yawkey said. "I don't want to be messing around with a loser in baseball any more than I would enjoy that sensation in any line of business. Baseball is my hobby. I have plenty of money, and I want to spend it the right way. Buying ball players and building a ball club is my idea of the right way to spend. And it is good business, as well as good fun."[2]

Foxx hit 41 home runs in 1936 to shatter the Red Sox team record of 29 set back in 1919 by Babe Ruth. Crowds increased at Fenway Park as the Red Sox remained in second place for much of the first half of the 1936 season and watched Foxx chase Ruth's home-run record. In early July, with Foxx and others launching so many home runs over the left-field wall, the Red Sox installed netting atop the wall to reduce the number of broken windows in the buildings along Lansdowne Street. Foxx broke Ruth's team record in late July.[3]

During the 1936 season, beer was sold for the first time at both Fenway Park and National League Park (nee Braves Field). To avoid crowd-control problems with intoxicated patrons, the spectator capacity of Fenway Park was capped at 38,000, which rendered the 47,000-plus crowds of 1934 and 1935 as forever the maximum attendance for a baseball game at Fenway Park. There was little concern with drunken crowds at the home of the Bees. Fans who loved the power-hitting style of the American League were not going to be coaxed to watch a Bees game, even though Bob Quinn ostensibly improved spectator viewing by moving the field 20 feet closer to the grandstand.[4]

The beer may have had some influence in making the fans at Fenway Park more impatient with the power hitters in the Red Sox lineup, and thus more vociferous. Sportswriters called these fans "wolves"—"not Canis lupus, but Canis fanus"—who howled at a slugger "when he did not succeed in making a supreme offensive gesture, like a home run or a clean hit with the bases full." The fans bayed at Foxx and Cronin in 1936 and in the coming years at Ted Williams.[5]

In a 1938 article entitled "Why a City Goes Baseball Crazy," Henry Harris attributed the fan frenzy for hitting to the dreams of young boys, now men, to be a professional ballplayer. "In a Jimmie Foxx, a Babe Ruth, or a Joe DiMaggio, they wistfully see themselves as they would like to have been," which encourages them to follow a hitter's batting statistics. Connecting this motivation with the expressive cheering at the ballpark, Harris wrote that fans get their exercise vicariously. "It gives the meek little guy (who is most of us) a perfect opportunity to let off steam. The man with the terrifying boss or the nagging wife, by the purchase of a ticket, buys the right to abuse authority (in the form of the umpire) as much as he wishes, so long as he keeps somewhere near the margins of decency. With the ticket, also, goes the privilege of second-guessing the manager (and thus becoming a master mind) and making as much noise as he wishes (often it is possible to get the limelight)."[6]

Of course, not all fans were always at the ballpark. "Nor is all the interest on the field," Harris wrote. "Gasoline stations and country stores throughout New England follow the play-by-play broadcasts [on radio]. Thousands more, who scarcely see three games a year, follow the accounts in the newspapers and the batting averages of their favorite players."[7]

Radio broadcasts switched from WNAC to WAAB for the 1937 season. John Shepard owned both stations, but he was expanding his national network affiliations, so he aligned WNAC and its Yankee Network with the NBC network and established WAAB with the new Colonial Network to affiliate with the Mutual Broadcasting System network. The Colonial Network had a dozen affiliated stations across five New England states (all except Vermont). Fred Hoey returned to the radio booth for 1937, following his temporary firing in the spat with General Mills, the sponsor of the baseball broadcasts. WNAC and the Yankee Network continued baseball coverage with a 15-minute program at 6:15 in the evening, where Hoey discussed the results of the day's ball games.[8]

Although Hoey and Shepard continued to have their differences before Hoey was fired once again (permanently) after the 1938 season, Hoey successfully cultivated baseball fans throughout New England. His voice also penetrated into upstate New York, where the Springfield, Massachusetts, radio station in the Colonial Network reached New York residents in the Albany area, who suffered from the radio boycott imposed by the owners of all three baseball clubs located in New York City that refused to broadcast their home games. The only radio broadcasts of baseball games that originated in New York state were of minor-league games.[9]

Radio broadcasts tapped in the region's growing middle class and a more robust working class. During the 1930s, the focus of business "shifted from production to distribution," exemplified by the notable "rapid increase in the importance of chain stores," which controlled one-quarter of the nation's retail sales in 1935, up from one-tenth in 1929. Independently owned small businesses were drying up, as seen in the Greater Boston area by the emergence of First National grocery stores and Howard Johnson's restaurants. While there were fewer self-employed individuals, there were more salaried office workers in the expansion of large corporations, which represented about two-fifths of middle-class workers by 1940, a broad classification that encompassed nearly one-half of the entire labor force. For hourly wage workers, the eight-hour day was institutionalized by the Fair Labor Standards Act, which provided for overtime pay for employees working more than 40 hours per week.[10]

In addition to more disposable income, many workers also had paid vacations, which became more common in the 1930s. Trips to the beach and mountains by New England residents were popular spots for a summer vacation, as were automobile trips to Boston to take in a ball game. Tourists helped to prop up attendance at weekday games of the Red Sox and Bees, not just weekend games. In 1936, attendance at Fenway Park was 626,000 spectators, the second highest seasonal total for professional baseball in Boston; the Bees drew just one-half that turnstile count. Two years later in 1938 another penultimate attendance mark was established with 646,000 paid admissions to Fenway Park.[11]

The expansion of the middle class, in combination with several traditional motivating factors plus two new elements, emerged in 1938 to influence more baseball fans to consistently root for the Red Sox than the Bees.

A big influence among traditional fan motivations was the American League style of play. Foxx hit 50 home runs for the Red Sox in 1938, with 175 RBIs, to set new Red Sox team records. Foxx also led the American League with a .349 batting average, as one of six members of the Red Sox that produced a greater than .300 batting average.

One of the new elements in 1938 was a Boston team that truly contended for the league pennant. For the first time in two decades, baseball fans in Boston contracted "pennant fever" for a protracted portion of the playing season, as the Red Sox battled the New York Yankees through July for first place in the American League. Although the Yankees won their third consecutive pennant in 1938, led by Joe DiMaggio, this pennant race helped to rekindle a faded fan element into a new motivation—the rivalry between the Red Sox and the Yankees, which engulfed fans during the next several decades.

This upper-income crowd in the box seats at Fenway Park shows the drawing power of the Red Sox in the late 1930s. While primarily men in business suits and fedoras, the composition of ball game crowds was beginning to include more women, as seen by several sitting in the third and fourth rows of the box seats (courtesy Boston Public Library, Leslie Jones Collection).

In July 1938, with the Red Sox only three games behind the first-place Yankees for most of the month, fans packed Fenway Park not only on the weekend but also during the work week. A Friday game with the Yankees drew 26,000 people and a Monday doubleheader with Cleveland attracted 29,000. Even with the Red Sox out of contention in August, a Ladies Day game at Fenway Park in late August attracted 26,000 people of both genders, as 12,000 women and girls crashed the gate to impede ticket sales for both females and males. Admission for Ladies Day was now the ten-cent federal amusement tax for a grandstand ticket, not completely free as it had been in years past. Many of the Ladies Day guests were forced to sit in the pavilion and bleachers, since there were not enough empty grandstand seats to accommodate one of the largest Ladies Day crowds ever seen in Boston.[12]

These elements, combined with a relatively new ballpark that has great sight lines for spectators, gave the Red Sox a supreme advantage over the Bees for the hearts of baseball fans in New England.

In 1939 the American League adopted night baseball, as Philadelphia, Chicago, and Cleveland installed lights to play night games. While the Red Sox played three night games during the 1939 season (one game in each of those three cities), Yawkey still had an institutional resistance to night baseball. But he softened his rhetoric in the following statement issued in August 1939: "There will be no night games at Fenway Park next season. We are not in favor of night games at any time, but if in 1941, the other clubs in the league vote for it, and the fans appear to demand it, why I suppose we could not reasonably stand alone in opposition to it." Translation: If every other club adopts night baseball, then the Red Sox will do it too.[13]

The Bees might also played three night road games in 1939, as Cincinnati, Brooklyn, and Philadelphia all played night baseball in the National League, which had inaugurated night games back in 1935. If not for their precarious financial situation, the Bees might have been willing to invest in a lighting system in Boston, given the positive indications that some baseball fans in New England now enjoyed night games. Minor-league baseball of the Class B variety returned to Hartford, Connecticut, in 1938 and to Springfield, Massachusetts, in 1939, both located 100 miles from Boston. Springfield had a permanent lighting system, while Hartford used a temporary system to stage a few night games.

From a twenty-first century perspective, it strains credulity that neither Boston club wanted to play night baseball to produce larger audiences than those generated for afternoon weekday games, which were ordinarily one-sixth the size of Sunday and holiday crowds. In 1939 the Red Sox averaged 5,000 for weekday games and 30,000 on Sundays; the Bees drew half those numbers and suffered a low of 474 spectators for the game on September 29. The Bees lived off the shrinking base of general baseball fans that supported both teams and a small group of dedicated Bees fans. However, the divide with dedicated Red Sox and Sox-leaning general fans was widening.

"Boston fans are apparently separating more into two distinct groups, than was formerly the case. The only strange feature of this is that it did not occur years ago," a fan living in Medford wrote in a letter to the editor published by the *Boston Globe*. "Anyone who is familiar with the other cities in which two rival ball clubs operate has seen this." In response, Maurice Albert, a Braves fan from Malden, wrote: "It saddens my heart no end to see the Bees and Red Sox rooters argue over who is rooting for the right team. I root for BOTH teams. After all, the Red Sox are in the American loop, playing the American League teams, and the Bees, in the National League, play National League teams."[14]

Ted Williams made his debut with the Red Sox in 1939 and hit 31 home runs in his rookie year, quite a feat for a left-handed hitter in a ballpark more suited to right-handed hitters. His first homer at Fenway Park came on April 23, when he powered the ball into the right-field bleachers, which were more than 400 feet from home plate. It was the first of six such blasts during the 1939 season; there were countless other hits that fell short of the fence into the glove of opposing outfielders. Fans loved the hitting and the newspapers loved the effervescent rookie, dubbed The Kid, especially the morning *Boston Record* and evening *Boston American*, both owned by the Hearst newspaper chain. This publicity created even more fans that wanted to follow the power-hitting style of play in the American League.[15]

As Boston baseball fans enjoyed the exploits of rookie Williams, World War II erupted in Europe on September 3, 1939, after Germany invaded Poland. When President Roosevelt spoke to the nation over the radio that evening, he declared American neutrality in the war, but signaled his support for the Allies of Britain and France that had declared war on Germany: "This nation will remain a neutral nation, but I cannot ask that every American remain neutral in thought as well. Even a neutral has a right to take account of facts. Even a neutral cannot be asked to close his mind or close his conscience." The American stance on military neutrality at the time—not choosing a side, but leaning to one side over the other—was similar to the nature of general baseball fans in Boston, who supported both teams but often had a leaning to one team over the other. Both general philosophies would evaporate during the postwar period, with American foreign policy and Boston baseball fans both decidedly backing just one side of their respective conflicts.[16]

While Americans digested the news regarding the emerging war in Europe on the morning of September 3, the Red Sox played the Yankees that afternoon at Fenway Park. Despite some modification to the Massachusetts Sunday baseball law over the years, the Sunday doubleheader still could be problematic.

With the score tied in the top of the eighth inning of the second game on September 3, New York rallied for two runs to go ahead, 7–5. The Yankees were threatening to score more runs with runners on second and third with one out. With less than ten minutes remaining before the execution of the 6:30 Sunday curfew, the Red Sox tried to stall for time by issuing the batter an intentional walk. However, the Yankee batter swung at the first two wide throws to try to strike out. Then in a hurry-up tactic, the two Yankee baserunners both trotted into home plate so they could be tagged out to put the Red Sox up to bat more quickly so that the eighth inning could be completed, or else the final score would revert to the 5–5 tally at the end of the seventh inning. Red Sox manager Cronin then executed his own stall by running onto to the field to argue with the home-plate umpire in "a time-consuming protest on the grounds that the Yankees were engaging in tactics that were probably illegal and certainly unfair ... and possibly even desecrating the Sabbath." When the umpire snubbed Cronin and ruled that play continue, the Fenway fans pelted the field with an assortment of soda bottles and other projectiles, which caused the umpire to declare the game forfeited to the Yankees.[17]

This travesty added more fodder to the movement to change the Massachusetts Sunday baseball law regarding its artificial ending time for a baseball game. Many churches no longer conducted evening services in addition to their morning ones, which was the rationale for the 6:00 ending time contained in the initial law in 1918, continued in the 1920 and 1928 amendments to the law, and extended to 6:30 in the revised law in 1931.

For the 1940 season, Jim Britt replaced Frank Frisch (who had replaced Fred Hoey for the 1939 season) for the Colonial Network radio broadcasts, to do "play-by-play of all Boston American League and National League home games except Sundays." Like Hoey, Britt had a very objective, straightforward manner to broadcasting a ball game; however, the college-educated Britt had a more "erudite and intelligent" approach to the selection of his words in comparison to the basic language used by Hoey. Although considered "a bright man with great diction and vocabulary," the well-spoken Britt could come off as arrogant or pompous, as if he were talking down to the radio audience. His dry wit at the microphone could go over the heads of his predominantly less-educated listeners. Even his tagline was articulate: "If you can't take part in a sport, be one anyway, will ya." For Shepard, the owner of the Colonial Network, Britt projected a more upscale image than did Hoey.[18]

Shepard added another new voice to the baseball radio coverage in 1940 with Jerry O'Leary hosting a 15-minute pre-game show, which typically ran at 2:45 before Britt came on air at 3:00 to do the ball game. Originally dubbed "Baseball Fans Interviews," the highly popular show was called "Play Ball" in its postwar period. O'Leary would roam the stands at the ballpark and randomly select contestants to pose baseball questions, which radio listeners had previously submitted to the show. People got $1 for each correct response, up to a maximum of $5 for a "home run" of four correct answers.[19]

Prior to the 1940 season, the Red Sox constructed bullpens in right-center field, dubbed Williamsburg, to be more receptive to fly balls hit by Ted Williams becoming home runs. The distance went from 402 feet to 380 feet in right center and from 332 to 302 feet down the right-field foul line, as the club took the opportunity to eliminate the pavilion section and convert it into a portion of the grandstand.[20]

In addition to shortening the home-run distance for Williams, Cronin also moved Williams to play left field (from right field where he played in 1939) and to the third spot in the batting order (from the fourth spot where he hit in 1939) to hit in front of Foxx, not behind him. Although all the moves were designed to help Williams as a hitter, he complained to sportswriters about his reduced number of RBIs by not hitting in the cleanup position. When he got off to a bad start at the plate in the 1940 season, the "wolves"

Ted Williams (left) in his rookie year with the Red Sox in 1939 chats with Eddie Miller) of the Bees, prior to a pre-season city series game between the two Boston teams. Williams became immensely popular among fans due to his hitting prowess and tempestuous feud with the Boston sportswriters (courtesy Boston Public Library, Leslie Jones Collection).

jeered him and the writers criticized him, which began a longstanding vendetta that Williams had with both groups.

An article in spring 1940 that faulted Williams for not visiting his parents over the winter "was a pivot point, turning what had been a simmering feud with sportswriters into a vitriolic campaign that he chose to wage his entire career," according to biographer Ben Bradlee, Jr. Another pivotal incident occurred in August when Williams complained to Austen Lake of the *Boston American* that he wanted to be traded to another team. The resulting furor made headlines for weeks in all eight of the Boston newspapers and the slew of suburban dailies. The baseball fans ate it up. Attendance at Fenway Park in 1940 was 716,000 people, establishing a new record for professional baseball in Boston, which was exceeded in 1941 (730,000 spectators) when Williams hit for a .406 batting average as the Red Sox once again fell short in the pennant quest to the Yankees.[21]

With such extensive competition for readers, the Boston newspapers "tried to bump, slam, elbow, and run around each other to get into the local living rooms and coffee shops," biographer Leigh Montville wrote about this external element that impacted Williams and his relationship with Red Sox fans. "No headline would jump sales any faster than a headline involving Ted and controversy." Sportswriters were under enormous pressure "for a fresh story on Williams because that's what their editors thirsted for, the only thing that would satisfy insatiable reader demand for all things Ted."[22]

"Oh, how I hated that Boston press," Williams wrote in his autobiography *My Turn at Bat* following his retirement from the Red Sox. "I've outlived the ones who were really vicious, who wrote some of the meanest, most slanderous things you can imagine. I can *still* remember the things they wrote … how I didn't hit in the clutch … was a draft dodger … wasn't a 'team man' … took too many bases on balls … so unfair." Williams had a difficult time ignoring the words spewed at him by sportswriters and the fans. "I admit I reacted to the fans, to what I thought was prejudiced and unfair abuse. There were always a few who paid their way in for no better reason than to let me have it. They eventually had to put special police in the left-field stands because some of the comments were so foul. They used to write how bad *my* mouth was. I was in kindergarten compared to some of those guys."[23]

Given the "wolves" in the stands and the fact that the *Boston Record* and the *Boston Post*, two staunchly Democratic papers, had the highest circulation among the Boston newspapers, the fan base for the Red Sox was turning more blue-collar. So was the *Boston American*, the sister paper to the *Record*, where Dave Egan was a sports columnist, a new iteration of the sportswriter who had traditionally just written about the events and not expressed an opinion. Egan was "an elegant writer, a provocateur, a contrarian who delighted in cutting against the grain seven days a week; if Ted was the darling of

Boston, Egan decided he had to knock him down." Columnists like Egan sold newspapers to the baseball fans. Williams despised Egan, but baseball fans eagerly scooped up copies of the *Record* to read Egan's latest indictment of Williams and dashed over to Fenway Park to both lash out at him while he played left field and gaped in awe of him while he hit in the batter's box.[24]

When the 1941 season began, the National League team took the field as the Bees but the team name soon reverted back to Braves, when ownership of the club changed on April 20. "I am heartily in favor of the change back to Braves," Quinn said, "and I hope it will encourage our players to perform the way the former Braves of 1914 did." Quinn and a group of 13 other men bought out the existing stockholders of the club. One of the new investors was Lou Perini, the owner of a local construction company, who was said to be "probably the most rabid of baseball rooters in the Boston Bees' syndicate." Perini would soon become the man who assumed the challenge to rebuild the Braves as a viable entity among Boston baseball fans. One of his first actions as a part-owner may have been to encourage Quinn to actively investigate the possibility of playing night baseball at Braves Field.[25]

With 11 of the 16 major-league baseball clubs playing night baseball in 1941, the Red Sox played five night games on the road and the Braves traveled to play six night games. While Yawkey was still staunchly opposed to night baseball, Quinn was warmer to the idea. Many baseball fans in Greater Boston watched the night games played in the revived New England League, which operated as a semi-pro league for the 1941 season, with aspirations for a return to minor-league status in 1942. Stadiums in Lynn, Massachusetts, and Manchester, New Hampshire, had permanent lights, while the teams in Pawtucket and Woonsocket in Rhode Island used portable lighting systems (the field for Woonsocket games was actually located in nearby Blackstone, Massachusetts). The Braves played two exhibition night games in 1941 to test the waters with New England baseball fans. After Quinn assisted the Braves' farm club in Hartford to install permanent lighting, the Braves played an exhibition night game at Hartford in early July. In August the Braves played a night game in Lynn, which attracted 7,500 fans.[26]

With more major-league clubs playing night baseball, the playing schedule began to feature more pre-scheduled Sunday doubleheaders. "Taking official cognizance of the growing practice of some clubs in arranging Sunday double-headers after the season starts, the American League schedule sets a precedent this year by definitely charting 16 Sabbath twin-bills in advance," *The Sporting News* reported. "Paralleling the action of the American League in making definite advance provision for Sunday double-headers, instead of waiting for individual clubs to arrange such dates after the season starts, the National League went even farther in that direction by charting 25 Sabbath twin-bills." In an editorial, *The Sporting News* wrote that "fans once more can depend upon the annual chart issued in the spring … their schedules will not look like Chinese puzzles before the season has progressed far" which will ensure "they need not alter their arrangements or run the risk of disappointment" in planning trips to the ballpark. The Red Sox had four Sunday doubleheaders pre-scheduled for 1941, while the Braves had one.[27]

There had always been a perception that a city had national economic status by being a two-team city, as one of only five such cities in major-league baseball and thus by extension one of the top five cities in the country. However, by 1940, Boston was the ninth largest city in America, down from seventh in 1920 and fifth in 1900. Boston was also just the seventh largest city in the American League (ahead of only Washington, D.C.) as well as the smallest of the five two-team cities. The minor-league cities of Los Angeles and Baltimore had larger populations than Boston.

Boston sportswriters actively encouraged the positive idea of a two-team city, with an annual dinner in February each year. The dinner was sponsored by the Boston chapter of the national Baseball Writers' Association, which replaced the now-discontinued Winter League banquet that had been sponsored by fans. This writers' banquet helped to sustain the image of bipartisanship through the inclusion of more local dignitaries such as Mayor Mansfield, who "spoke of the commercial benefit which the two major-league clubs are to a city like Boston."[28]

Quinn had always been a supporter of the two-team city. Yawkey initially also backed the concept, as seen in a statement he issued in 1935 advocating for Boston to be a two-team city, when the Braves signed Babe Ruth. "I think it was a great move for the Braves. It should not only help the Boston National League ball club, but also be of great benefit to a great baseball city—one which surely can support two baseball teams and support them well." He added politely that the Braves needed the assistance: "Baseball these days has several new obstacles in New England. There has been a wonderful response by the fans to the Red Sox as we have striven to rebuild them, and Ruth's coming back to the town where he first played … should [help] his new club and to the cause of baseball in one of the country's outstanding baseball districts."[29]

However, Yawkey had limitations regarding the benefit of being part of a two-team city. He made it clear in 1939 that he would not be sentimental and allow the Braves to play at Fenway Park if that was a necessary condition to maintaining Boston as a two-team city. "We built the park for our own use and with no idea of sharing it with a tenant," Yawkey pronounced in regard to rumors that the National League team might play at Fenway Park. "So the report that we were to take one [tenant] in is definitely off and has no foundation in fact." While the two teams in St. Louis and Philadelphia shared one ballpark, there would be no sharing in Boston.[30]

By 1941, in the fourth-largest two-team city of St. Louis, there was serious talk of the Browns relocating to Los Angeles. However, the entry of the United States into World War II in December 1941 quashed that discussion.[31]

With increasingly dim prospects for Boston as a two-team city, the Braves might have considered a relocation to another city within the next few years had the war not intervened.

◆ 16 ◆

Doubleheaders
in the War Years

With America's entry into World War II following the Japanese invasion of Pearl Harbor on December 7, 1941, there was great uncertainty whether baseball would continue at Fenway Park and Braves Field during the expected multi-year duration of the military conflict. There would be a shortage of capable ballplayers, through enlistment or conscription into the military and those deciding to take a war-industry job. Would the federal government proclaim baseball to be a non-essential industry (as it did in World War I) and force it to shut down? If not, would fans (those not in the military service) continue to pay good money to watch less-talented ballplayers?

President Franklin Roosevelt addressed the first question with his "green light" letter sent to Commissioner Landis in mid–January 1942, which created the principle that continuation of baseball was good for the morale of the country. "I honestly feel that it would be best for the country to keep baseball going," Roosevelt wrote. "There will be fewer people unemployed and everybody will work longer hours and harder than ever. And that means that they ought to have a chance for recreation and for taking their minds off their work even more than before." Those on the homefront could attend games, listen to them on the radio, and read about them in the newspapers. Those overseas could maintain an interest in baseball through news accounts and letters from home.[1]

As for the second question, fans in Boston did tolerate wartime baseball, as it morphed more into entertainment (and nearly a farce by 1945) than high-level athletic competition. Baseball, which clothed itself with the stars and stripes, herald itself as an institution (i.e., the National Pastime) that American soldiers were fighting to preserve. Fans responded to this wave of patriotic fervor tinged with blatant corporate self-interest, as both the Red

Sox and Braves, like all major-league clubs, struggled to endure the duration of the war.

Roosevelt's sanction of wartime baseball produced a renewed sense of mutuality between the Red Sox and Braves, a deeper embracing of the informal cooperative arrangement that the two baseball clubs had periodically pursued in the past. "We all feel that baseball will do its full share toward the entertainment and recreation which Mr. Roosevelt has prescribed," Braves president Bob Quinn told sportswriters in January 1942. "The problem, if there is a problem, is how to do this in the best way." Quinn and Red Sox general manager Eddie Collins collaborated to consider the best way to tackle a number of wartime operating issues that confronted both clubs, in order to handle them in a common manner. Free admission of servicemen to the ballpark was the first issue Quinn and Collins tackled, with the free tickets to be distributed by the morale officers at the various local military operations.[2]

The two baseball clubs also agreed to raise money for the Army-Navy Relief Fund, by playing exhibition games against military-base teams. The Red Sox played their first such game on May 23, 1942, when a small crowd of 12, 000 people watched the game under dark skies as "second class seaman Ted Williams signaled his enlistment in the Naval Air Corps by hitting his 10th home run of the season." The Braves used more marketing muscle to attract 25,000 for their war-relief game that year on June 25, which resulted in more than $28,000 being contributed.

In addition, the clubs conducted scrap drives to recycle material for the war effort. At Fenway Park on September 27, 1942, more than 3,000 spectators received free admission by bringing a total of 46,850 pounds of metal for the war effort. As was typical during the war, attendance was reported in three tiers: 18,622 paid, 1,042 servicemen (free admission), and 3,251 other (complimentary tickets, most often applied to Ladies Day).

Game scheduling was also a discussion point, to accommodate war workers and servicemen, through doubleheaders and twilight games. The Red Sox and Braves played twice as many doubleheaders in 1942, and triple in 1943, than they did in 1941, to minimize travel by suburban fans that were now coping with government gasoline rationing to conserve fuel for the war effort. Close to two-thirds of all ball games played in Boston during 1943 were part of a doubleheader. The Sunday doubleheader became the prime attraction in Boston baseball during the war, especially with the radio ban on broadcasting Sunday games still intact.

The Red Sox experimented with twilight games in 1942, scheduling a 6:00 start for the July 3 game with the Yankees, which attracted 21,000 paying patrons and 1,700 servicemen. Interest lessened in twilight games in 1943, though, when only 8,000 attended the June 8 twilight game against the Yankees and 4,000 at the June 13 game with the Athletics. The Braves seemed to be resistant to the idea of twilight games.

President Roosevelt had also encouraged more night games during the war so that day-shift workers could attend games occasionally, so the two leagues doubled the allowable number of night games from seven to 14. Since both Fenway Park and Braves Field were not yet fitted with artificial lighting, this didn't impact Boston fans. Even if they had lights, the two ballparks would have remained dark due to the dim-out restrictions enforced along the East Coast, which curtailed night baseball in New York City during the early war years.

With the Braves playing more road games at night, the Braves extended their research on night baseball to consider the idea for postwar games at Braves Field. On August 20, 1942, the Braves played an exhibition game in Pawtucket, Rhode Island, at the newly constructed Municipal Stadium (renamed McCoy Stadium in 1946), one of the first ballparks in eastern New England with permanent lighting. A crowd of 10,000 watched the semi-pro Pawtucket Slaters defeat the Braves. The next day the Braves played a night game in Springfield, Massachusetts, against the minor-league team there in the Eastern League.[3]

Attendance records were set in 1942, when, for the first time, more than one million people attended baseball games in Boston. The combined attendance at Fenway Park and Braves Field was 1,015,000 people, with the Red Sox establishing an all-time high of 730,000 spectators (not counting servicemen) while the Braves attracted 285,000. While these attendance figures indicate an increasing number of partisan Red Sox fans, characterized either as dedicated or Sox-leaning, there remained a sizeable number of pure general baseball fans that supported both teams on a non-partisan basis.

One such traditional general baseball fan was Lillian "Lolly" Hopkins, better known as "the Woman with the Megaphone," who vocalized comments at managers, umpires, visiting players, and the official scorer through a megaphone, a different color at each ballpark. "Three times a week she comes to Boston from Providence, where she lives, to see the Red Sox and Braves play," Harold Kaese wrote about Hopkins in a 1943 article entitled "'Megaphone Lolly' Enlivens Games of Sox and Tribe." It didn't matter to Hopkins which team was playing in Boston when she made the 100-mile round trip to the ballpark. "I usually come up Wednesdays, Ladies Days and Sundays," Hopkins told Kaese between games of a Sunday doubleheader. "This morning I left the house at 7:50, went to church, and got the train. I'll get the 8 o'clock train tonight and be home by 9:30." Concluded Kaese: "Mrs. Hopkins (Lolly) is a FAN in capital letters."[4]

"You know where to look for her at both parks," Kaese wrote about the quintessential general baseball fan in Boston. "At Fenway Park it is Section

Lolly Hopkins, shown in this photograph with her trademark megaphone, was the quintessential general baseball fan, who supported both Boston teams on a non-partisan basis. With reserved seats at both Fenway Park and Braves Field, Hopkins typically made three trips each week to watch whichever Boston team was then playing at home (courtesy Boston Public Library, Leslie Jones Collection).

14, Row 1, Seat 24. At Braves Field it is Section M, Row 1, Seat 1." Hopkins liked to sit behind first base, because that was the angle she was accustomed to watching baseball, since "that's where we used to sit when I was a little girl and my father brought me up from Providence to see games at the Walpole-st. and Huntington-av. parks." However, Hopkins, as a fervent supporter of both the Braves and the Red Sox, was becoming an endangered species in Boston.[5]

More reflective of the coming majority of baseball fans in New England was a woman who took a different route during the war years. Elizabeth "Lib" Dooley became a dedicated Red Sox fan in 1944 when she purchased her first season ticket to Fenway Park. Although she and her father (John Dooley) had been lifelong general baseball fans of both teams, the younger Dooley eventually choose the Red Sox. In one of life's difficult choices, she wrote that she "could have gone either way regarding my choice of where to purchase season tickets," but she choose the Red Sox because the box seats at Fenway Park were more comfortable than those at Braves Field. As a teacher in the Boston school system, Dooley could carve out the time to go to the ballpark in the late afternoon. After purchasing her season ticket in 1944, she "didn't miss a Red Sox home game for the next half-century," attending more than 4,000 consecutive games at Fenway Park.[6]

While President Roosevelt had fostered the continuation of professional baseball during the war, he was also clear that ballplayers would receive no favoritism when it came to military service. This hit home with Boston baseball fans in 1943 with the departure of Ted Williams, Warren Spahn, and many other ballplayers for military service.

In 1943 the federal government instituted more severe restrictions in gasoline rationing, which made public transportation virtually the only way for suburban baseball fans to get to Braves Field or Fenway Park. The three gallons of gasoline per week for a car with an "A" sticker enabled everyday people to get to work, but didn't leave much in the gas tank for pleasure trips. "Driving to baseball games was out in the East," William Mead wrote in *Even the Browns: The Zany, True Story of Baseball in the Early Forties.* "Most families could not afford to squander their meager gasoline ration on trips to the ball park."[7]

War workers with a "B" sticker got eight gallons of gasoline, but even with the extra gasoline many had a difficult time attending ball games, since the first shift at most war plants ran from 7:00 in the morning to 3:00 in the afternoon, the ending time coinciding with the start of the game at Braves Field and Fenway Park. Sunday was the most convenient time for first-shift workers to attend a ball game, although they could catch the second game of a doubleheader played during the week, which typically started around 3:45.

Workers on the swing shift had an even more challenging task to watch a ball game during the work week, since they worked from 3:00 in the afternoon to 11:00 at night. To accommodate the swing shift, a few major-league teams played morning games, most prominently in Philadelphia where the teams dabbled in swing-shift doubleheaders that combined a morning game with an early afternoon game.

The Red Sox experimented with a morning game on May 27, 1943, when they rescheduled the rained-out game on May 26 for 10:30 in the morning prior to the scheduled afternoon game that day. "But it will be no bargain—they'll be a separate admission charge for each game," the *Boston Globe* reported. "The Red Sox are to play baseball this morning right after breakfast. The morning game was scheduled so that war workers who go to work on the 3–11 p.m. shift can take in a game. Whether they'll roll out of bed sufficiently early to take it in remains to be seen." They stayed in bed. Only 2,027 fans showed up for the first non-holiday morning game in the history of professional baseball in Boston. The *Globe* reasoned that the meager attendance resulted "because the Red Sox—with an amazing lack of promotional flare— kept the game a secret until the last moment." The *Globe* also noted another flaw in the plan for the morning game: "Guys who have worked all night and other guys who've jumped out of bed on six hours sleep don't like frankfurters for breakfast." While morning games were still played on the Patriots Day holiday in Boston, they were not popular at other times.[8]

The May 27 twin bill was a precursor of more separate-admission two-game sets in the postwar years, when the Red Sox, then with lights at Fenway Park, sought to squeeze as many fans as possible into the ballpark by conducting what became known as a day-night doubleheader.

Even the 2-for-1 doubleheader wasn't a perfect solution to the wartime challenge of attracting spectators to the ballpark. Darkness could still prematurely curtail the second game of the twin bill, even though the first game started at 1:30, and on Sunday there were only five hours to play both games due to the 6:30 curfew in the Sunday baseball law. The Massachusetts legislature provided the Red Sox and Braves with some wartime relief on the Sunday curfew, when a new law allowed the second game of a Sunday doubleheader to be completed after 6:30, if that game started prior to 4:30. The law was written, though, to expire when the war ended.[9]

Besides the travel issues for fans in 1943, baseball clubs experienced their own transportation challenges, since the federal government curtailed personal train travel in order to more efficiently move military personnel around the country. Because train accommodations were in short supply, teams often had no flexibility in travel times between cities. The National League responded to this problem by creating the suspended-game rule, which postponed completion of a game to a later date rather than have that game end abruptly with the score reverting to the last completed inning. As Boston fans too often witnessed, the curfew in the Sunday baseball law unintentionally encouraged teams to engage in stalling and other similar acts of skullduggery when a game artificially stopped at the 6:30 curfew. With a suspended game, the game was resumed at the point of stoppage the next time that the opponent visited the home team.[10]

This suspended-game rule was first applied in Boston on July 18, 1943, when the second game of the Sunday doubleheader at Braves Field was stopped by the Sunday curfew. The twin bill ran long because the first game went 11 innings. In the second game, when the Braves had scored three runs in the sixth inning to tie the game, 4–4, they still had the bases loaded with one out "when the gong struck at 6:29 and the umps called it a day for fans and ball tossers alike." If the game had occurred in 1942, the score would have reverted to a 4–1 victory for Brooklyn. "The boos compared favorably, however, with the pop bottles that might have flown through the air if the game had reverted in Brooklyn's favor," the *Boston Globe* remarked about the Dodgers likely engaging in some stalling shenanigans without the suspended-game rule. "It really worked out great compared with some of the games we used to have. There wasn't any stalling," one of the umpires said after the game. "Everything Brooklyn did was strictly legitimate. Knowing the game was going to be finished anyway [at a later date], nobody was under pressure." The game was resumed two months later on September 13, when the Braves won, 7–6, in ten innings.[11]

Single games during the week were also subject to the suspended-game rule. For example, on August 1, 1944, the game with Pittsburgh at Braves Field was stopped at 5:00 after eight innings to enable the Pirates to catch a train to get to Pittsburgh for its August 2 game. This suspended game was resumed on September 25, when just 463 people paid their way into Braves Field.[12]

For fans listening to wartime baseball on the radio, the broadcasts returned to WNAC and the Yankee Network in June 1942, from WAAB and the Colonial Network, when John Shepard sold his radio station operations to General Tire and Rubber Company. Jim Britt continued to man the microphone to do the broadcasts for the remainder of the 1942 season until he joined the Navy that fall. Tom Hussey filled in for Britt until he returned from the war to resume radio broadcasts in 1946. George Hartrick substituted for Hussey as the number-two announcer. When pre-game host Jerry O'Leary also went into the military, Leo Egan filled in for the 1943 season, doing interviews exclusively with servicemen in the stands. The pre-game show was then shelved until after the war.[13]

There were more radio broadcasts of telegraphic recreations of road games during the war, since both Boston teams more often had open dates due to the number of doubleheaders, travel issues, and military exhibition games. For example, WNAC aired a recreation of the Red Sox road game on August 26, 1943, when the Braves were in Rhode Island to play a doubleheader against two service teams. Like most radio stations that engaged in baseball game recreations, WNAC used the Western Union "paragraph one" telegraph service, which provided a condensed pitch-by-pitch description, in Morse Code, of a ball game. A telegraph operator at the radio station received the dots and dashes, converted them into letter-number combinations, and then sat at a typewriter to translate them into words. For example, S1C meant "strike one called" and B2L meant "ball two low." The radio announcer would then create a more elaborate description from these snippets of information. Hussey did most of wartime recreations in a very staid way, not trying to fool the audience with fake crowd noise in the background or whacking a piece of wood to simulate bat hitting ball.[14]

Fans also had to tolerate curtailed newspaper coverage of the ball games, beginning in 1944, given the paper shortage the country faced. Editors devoted most of the limited space to the news about the war and printed only brief accounts of the ball games.

A major shakeup in the ownership of the Braves occurred in January

1944, when three existing stockholders—Lou Perini, Guido Rugo, and Joseph Maney—purchased enough stock from the other investors to obtain a controlling interest in the Braves. Perini took a lead role in influencing changes within the baseball club during the war, and would have a major impact in the postwar years.[15]

Perini encouraged Quinn, still the Braves president for the moment, to play more twilight games, to try to increase attendance by attracting first-shift war workers. The Braves, though, seemed to be snakebit when they announced their first twilight game would be played on June 20, 1944. That game was rained out, as was the rescheduled game the next day. The Braves finally got to play a twilight game on June 22, as the second part of a doubleheader where the first game began at 3:15. However, the first game went 15 innings, so the twilight game did not begin until 7:00. There was only time for an hour and ten minutes of game time before darkness set in. Those few remaining fans at that hour saw Jim Tobin throw a no-hitter in the five-inning game.

When a U.S. victory in Europe seemed assured following D–Day on June 6, 1944, Perini began to make preparations for postwar baseball when he could resurrect the Braves franchise. Beyond improving the product on the field, Perini's top priority was to play night baseball at Braves Field. This alternative became more practicable when the major-league owners voted to allow unlimited night games during the 1944 season, rather than be constrained to 14 games (or 21 games in a few special circumstances). Installing lights to play just 14 games didn't make complete economic sense to Perini, even if spectators packed Braves Field for those games, but double that number would be more financially viable.

Perini expanded the research on night baseball, since he could hardly fail to notice the attendance spike at road games played at night by the Braves in 1944. To help validate that fans in New England accepted the idea of night baseball, the Braves played exhibition night games at Pawtucket, Rhode Island, on July 13 and in Lynn, Massachusetts, on September 19. Crowds packed the ballpark in both working-class cities, which at the time supported semi-pro teams in the New England League.[16]

One reason to conduct night baseball at Braves Field was to lessen the reliance on Sunday doubleheaders. Perini feared that postwar spectators would continue to expect a doubleheader on Sunday, when a large crowd could be anticipated for just a single game. Another reason was that attendance for night games might be a large multiple over the present small crowds at weekday games, possibly ten times larger. In order to compete with the Red Sox, Perini was targeting a different audience for night games than normally attended non–Sunday daylight games, in the prewar years, at either Fenway Park or Braves Field. Given Yawkey's aversion to night baseball, Perini looked to achieve a significant competitive advantage with night baseball attracting this brand new group of spectators.

The 1945 baseball season was challenging for Boston baseball fans, since both the Red Sox and Braves needed to deploy players who were either too young or too old for military service, or those who had been deemed 4–F as physically unfit for military duty. Travel restrictions canceled the All-Star Game slated for Fenway Park in 1945. As a substitute, the Braves and Red Sox played an exhibition game on July 10, where 22,000 watched at Fenway Park to contribute $70,000 to the United War Fund. Following V–J Day in August, attendance spiked as several star ballplayers returned from the war to play for visiting teams at Fenway Park. Bob Feller pitched for Cleveland in an afternoon game with the Red Sox on September 5, which drew 10,000 fans; Hank Greenberg played for Detroit in a Sunday doubleheader with the Sox on September 9, when 30,000 jammed Fenway Park.

Perini became president of the Braves in March 1945, replacing Quinn, who said, "Now is the time for baseball to make full preparations for the conduct of its business following the close of the war." Quinn's son, John Quinn, was promoted to general manager of the Braves the same day. Following V–E Day in May, Perini advanced the night baseball plan and on July 18, 1945, received approval from the War Production Board to install lights at Braves Field, under a "plan to put up lights next spring and play night games next season."[17]

While the plan to stage night games at Braves Field became a reality for the 1946 baseball season, night baseball turned out to be the beginning of the end for Boston as a two-team city.

◆ 17 ◆

Braves Initiate
Night Baseball

During the winter of 1946, as workmen erected light towers at Braves Field, many ballplayers on both the Braves and Red Sox prepared to return to the baseball diamond following the completion of their wartime military service obligation. Ted Williams and Johnny Pesky returned to the Red Sox following their tours of duty, as did Johnny Sain and Warren Spahn of the Braves.

In addition to the returning ballplayers, Red Sox owner Tom Yawkey and Braves president Lou Perini expected a postwar resurgence of spectators during the 1946 season as the country returned to normalcy. But even their wildest hopes were exceeded. At the final game of the preseason city series, attendance was 33,279 at Fenway Park, which was double the largest prewar turnout for the exhibition series. This presaged large regular-season crowds, which packed both Fenway Park and Braves Field, as each club nearly doubled its previous record attendance.

For the Red Sox, the 1946 schedule mirrored the prewar 1941 one, with doubleheaders slated for Sundays and holidays and single games played in the afternoon during daylight. On the other hand, the Braves had 20 night games scheduled for Braves Field, the first-ever nocturnal baseball games in Boston, to go with the standard fare of Sunday and holiday doubleheaders, with the remainder as day games in mid-afternoon.[1]

Perini went solo for night baseball, rather than pursue the venture jointly with Yawkey, in contravention of the informal cooperative arrangement in which the two clubs agreed to one common policy for Boston community-related issues such as game times and radio broadcasts. While Perini did offer Yawkey the use of Braves Field in 1946 so that the Red Sox could also play night games, Yawkey politely declined. In early May the Red Sox announced that lights would be installed at Fenway Park to play night games during the 1947 season, despite Yawkey's longstanding disdain for night baseball.[2]

The Braves and Red Sox did collaborate in the setting of ticket prices, which increased for box seats ($2.40 from $1.80) and reserved grandstand seats ($1.80 from $1.60), but remained the same for general admission grandstand ($1.20) and bleachers (60 cents) as well as the pavilion sections at Braves Field (95 cents). The price increases were set in expectation of postwar demand not only to watch baseball but also to buy tickets in advance.[3]

Fans flocked to the season-opener for both teams. On April 20 at Fenway Park the 30,462 spectators established an attendance record for a non-holiday season-opener in Boston. Another 32,679 people came the next day, Easter Sunday, to watch a doubleheader between the Red Sox and Philadelphia Athletics. This Sunday doubleheader set in motion the end of the 6:30 Sunday curfew under Massachusetts Sunday baseball law, when the Red Sox lost the second game of the doubleheader because the game was forced to conclude after five innings. The Massachusetts legislature modified the Sunday baseball law in mid–May to allow baseball games to continue beyond 6:30, but with one proviso: "only so long as the game can be played without the aid of artificial lighting."[4]

For the season-opener at Braves Field on April 16, the crowd of 18,261 was the largest opening-day assemblage in recent memory at that venerable ballpark. Even the fresh green paint that stained the clothing of many spectators that day did not deter continued patronage during the 1946 season. The facelift at the 30-year-old ballpark was just one of several enhancements unveiled by the Braves in 1946 to attract spectators, beyond the incorporation of night games into the playing schedule. One of the more visible changes was the new uniform worn by Braves players, which sported the now-familiar tomahawk logo on the front of the jersey.[5]

Newly hired publicity director Billy Sullivan created the yearbook, which was called a sketch book at the time, so fans could learn more about the ballplayers. He also produced a monthly newsletter that was mailed to thousands of fans to keep them abreast of team developments. Sullivan also increased communication with the sportswriters by distributing a daily briefing with up-to-date statistics and information, which indirectly made fans more informed.[6]

Perini did not try the foolhardy strategy to convert dedicated Red Sox fans, who were known to be "intelligent, knowing, patient and moderate," with an emotional attachment to the team ranging "somewhere between the weird fanaticism of the Brooklyn fan and the blasé sophistication of the Yankee fan." Instead, Perini tried to gain a bigger share of the large group of general baseball fans, hoping to convert them into dedicated Braves fans, or at least Braves-leaning general fans. In his sights, too, were the Sox-leaning general fans, many of whom were listeners of radio broadcasts and readers of the sports page, but infrequent attendees at the ballpark. Perini also looked to attract intermittent fans, hoping to convert them into Braves-leaning general baseball fans. Not much attention was paid in the past to the intermittent fans, who mostly expressed an interest in Saturday or Sunday contests. Since men were the primary fans at the ballpark, Perini also aimed to develop more women into baseball fans.[7]

In postwar Boston, Yawkey continued his prewar strategy to put a hard-hitting, winning Red Sox team on the field to appeal to general baseball fans and his modestly large group of dedicated fans. To Perini, though, a ticket sold was ticket sold, and wasn't dependent upon the buyer's baseball disposition. He went after the general baseball and intermittent fans by deploying his strategy to play night baseball.

The first night game at Braves Field was staged on Saturday, May 11. Attendance at this night game was 35,407, the largest crowd since 1933. There were fireworks before the game, neon foul poles, and special sateen uniforms that were designed for better visibility at night. Night games started at 8:30 during this era, because it was important to distinguish these games from day games (which were prohibited from being completed under the lights).

Another promotion by the Braves was specifically targeted to night games. Sullivan organized a bus package to transport fans to night games at Braves Field from outlying areas of Greater Boston such as Lowell, Haverhill, Brockton, and Attleboro, to make it easier for fans to get to night games who likely otherwise would not attend. A $3 ticket on the "Braves Field Express" provided round-trip transportation and a reserved grandstand seat. Thirty buses brought 1,000 fans to the first night game.[8]

WNAC, with Jim Britt at the microphone, continued doing the radio broadcasts of both Braves and Red Sox games in 1946, which were sponsored for the first time by a brewery, Narragansett. However, WNAC declined to broadcast the night games, since it was obligated to air the evening network programs of the Mutual Broadcasting System. The Braves had to arrange for WMEX to do the radio broadcasts of the night games during 1946, with Frank Fallon doing the play-by-play rather than Britt. Besides losing some of the local audience in Greater Boston, the big negative was the lost audience throughout New England because the night games were not distributed through the stations of the Yankee Network.[9]

Radio broadcasts of Sunday games were still not allowed by either club in 1946, under the longstanding application of the informal cooperative arrangement between the two clubs to maximize ballpark attendance on Sunday. WNAC liked the policy too, since the station didn't want to disrupt its Sunday afternoon programming. There were some exceptions, though, such as May 26 game against the Yankees when the Red Sox were assured of a sellout at Fenway Park (although WNAC broadcast only the first game of the doubleheader, with WMEX doing the second game).[10]

Night games at Braves Field were well attended, with an average 30,000 crowd per game; the August 5 game against the Brooklyn Dodgers drew 42,409 spectators. Night baseball outdrew Sunday doubleheaders at Braves Field, actually reducing their attendance due to the Saturday night games. The Braves converted four day games in September into night games to provide additional opportunity for fans to experience night baseball.

During the summer the Braves distributed a survey questionnaire to Braves Field patrons to get their input on potential improvements for the 1947 season. Prizes were offered as an incentive to respond to the survey. Top prize was an automobile, with special prizes for men of a pair of season tickets, for women of 30 pairs of nylon stockings, and a bicycle for children. Leslie Russell of Watertown was the lucky winner of the new automobile. "Not much that I can say," Russell told sportswriters. "Guess the biggest thing in this

The Braves were outfitted in special sateen uniforms for night games at Braves Field, illustrated in this photograph by manager Billy Southworth (left) and pitcher Clyde Shoun. The satin-like fabric was designed for fans to see the ballplayers better under the artificial lighting at Braves Field (courtesy Boston Public Library, Leslie Jones Collection).

little world is a great piece of luck." William Slater of Worcester won the season tickets, Mrs. Roger Stokey of Cambridge won the nylons, and Sheila Finn of East Boston won the bicycle. The Braves received 50,000 responses to the survey, which inspired Appreciation Day and other automobile giveaways during the next few years.[11]

The combination of night baseball and the first decent Braves team since 1933 should have given the Braves an edge over the Red Sox in attracting fans. However, because the Red Sox dominated the American League in 1946, they attracted 1.4 million spectators to Fenway Park, while the attendance at Braves Field was just less than one million at 969,000 people.

Boston rapidly evolved into an American League town in 1946, as baseball fans sought to follow the hitting exploits of Ted Williams and Rudy York propel the Red Sox to their first pennant in 28 years. The combination of winning team, power-hitting, and ballpark intimacy was a powerful fan motivation, which created a wealth of dedicated and Sox-leaning fans to make a significant inroad into the traditional base of general baseball fans that followed both teams in Boston. The Red Sox blasted through their previous record for attendance (730,000 in 1942), which they accomplished, amazingly in retrospect, by playing all their games in daylight. A large portion of the total attendance at Braves Field resulted from night games.

One example of the crush of people seeking entry into Fenway Park in 1946 was Joe Boucher, a construction engineer from Albany, New York. Boucher went to the Sunday game on June 9, when Ted Williams poked a mammoth home run that landed 33 rows up into the right-field bleachers, on top of the head of Boucher. Gale-force winds that day assisted the flight of the ball, which the Red Sox later calculated to have traveled 502 feet. "How far away must one sit to be safe in this park?" Boucher, who was unhurt, joked after the game. "I am a great baseball fan and I am a Red Sox rooter. I've worked here since the start of the war. This is the first time I've sat in the bleachers. I couldn't get into the grandstand." Today, that seat is painted red—known simply as "the red seat"—and "sits in a sea of green ... a fleck of red paint on an otherwise lush green canvas."[12]

With a large lead in the American League pennant race by mid–August, the Red Sox announced their plan for fans to obtain World Series tickets. Two tickets for only one game was the limit per person. This policy provided the maximum opportunity for fans to attend a World Series game, which would number far fewer under the traditional block-of-three-games approach. Only about 20,000 grandstand seats would be available for each game. There was no advance sale of the 8,500 bleacher seats, which would be sold at the ballpark on the day of the game only. Standing-room tickets for 1,600 people would also be sold one hour before game time.[13]

The Red Sox accepted applications only by mail, which needed to be postmarked after 12:01 in the morning of September 10. This encouraged an inordinate number of people to line up before midnight at the South Postal Annex in Boston, in order to get the earliest possible postmark. "By auto, train, and bus, thousands of baseball fans poured into Boston from all over New England last night to enter the mad race for World Series tickets at the midnight 'zero hour.'" There was an overwhelming demand for tickets, as the Red Sox received half a million applications for the 60,000 available reserved seats. After the Red Sox clinched the pennant on September 13, the tickets were mailed to the lucky names selected in the lottery for World Series tickets. Since there was roughly a 15-to-1 chance at getting a pair of reserved tickets, there were numerous complaints voiced by disappointed fans.[14]

The line for bleacher tickets for the first game in Boston started 34 hours before the ticket window was slated to open at 9:00 on Wednesday morning of the third Series game. Grover Gilmore, "an ardent baseball fan" who lived in the Back Bay, was first in line at 11:00 on Monday night, sitting in a candy-striped beach chair. By midnight Tuesday, there were 400 people in line, waiting in 45-degree weather. Gilmore got his bleacher ticket, but he reportedly fell asleep during the game from the effects of his lengthy vigil.[15]

The Red Sox split the first two games of the World Series in St. Louis, and then won two of the three games played at Fenway Park. Needing only one win in the last two games in St. Louis, the Red Sox lost both games. The Cardinals scored the winning run in the seventh game with two outs in the bottom of the eighth inning, when Enos Slaughter dashed home from first base on Harry Walker's line drive to left-center field, after shortstop Johnny Pesky allegedly hesitated on the relay from Lee Culberson as Slaughter beat Pesky's throw to home plate. A generation of Boston baseball fans clung to the belief that Pesky "held the ball," based on the radio broadcast of the seventh game.

Fans listened to the radio account of the World Series games on WNAC, which broadcast the Mutual Broadcasting System's production of the games, which were called by Jim Britt and Washington Senators broadcaster Arch McDonald. Unlike the last World Series contested by Boston teams in the 1910s, there was no re-creation of the games in theaters or mobs of people on Newspaper Row being fed information from telegraph reports. The World Series in 1946 could easily be consumed via radio broadcast in the comfort of one's own home. If a community atmosphere was desired, there were a few public places, like the Hatch Shell along the Charles River in Boston, where the radio broadcast was distributed through a public address system.[16]

The Braves capitalized on the renewed interest in baseball in Boston. Because many Red Sox fans were not able to secure World Series tickets, the Braves instituted a policy for the 1947 season that every season-ticket holder had the right to buy a World Series ticket if the Braves won the National

League pennant. In addition to the standard 77-game reserved-grandstand ticket package for all home games, the Braves also made available three other smaller-sized season-ticket plans for the 1947 season. One alternative was a package of two tickets for opening day, 12 Sundays, two holidays, and the first seven night games. The other two alternatives were all night games and 25 general-admission tickets.[17]

An increased number of night games were carded by the Braves for the 1947 season, to respond to one of the more popular results from the fan survey as well as the Red Sox initiating night baseball at Fenway that season. The Braves slated 28 night games at Braves Field, while the Red Sox included 14 night games on the schedule at Fenway Park. In the Braves' survey, 70 percent of fans wanted 28 or more night games (38 percent wanted 28 and 32 percent wanted more than 28) while 22 percent favored 21 night games and just 8 percent were content with just 14 games.[18]

As part of the informal cooperative arrangement, the Braves coordinated with the Red Sox to have all night games begin at 8:30 in the evening. Both teams also agreed to start afternoon games at 2:00 during the 1947 season, rather than the 3:00 commencement that the teams had used for decades. In the Braves' survey, 90 percent of fans wanted an earlier than 3:00 start, presumably to get home for dinner at a more reasonable time.[19]

Sunday doubleheaders were reduced in 1947, since Sunday drew well enough with just one game, so the 2-for-1 promotion had little impact to attendance. Because the Braves played night games on Saturday, this diminished the demand to attend two games on Sunday. The Massachusetts legislature had apparently locked the barn door after the horse was stolen, because, in practicality, the revised Sunday baseball law passed in 1946 was no longer needed.

The Braves tinkered with the traditional holiday schedule on Patriots Day, scuttling the twin bill of separate-admission morning and afternoon games in favor of a conventional doubleheader in the afternoon. One reason was the poor attendance for the morning game. Also, the rationale for the twin bill had less applicability to Braves Field than it did to Fenway Park. The Boston Marathon course was a mile from Braves Field, so there was no special reason to have an intermission so that fans could watch the runners, unlike Fenway Park that was very close to where the runners passed through Kenmore Square.

Although the Red Sox continued the twin bill tradition on Patriots Day for several more years, the team did opt to play just a single game on Bunker Hill Day in 1947 rather than the doubleheader normally played on that Boston holiday. Both teams continued to stage doubleheaders on the three national holidays.

The Braves also experimented with a different way to handle the makeup of a rainout rather than staging a 2-for-1 doubleheader. On July 10, 1947, the Braves played a separate-admission day-night twin bill against Cincinnati, with the afternoon game the makeup and the evening game the regularly scheduled night game. This technique had been pioneered in Brooklyn during the 1946 season. The Braves drew a combined 37,000 for both games, with 27,000 at the night game and 10,000 at the afternoon game.[20]

Billy Sullivan, the publicity director for the Braves, was still a busy man. In a novel move in major-league baseball, the Braves created a 30-minute film of highlights from the 1946 season, which the club made available to local civic groups to spur interest in the team. The Braves also partnered with the Somerset Hotel in Kenmore Square to promote a combination package of dinner and a ball game. Dubbed the blue-plate special, the $4.50 package also included cab rides to the ballpark and back to the hotel. Fried clams were now sold at the concession stand at Braves Field, in addition to the traditional ballpark fare of hot dogs and popcorn. One wag quipped that the promotion most desired, but not offered, was a parking space near Braves Field that allowed the spectator to drive away from the ballpark in less than one hour after the game ended.[21]

The Braves did their best to improve the automobile parking situation by negotiating a lease in July 1947 to use the outdoor space at the Commonwealth Armory, next door to Braves Field. The Braves had to work through the Massachusetts legislature to pass a special law to allow the state to rent the Commonwealth Armory when it was not being used for military purposes.[22]

All of these promotions appealed most to intermittent fans, who were a predominant part of the spectator audience for night games at Braves Field in 1946 and 1947, rather than necessarily the dedicated or general baseball fan that was more interested in the baseball game itself. These promotions exacerbated the shift of general baseball fans to Sox-leaning status, and eventually to become dedicated Sox fans, especially after night baseball arrived at Fenway Park in 1947.

Yawkey sought to appeal to baseball purists, the dedicated and general baseball fans, rather than the intermittent enthusiasts that the Braves now targeted, who had to endure increased signage on the outfield fences at Braves Field while they consumed fried clams at their seat purchased as part of one of the club's mini-season-ticket plans. Yawkey did not compete with the Braves for that those new fans. As construction progressed on the lightning system at Fenway Park and the creation of roof seats reconstituted from the temporary press box built for the World Series, Yawkey removed the advertising signage from the left-field wall and had it painted green to match the rest of the ballpark. This differentiated the Red Sox from the Braves, because the Sox promotions were baseball-oriented, with the only possible exception being the roof seats.[23]

This innocuous decision in 1947 later resulted in the left-field wall being called the "Green Monster," a label that was bestowed sometime during the 1960s. The distinctive shade of green has changed slightly over the years since Yawkey decided to remove the advertising. In 1947 the color was called Dartmouth Green, but in the 1960s was modified to be Statler Green. During the early 1970s the color became Fence Green, when the California Paints Company in Andover, Massachusetts, began providing the paint mix to the Red Sox. In 2014, the paint color was sold to the general public for the first time, when the Benjamin Moore Company began marketing Fenway Green paint.[24]

With more night games in 1947, the Braves and Red Sox transferred the radio broadcast coverage to WHDH, an independent radio station that had recently been purchased by the *Boston Herald* newspaper. Since WHDH had no network affiliation, there was no concern with broadcasting night ball games as there was at WNAC. Additionally, with no lucrative Sunday programming to disrupt, WHDH was willing to air broadcasts of Sunday ball games. With regular sellouts on Sunday anticipated at both ballparks, the Braves and Red Sox had few attendance-reduction qualms for 1947 and thus approved regular Sunday radio broadcasts for the first time since the 1931 season.[25]

Although the switch from the Yankee Network affiliated with WNAC to a new network put together by WHDH was initially an obstacle to baseball fans in outlying areas of New England, once fans got used to dialing in a new station to listen to ball games they discovered a dramatic increase in the number of games being broadcast, with all night and Sunday games now available over radio. WHDH also continued the tradition of doing telegraphic recreations of a road game when there was no home game in Boston, such as the Braves game at the Polo Grounds in New York City on May 9, when there was no game that day at Fenway Park. Both clubs hoped to convert this expanded radio audience into spectators for a Saturday, Sunday, or night game.[26]

Night games were inaugurated at Fenway Park on Friday, June 13, 1947, when 34,510 spectators watched a ball game under the recently erected light towers. Consistent with Yawkey's emphasis on the quality of the ball game, the Fenway Park lighting system was said to be one of the two best in the major leagues. However, since "Yawkey is strictly in the baseball business" and despised door-prize promotions, he ensured that the arc lights, as much as possible, provided for the same top-flight game as would played during daylight, not just appealed to a new group of spectators. "If it weren't for public demand, owner Tom Yawkey would never have installed the giant towers over his orchard," the *Boston Globe* noted. Like the owners of the Detroit Tigers and Chicago Cubs, "Yawkey believes that baseball should be played under sunlight, not arc lights."[27]

The evening games of the Red Sox were very popular, attracting more than 30,000 for all but one game in 1947. The Braves, on the other hand, averaged around 20,000 for their night games in their second year of night baseball. In addition to larger crowds at night and on Sunday, the Red Sox also had a decided advantage over the Braves for day games during the workweek. Attendance for afternoon games at Fenway Park was triple that for similar games at Braves Field. The Red Sox had a strong draw among businessmen as well among women fans that flocked to Ladies Day games for the bargain price of the tax and a small service charge. The Ladies Day game on June 23 attracted 9,813 women, which enlarged the afternoon audience to more than 30,000 people. The crush of day-of-the-game ticket purchases caused the Red Sox to institute a new policy that required discounted Ladies Day tickets to be purchased in advance. Boston and Cleveland were the last two major-cities to conduct regular Ladies Day events.[28]

In 1947 more spectators went through the turnstiles at Fenway Park than at Braves Field, even though the Braves challenged for the National League lead from the beginning of the season and took over first place in mid–June, before fading from the pennant race in August to finish in third place. For the entire season, 1.4 million people went to Fenway Park while 1.2 million went to Braves Field, despite all the promotional dollars spent by the Braves.

When attendance at Braves Field was projected to hit one million customers on August 20, the Braves offered their first Appreciation Day to honor one lucky fan with a new automobile. More than 36,000 people showed up; 24,638 paid, with 6,248 free on Ladies Day passes and another 5,120 cut-rate tickets for kids with Knot Hole Gang passes. "The fans stayed to the bitter end," the *Boston Globe* sarcastically commented on the 16–10 loss to Pittsburgh. "Not because they appreciated the poor brand of baseball. Not because they had much hope of the Braves coming back with one of their patented thrilling ninth inning rallies. They were in the market for a new car."[29]

John Ragucci, a 21-year-old from Everett, was selected from the barrel of 30,886 ticket stubs (the under-18 Knot Holers were ineligible) to win a new Packard automobile. Ragucci raced to home plate to shake hands with Perini, who asked him how he felt to own a new car. "Great! Great!" Ragucci responded. The second, and last, question posed was: "What are you going to do with it?" Perini was a bit rattled when Ragucci enthusiastically responded: "I'm going to raise hell with it!" As a surprise for the fans, Perini gave away a second car that evening, which was won by 48-year-old John Howell of Everett, who had a more subdued reaction than Ragucci.[30]

Perini conducted a second fan raffle in 1947 at the last home game in Braves Field, among all the ticket stubs from the last ten home games of the 1947 season. One lucky fan won a spring training trip to see the Braves in

Bradenton, Florida, in March 1948, which came with $500 in spending money. Portable radios were awarded as consolation prizes to dozens of fans.[31]

The raffles on Appreciation Day and at the last home game became staple promotions at Braves Field through the 1950 season.

Fan interest in Boston reached new heights in 1948, when both teams were involved in the pennant chase, and nearly played each other in the World Series, which provided the Braves with their best opportunity to generate a core of dedicated fans.

◆ 18 ◆

Trying to Mint
Braves Fans

While the Red Sox focused on strengthening the team on the playing field, the Braves rolled out more fan-friendly items for the 1948 season, with roof seats and a new scoreboard. Perini clearly had his sights set on ballpark spectators who were less familiar with the game and sought amenities beyond watching a good baseball team.

The rooftop Sky View seats were created from the former football press box and season tickets for these seats retailed for $200. Perini originally envisioned an outdoor café next to the seating area, but there wasn't enough space. Instead, there was seat service provided by "boys in snappy uniforms" taking orders from patrons, not a vendor hawking peanuts and popcorn. The Sky View patrons had an excellent view not just of the playing field but also the new all-electric scoreboard, which contrasted to the largely manual scoreboard at Fenway Park. There was so much information displayed on the scoreboard that one sportswriter quipped "the new electrical encyclopedia would show everything about the ball game except the batter's heart beat."[1]

The Braves also expanded their community service efforts in 1948 when several Braves players participated in a ten-minute segment of the "Truth or Consequences" radio show on May 22 that focused on a 12-year-old cancer patient at Children's Hospital in Boston. The idea was to drum up interest among listeners to contribute to the Children's Cancer Research Fund so that Dr. Sidney Farber could help other cancer-stricken children.

While the actual patient was real—and a dedicated Braves fan—his identity was kept anonymous and a generic "Jimmy" was deployed as his name for the radio broadcast. "He's a swell little guy," host Ralph Edwards remarked, "and although he cannot figure out why he isn't out with the other kids, he does love his baseball and follows every move of his favorite team, the Boston

Braves." After talking with the boy about the Braves, Edwards then asked, "Have you ever met Phil Masi," the Braves catcher. When Jimmy replied, "No," Masi then entered the hospital room and introduced himself to Jimmy. "Who's that, Jimmy?" Edwards asked. Radio listeners heard Jimmy gasp and shout, "Phil Masi!" After meeting several more ballplayers, the gathering ended with the players and Jimmy singing, off-key, the song "Take Me Out to the Ball Game." Edwards concluded the segment by appealing to listeners to contribute money to the Children's Cancer Research Fund.[2]

The interaction between "Jimmy" and the Braves players was so successful in raising money that the cause was soon labeled the Jimmy Fund, as an easily remembered, warm-hearted slogan compared to the longer, somewhat sterile Children's Cancer Research Fund. The Braves had a prominent place in the June 26 celebration of Jimmy Fund Day throughout Massachusetts. Third baseman Bob Elliott raffled off prizes at a rally on Boston Common, which included Braves t-shirts, a portrait painted of the winner's favorite Braves player, and an autographed baseball by the Braves (won by 11-year-old Donald Bresnahan of Roxbury). Other Braves players traveled to towns around the state before returning to Boston for the Saturday night game at Braves Field.[3]

Radio announcer Jim Britt hosted many Jimmy Fund events during his time in Boston, boosting donation levels by using his popularity among Boston baseball fans. Britt and number-two-man Tom Hussey had a sizeable listening audience for their WHDH broadcasts of Red Sox and Braves games through the well-established radio medium, as 95 percent of American households now owned a radio. Fans also enjoyed listening to Jerry O'Leary, who conducted a popular pre-game show called "Play Ball" that was a prelude to the game broadcast. O'Leary roamed the stands of the ballpark to ask spectators trivia questions to win a small cash prize. O'Leary, an advertising executive in his day job, explained the popularity of his show as "the lure of baseball and the current craze for quiz programs."[4]

However, a new communication medium—television—was just taking hold in Boston. On June 9, 1948, WBZ became the first television station to operate in Boston. Less than a week later, WBZ televised its first baseball game on June 15, when the Braves played the Chicago Cubs at Braves Field in a Saturday night game. The baseball telecasts alternated between WBZ and WNAC, which began operating on June 21. Very few people saw the initial telecasts from Fenway Park and Braves Field in 1948. The two television stations had just a 40-mile reception area for the approximately 3,500 television sets that had been installed in the Greater Boston area, about half of which were in taverns, hotels, and restaurants.[5]

The inception of televised ball games disrupted the radio coverage of the games. Britt and Hussey were deployed to handle both mediums by splitting their time at the respective microphones for radio and television. Hussey handled the first and last three innings of each game on TV, while Britt did the middle three innings. When one announcer was doing television, the other did the radio coverage, with Leo Egan helping out on radio as needed. Bump Hadley did commentary for the televised games.[6]

Television was a novelty, so televised baseball was simply an experiment. "Everyone knows that baseball feared radio when it came into being," Braves general manager John Quinn said at the time. "But it didn't hurt the game. We'll just have to give it a try and see what happens." However, things did not turn out the same as the impact of radio. Television became a new community within the private home, supplanting the need for public venues like the ballpark and movie theaters to have a community experience. Soon, "the normal way to enjoy a community experience was at home in your living room at your TV set."[7]

The first televised baseball game in Boston on June 15 was the Braves' first game back home following a road trip, where the team had moved into first place in the National League standings. While the newfound success of the Braves did entice more fans to go to Braves Field that June, more people went through the turnstiles at Fenway Park even though the Red Sox were then in sixth place. The Red Sox drew 33,000 fans for a night game on Tuesday, June 8, while a week later on June 15 the Braves drew only 24,000 for a night game. On Friday night, June 11, the Red Sox drew 38,000 while a week later the night game on June 18 at Braves Field drew 30,000. This stark contrast, which continued through the remainder of the season, indicates the inherent challenge faced by Perini and the Braves to gain an advantage among Boston fans.

Based on the American League style of play, the Red Sox had a good base of dedicated fans from the prewar days. The Sox minted more dedicated fans in the postwar period through the transformation of Sox-leaning general baseball fans who disliked the perceived "hokey" promotions of the Braves. Many intermittent fans became Sox-leaners for the same reason. A fixation with the game on the field led many fans to want to be associated with the baseball-focused Red Sox. While Perini had some success in converting intermittent fans and Sox-leaning general fans into Braves-leaning fans, especially among women and children, he seemed to be more successful in developing new intermittent fans.

If the Braves had been the only Boston team to produce great results on the ball field in 1948, their success with Boston fans might have turned out differently. However, the sixth-place Red Sox turned into the first-place Red Sox when the team won a dozen consecutive games in mid–July. On the morning of July 26, both the Braves and Red Sox held first place in their respective leagues, the first time that had occurred since September 1916. The winning streak encouraged fans to flock to Fenway Park. The Red Sox staged separate-admission day-night doubleheaders on July 15 and July 21 to shoe-horn as many eager fans as possible into the ballpark. "It will be possible for 70,000 lucky fans to see the magnificent Red Sox on these dates, instead of only 35,000," one wag put it. "Oh, lucky Boston fans, to be followers of such benevolent despots!"[8]

Appreciation Day at Braves Field on Sunday, August 8, might be considered the beginning of the end for the Braves in Boston, when 41,527 spectators packed the ballpark for a game against the hapless Chicago Cubs for a chance to win a free automobile. Two free cars were raffled off, with the winners (Edward Coffey and Ronald Hiltz) both residents of suburban Belmont. Two television sets and three trips to the World Series were also given away, won by a mix of two Boston residents (Brighton and Roxbury), two from the suburbs (Watertown and Wollaston), and one from out of state (Tiverton, Rhode Island). Among these latter five winners, two were women and just three were men. Lolly Hopkins, a true general baseball fan who was recognized as the number one fan of both teams, drew the prize-winning ticket stubs from a large barrel, to commemorate the Braves drawing one million spectators for a second consecutive season.[9]

Many of the people at Braves Field that Sunday afternoon were disinterested in the actual ball game, simply waiting around until the game ended for the winning ticket stubs to be picked. "Ted Williams may be the biggest drawing card at Fenway Park, but at Braves Field the No. 1 attraction is a free automobile," the *Boston Globe* slammed the Braves' blatant promotion aimed not at baseball fans, but rather at entertainment-oriented folks. Some of the overflow crowd was herded into a roped-off area in foul territory in left field, where "people idled on the grass," "men slept and even snored," and "small groups sprawled lazily around portable radios." It was not the type of crowd that would normally be seen at Fenway Park for a Red Sox game.[10]

With pennant contenders at both Fenway Park and Braves Field in 1948 for the first time in a generation, the environment appeared perfect to solidify the traditional base of general baseball fans that supported both Boston teams. However, just the opposite occurred, with a bifurcation of general baseball fans into partisan, dedicated fans that exclusively followed either the Red Sox or the Braves. Unfortunately for the Braves, that fan passion translated mostly into the formation of dedicated Red Sox fans. The broad label of "Boston baseball fan," still in wide newspaper use in 1946, began to disintegrate as a characterization of the majority species in Boston fandom by 1948, when the more narrow term "Red Sox fan" became a much more common occurrence. People like Lolly Hopkins who rooted faithfully for both teams were becoming dinosaurs. The headline "Split Between Sox–Braves Fans Growing Wider" in a May 1949 edition of the *Boston Globe* said it all, signaling the demise of the Braves as a business-viable team in Boston.[11]

Despite the success of the Braves on the field during the three seasons from 1946 to 1948, there were still very few dedicated Braves fans. Even those people who characterized themselves as a pure Braves fan were, upon further prodding, really Braves-leaning general baseball fans.

One unnamed "Braves fan" interviewed in 1948, who vowed that he didn't root for the Red Sox, provided an apt methodology to differentiate between dedicated fans in both camps. "Braves fans root for the Braves. Red Sox fans root for the Red Sox," the man stated the obvious, but then added his litmus test: "Red Sox fans don't know the Braves exist. They're indifferent. But Braves fans like me—we root against the Red Sox." Although this man thought he was describing Braves fans as being more rabid than Red Sox fans, he actually depicted Red Sox fans as being more rabid. Dedicated Red Sox fans did not care about the Braves. However, Braves fans did follow the Red Sox, but just rooted against them. This man was a Braves-leaning general baseball fan, part of the old duopoly in Boston.[12]

A self-described "ardent Braves fan," Earl Mokler, a 38-year-old from Somerville who owned a trucking company, traveled to Florida in 1948 to watch the Braves in spring training. In an interview, Mokler was very conversant about the players on both teams, although he was less enthusiastic about the Red Sox, but then admitted: "I'd see them more—if I could get good seats. I've had the same seats at Braves Field for seven years." Mokler was another Braves-leaning general baseball fan.[13]

Esther MacMillan of Brookline was another hearty Braves fan, who attended games at nearby Braves Field and often had to arbitrate disputes between her two teenaged sons, James who was a Red Sox fan and Joseph who was a Braves fans. "I like the Braves best, but I'm not against the Red Sox either. I'm for them against any team, except the Braves," MacMillan said, before summing up the situation perfectly by adding, "I guess I'm a Boston fan."[14]

Even some dedicated Red Sox fans tried to disavow this label, since it was so opposite to past convention. "Though it is common knowledge in Northampton that Mrs. Coolidge suffers as acutely in the misfortunes and failures of the Red Sox as does any true-blue fan, she doesn't like to go officially on record as favoring any one team," one writer wrote about Grace Coolidge, the wife of the late former president Calvin Coolidge. "I'm an American League fan," she said diplomatically, "but I'm rooting for both Boston teams." The remainder of the article showed, however, that she clearly favored the Red Sox.[15]

Beginning in 1948, it was a one-way street for "Red Sox fans," due to the increasing number of dedicated ones and a higher standard for Sox-leaning general fans. For "Braves fans" it continued to be a two-way street, as they just could not forsake at least a minor interest in the outcome of Red Sox games or the temptation to watch a game at Fenway Park. This represented a recipe for future disaster, even as the prospects for an all-Boston World Series in 1948 loomed on the horizon, as indicated by this mid–September front-page banner headline in *The Sporting News*: "All-Boston Series Frenzy Sweeps Hub."[16]

Joking about the potential all-Boston World Series started early in the 1948 season, with one sportswriter in April quipping, "We should worry about whether or not the World Series games will all be played at Braves Field, the larger park." By July humorous concern was voiced about the impact to Boston fans: "Barbers with Braves inclinations will give Red Sox fans hedge-clipper haircuts. And can you imagine what will happen to the Braves fan who confesses his preference to a Red Sox dentist?" The writer concluded that "nonpartisan fans should stay home ... not even neutral fans will get past the barricades during a Red Sox–Braves World Series."[17]

As the Braves lengthened their lead in the National League in mid–September, Gerry Hern wrote an article for the *Boston Post* that neatly summarized the Braves pitching strategy, which was entitled: "Braves Boast Two-Man Staff: Pitch Spahn and Sain, Then Pray for Rain." While the *Post* was defunct eight years later, that title lived on to become a literary classic in baseball.[18]

In mid–September the Braves mailed letters to season-ticket holders about how to obtain World Series tickets, which was part of the promise the club had made to buyers of any of the four season-ticket plans. "The Braves are giving first consideration in October to those who had confidence in the club last winter," Quinn announced, along with the restriction that fans could buy only two tickets for one game, the same policy that the Red Sox had for the 1946 World Series. Grandstand and pavilion seats sold out 36 hours after the announcement; 1,500 bleacher seats and 2,500 standing-room tickets would be sold later.[19]

When the Braves clinched the National League pennant on September 26, the team prepared for its first World Series since 1914. The World Series in 1948 was scheduled to be played on consecutive days over a seven-day period, beginning on Wednesday, October 6, with no travel days. The first two games were slated for the National League ballpark. While convenient for the Braves to play the Red Sox or the Yankees, two of the three teams battling down to the wire for the American League pennant, this schedule would result in grueling train trips if Cleveland, the third contending team, won the pennant.

Many of the Braves players actually rooted for Cleveland to win the American League pennant, rather than the Red Sox that would have set up an exciting streetcar series between the two Boston teams. "So far as baseball rivalry is concerned, I would like to play the Red Sox," infielder Alvin Dark told a sportswriter. "But for business reasons, I naturally would want to see Cleveland win the pennant." Cleveland played in an 80,000-seat stadium, which would mean an additional $2,000 for each Braves player in their World Series paycheck, compared to receipts from the much smaller Fenway Park.[20]

With so much interest in the Red Sox, WHDH broadcast several re-creations of Red Sox road games during mid–September, when the Braves did not play at Braves Field. WHDH even broadcast a live road game from Yankee Stadium on Friday, September 24, when the Braves were idle due to a college football game between Boston College and Wake Forest at Braves Field.[21]

On the last day of the 1948 season, the Red Sox defeated the Yankees and the Indians lost to the Tigers, which created a tie for first place between the Red Sox and Indians. The tie was settled in the first-ever playoff for the American League pennant, a one-game, sudden-death game on Monday, October 4, at Fenway Park.

While the Red Sox were already in Boston, the Indians had to endure an all-night train ride from Cleveland and did not get into Boston until 10:00 in the morning of the playoff game, which started at 1:00 that afternoon. The fact that many of the Indians were tired and hung over did not seem to matter, as they pummeled the serves of journeyman pitcher Denny Galehouse, whom Red Sox manager Joe McCarthy surprisingly had selected to pitch for the Red Sox. Cleveland easily defeated the Red Sox in the playoff game to win the pennant and meet the Braves in the World Series. Cleveland defeated the Braves in the World Series, four games to two.

The World Series seemed to be anti-climatic in Boston, though, with the failure of the Red Sox to qualify for it. On the day of the American League playoff game, Harold Kaese of the *Boston Globe* had prophetically written: "No World Series—whether it be between the Braves and Red Sox or (Booh!) the Braves and Indians—can equal the thrills of a close pennant race, such as the one which will be decided by today's playoff between the Red Sox and Indians at Fenway Park." Three million spectators attended baseball games in Boston in 1948, 1.55 million at Fenway Park and 1.45 million at Braves Field. Despite winning the National League pennant, the Braves were once again outfoxed at the box office by the Red Sox. The ability to mint dedicated Braves fans turned out to be more challenging than Perini had originally believed.[22]

Dave Stein, a teenager who sold souvenirs at Braves Field during the World Series, exemplified the dilemma faced by many would-be dedicated Braves fans. "I'm a Braves fan and Johnny Sain is my favorite player in the National League," he told Elizabeth Watts of the *Boston Globe*. But Stein put Ted Williams at the top of his list of all ballplayers, despite his moody ways, because "he's still entitled to do what he wants as long as he plays ball the way he does." His favorite team was the Braves, but his favorite player was on the Red Sox. Stein admitted that he didn't make much money at Braves Field during the World Series. "The most money I made was at a double-header at Fenway Park when the Sox played the Indians," Stein told Watts. "The fans really loosened up then." Braves Field was where his heart was, but Fenway Park put money in his pocket. These were tough choices for a 14-year-old in postwar Boston.[23]

Most people in Boston followed the 1948 World Series on WNAC radio, which carried the Mutual Broadcasting System network broadcast done by Jim Britt and Yankees broadcaster Mel Allen. The first two games, at Braves Field, were telecast in Boston on both WNAC-TV and WBZ-TV, since the Mutual network used as many television stations as possible to maximize the television exposure. Brooklyn broadcaster Red Barber was at the microphone for the telecasts. However, the middle three games from Cleveland were not televised in Boston due to technical complications that prevented signals from being transmitted from Cleveland to the East Coast (coaxial cables were not yet state-of-the-art for long distance signal transmission).[24]

Boston-based Gillette Company, which sponsored the World Series broadcasts and telecasts, set up 100 RCA-donated television sets on the Boston Common, which were watched by an estimated 10,000 fans. The picture quality was poor, though, showing the pitcher at the top of the screen and just the batter's head at the bottom of the screen. No bat, catcher, or umpire was shown. The inexperienced cameramen were often late showing plays to the infield. There were no shots of the outfield or the crowd, despite pleas to the production crew from telecaster Barber. The radio broadcasts by Britt and Allen were much more informative.[25]

The Braves might have been better off playing the Red Sox in the 1948 World Series to ensure a brighter future with baseball fans in Boston, because in 1949 television would begin to impact the future of the Braves in Boston.

Television and
Suburban Fans

In January 1949, basking in the glory of its 1948 National League championship, the Braves made a public commitment to stay at Braves Field when president Lou Perini announced that the club had purchased the ballpark (no longer leasing it from the Gaffney estate) and unveiled his plan for future improvements to Braves Field.

For the 1949 season, the Braves permanently added the 600 box seats temporarily built for the World Series and also took over the concession stands from the Harry Stevens Company to focus on regional items like fish cakes on Friday night, baked beans on Saturday, and clam chowder to replace the aroma-displeasing fried clams. Longer term, the Braves planned to expand the ballpark to hold 50,000 spectators by adding new bleachers behind the outfield wall, have a railroad station behind left field so more fans would take the train to the game rather than drive an automobile, and construct a footbridge over the Boston & Albany railroad tracks to connect to a parking lot along the proposed Storrow Drive for fans desiring to drive to the game.[1]

Left unsaid by Perini was that his long-term plan was premised on the implementation of the "Master Highway Plan for the Boston Metropolitan Area," produced in 1948 by the Massachusetts Department of Public Works. This plan would enable people living in the suburbs to more easily travel by automobile to and from downtown Boston, and, by extension, to and from Braves Field. Perini had confidence that these highways would be built, since he was well acquainted with William Callahan, the new state transportation chief under the new governor, Paul Dever, who had won the November 1948 gubernatorial election.

The "Master Highway Plan" recommended the construction of eight limited-access highway "spokes" emanating from a "hub" in downtown Boston, with a ninth expressway, the inner belt, circling downtown Boston in a two-mile radius. Of most interest to Perini were the proposed western expressway and the inner belt that connected all the spokes (which had an interchange planned for the Cottage Farm area, near Braves Field). Without these highways into Boston, people living in the suburbs would be very reluctant to travel to Braves Field to watch a ball game. In this sense, limited-access highways were essential to the continued financial success of the Braves club.[2]

Perini alluded to this foundational element in his comments to sportswriters, when he said that his plan was would go forward "only if conditions warrant it." Perini only vaguely amplified what conditions he meant, saying "the nation's population is increasing" and "interest in baseball is increasing." Perini seemed to be referring to the population shift from the inner city to the suburbs, but, in retrospect, he could also have been referring to moving the Braves from Boston to Milwaukee, the home of the Braves' top farm club, where the plan for a publicly funded stadium was moving forward at a brisk pace.[3]

In discussing the plan with sportswriters, Perini also said that he had spent "five years examining other locations all over greater Boston" before deciding to refurbish Braves Field. One of the locations examined was Fenway Park, which Perini considered renting from the Red Sox back in 1945. Red Sox owner Tom Yawkey, though, was not enamored with Perini's idea, which reportedly was posed to Yawkey by Braves general manager John Quinn. In a *Saturday Evening Post* article in 1947, Harold Kaese of the *Boston Globe* disclosed the meeting, writing that "as much as Yawkey liked Quinn, son of the man who had sold him the Red Sox, he would not yield a square inch of Fenway Park, except when the Braves were in a spot." A quarter-century later, Quinn acknowledged the meeting and remarked that he wasn't surprised at the reaction he received from Yawkey, saying, "He's a funny guy. What's his, he wants for his own."[4]

Perini also contemplated building a new ballpark in suburban Framingham. It was likely no coincidence that the briefing of sportswriters about the future of Braves Field was held in Framingham at the corporate office of Perini Construction. Located 20 miles west of Boston, Framingham, along with the neighboring town of Natick, was the epicenter of suburban development in the Greater Boston area in the late 1940s. Framingham was an ideal candidate for the location of a suburban ballpark, beyond Perini's local knowledge of the area, due to the prognosis for new construction and transportation development. The town had grown to be a regional railroad hub as the midway point between Boston and Worcester on the Boston & Albany Railroad. It was also the midpoint for automobile traffic on what used to be known as the Worcester Turnpike, now better known as Route 9, a divided highway that was the last major state highway project, built in the 1930s by the Perini Construction Company.[5]

Braves president Lou Perini (second from left) smiles during pre-game festivities at Braves Field, as an unidentified dignitary throws out the ceremonial first pitch. Perini initiated night baseball in Boston and gave away automobiles in promotions to attract fans to Braves Field, as he tried to compete with the Red Sox (courtesy Boston Public Library, Leslie Jones Collection).

To respond to the postwar housing shortage, Framingham had a great deal of undeveloped acreage within its 25 square miles. Highways were the new barometer to decide the location of commerce and housing, not rivers or railroads, as housing developers like the Campanelli brothers bought farms and meadows in Framingham and Natick to build numerous housing subdivisions with idyllic names such as Cherryfield and Deerfield. Designed to appeal to middle-class workers, these ranch and split-level houses were modest 2- and 3-bedroom detached homes, with a prominent picture window in the living room overlooking the front yard and well-equipped kitchens with modern appliances.[6]

The 1948 opening of a General Motors assembly plant in Framingham helped to spur growth, as did the 1951 opening of Shoppers' World, the first shopping mall east of the Mississippi River. "The flight to suburbia reflected a profound rejection of the city. It seemed completely out of date," James O'Connell wrote in *The Hub's Metropolis: Greater Boston's Development from Railroad Suburbs to Smart Growth.* "The neighborhoods built in the 19th and early 20th centuries were deteriorating. Boston's industries suffered a deep depression, and vacant factories were everywhere." Symbolizing this suburban flight was the Jordan Marsh department store, which had a long presence in downtown Boston, but now was an anchor tenant at Shoppers' World in the store's first foray outside of downtown Boston.[7]

This was all happening before the transportation developments that magnified the growth prospects for Framingham. Callahan implemented the suburban aspects of the state's 1948 master highway plan, "to provide ready [automobile] access to the North and South Shore recreational and residential areas," before tackling the more expensive highways within the city of Boston. Construction of the circumferential highway in a ten-mile perimeter around Boston, now known as Route 128, began in 1950, and the first stretch between Lynnfield and Wellesley (which linked to Route 9 that went to Framingham) opened in August 1951. While initially panned as a "road to nowhere," authors Susan Rosegrant and David Lampe noted in their book *Route 128: Lessons from Boston's High-Tech Community* that the highway quickly became "an incubator for computer entrepreneurs than soon led to a high-tech boom in the 1960s."[8]

The east-west tollway, now known as the Massachusetts Turnpike, opened in 1957, with an exit in Framingham adjacent to the industrial park where Perini wanted to build the suburban ballpark. The tollway then ended at Route 128, and was not extended into Boston until 1965. The consolation prize for Perini was that his construction company built much of the turnpike.[9]

Since the construction of a suburban ballpark would have made the most economic sense if the Braves and Red Sox shared the facility, Perini tried to enlist the Red Sox as a joint tenant, but again Yawkey refused to share ball grounds. The land in Framingham slated for the proposed ballpark was used to build a highly successful industrial park. "I guess the industrial park turned out to be a better thing for Framingham because of the tax revenue," said Don Croatti, a Sox-leaning general baseball fan that went to games at both Fenway Park and Braves Field as a teenager, who later worked for two decades as the town's treasurer-collector.[10]

While Perini had accurately pegged the suburbs as a trend to respond to for the future, he didn't foresee the massive impact that television would have to American society in the short term. The 1948 experiment to televise ball games from Fenway Park and Braves Field had minimal, if any, impact on attendance. Like radio 25 years earlier, television was seen as an advertising technique to increase patronage over time. However, in 1949, the impact of television arrived much faster than had the impact of radio, and produced a much different result. The initial impact was the construction of new perches for television broadcasters and cameras at Fenway Park.[11]

Television sets were not yet a fixture in the American home in 1949, when just two percent of U.S. households owned a TV set. However, televised ball games helped to spur the acceptance of television in the days before network programming filled the airwaves. "Television did not create baseball, but baseball helped to create television," James Walker and Robert Bellamy wrote in *Center Field Shot: A History of Baseball on Television.* "Newly minted television stations were not the only ones that needed baseball to fill their broadcast hours. Television manufacturers needed appealing programs to push consumers to buy their first set."[12]

Watching a ball game on one of the early television sets wasn't all that enjoyable for baseball fans. The screen was very small and the reception quality of the black-and-white picture depended upon the positioning of the house vis-à-vis nearby hills and the aiming of the TV antenna. There wasn't much for fans to see even with a quality TV picture, just the pitcher and the batter, and portions of those players might be cut off. There were only two cameras to follow the action once the ball was in play, and they often were late in capturing the play. Announcers added little to what viewers saw on the television screen, since they were instructed to watch the TV monitor in the booth, not the game on the field, to just describe what they saw on the screen. In 1949, there appeared to be little worry that televised baseball games would ever have much impact on attendance at the ballpark.[13]

In one respect, television actually increased baseball exposure, when a quiz show featured ballplayers from the Braves was aired in September 1949 as part of the fund-raising campaign for the Jimmy Fund to encourage Boston baseball fans to contribute to the effort to cure cancer in children. It was great publicity for the Braves, showing their community spirit, which they hoped would also translate into box-office receipts. While the Braves' association with the Jimmy Fund did increase its public visibility, especially when contrasted with the Red Sox, its charitable efforts attracted more intermittent fans than general baseball fans. It was good for the short term, but unless these new fans could be converted into dedicated or at least Braves-leaning general fans, it didn't have attractive long-term implications. Therefore, the continued strong attendance at Braves Field in 1949 was illusionary as a measure of the Braves' prowess in capturing general baseball fans.[14]

All of the home games played by both the Red Sox and Braves during the 1949 season were on television, divided evenly between WNAC and WBZ. The sponsorship of the telecasts was split among Narragansett beer (all games), Atlantic gasoline (half of the games), and the New England Chevrolet Dealers Association (half of the games). Since most television sets in 1949 were located in taverns, the beer commercials were targeted to an appropriate audience. Clearly, though, the latter two organizations believed that advertising on the televised ball games would appeal to automobile owners, or at least aspiring purchasers, who lived in the suburbs.[15]

There were no hints of concern with television prior to the beginning of the 1949 season, as the "demands for season tickets and mail orders for special games exceed[ed] anything in the history of Boston baseball" at both Fenway Park and Braves Field. There was, though, a bigger demand at Fenway Park where all the box seats were sold out for the season and the club stopped ticket sales for certain big games to save a reasonable allotment for day-of-game sales "in order to accommodate as many people as possible."[16]

Both clubs also arranged their playing schedules to maximize attendance at their 77 home games. The Red Sox limited Sunday doubleheaders to the July–August period, mostly against the less-talented teams from Philadelphia and Washington, and staged three day-night doubleheaders. The Braves increased the number of night games to appeal to suburban fans. While the Red Sox succeeded in increasing attendance at Fenway Park to 1.6 million fans in 1949, the Braves suffered a 25 percent decline in attendance down to 1.1 million.

The eight night games played at Braves Field during the first long home-stand from late April to mid–May drew smaller crowds than night games had the previous three seasons, as a chilly breeze blew off the Charles River to annoy fans. Then the parking problems erupted, since the 3,000 parking-lot spaces within the vicinity of Braves Field were woefully inadequate to handle the number of people attending night games. The state tried to halt parking at the Commonwealth Armory, adjacent to Braves Field, which would have taken away 700 parking spaces and forced many people to try to park their automobiles on the residential streets of upscale Brookline. There already were numerous complaints from Brookline residents voiced in the letters to the editor section of the newspapers. "Mr. Perini's night games are a constant invitation to the hoodlums who drink beer, throw the bottles and cans on our front lawns, break windows, park cars on our lawns and private driveways, and invade the quiet of our homes," Cecilia Haskell wrote to the *Boston Globe*. "Isn't it time to restore baseball to a daytime activity and allow the residents of Brookline the opportunity to enjoy their homes at night without benefit of blazing lights from Braves Field, constant horn-tooting, and the general bedlam which comes when the management has not made parking provisions for its customers?"[17]

Despite a disappointing season on the ball field and its sundry challenges with the external amenities at Braves Field, the Braves passed the one million mark in attendance in late August. The winners of the Appreciation Day raffle of two new automobiles were Ralph Pullo of Allston and Alfred Villa of Brighton. Ironically, in hindsight, four new television sets were also raffled off, which were won by two fans from the suburbs and two from Boston neighborhoods, including eight-year-old Martin Kantrovitz of Dorchester. In a sign of future concern, though, more raffle winners lived in the Boston neighborhoods than in the suburbs. In another sign of concern at the spring-training raffle on the last day of the season, October 2, with only 3,700 fans in attendance, the first two ticket stubs drawn as winners had already left Braves Field and couldn't claim their prize immediately. They were given a few days to claim the prize, or it would go to the person with the third stub drawn, who was still at the ballpark. The absent raffle winners may have been general baseball fans who were listening to the radio broadcast of the Red Sox–Yankees game then being played in New York City (see below).[18]

The Red Sox continued to be wildly popular, as the team battled the New York Yankees in a hot pennant race that went down to the last two games of the season to determine the American League pennant winner. The Red Sox had a one-game lead when they arrived at Yankee Stadium to play the Yankees in those last two games of the 1949 season, and needed to win just one of the two games to be crowned American League champion. The Sox failed to accomplish that task, though. On Saturday, October 1, the Red Sox lost, 5–4, on a home run by the Yankees in the eighth inning, then lost on Sunday, 5–3, when right-fielder Al Zarilla dove for the fly ball off the bat of light-hitting Jerry Coleman in the eighth inning, but missed catching it by inches. Second baseman Bobby Doerr retrieved the errant ball, but not before three Yankees had crossed home plate. A three-run rally by the Red Sox in the top of the ninth inning fell short of victory.

"This ending had been even worse than 1948's. For two years in a row they had come so close, and ended up with nothing," David Halberstam wrote about the Red Sox in *Summer of '49*. "They had played *309* regular-season games over the two seasons and had ended up a total of one game behind the two pennant winners in that period." Even worse was that the defeat was the third in a trio of mishaps that had befallen the Red Sox over the four-year period from 1946 to 1949 and deprived them of a World Series championship. For decades, this series of losses haunted the team, the fans, and especially Pesky, Galehouse, and Zarilla.[19]

This was the start of the reputed Curse of the Bambino, where the season-ending games of 1948 and 1949 "were the forefather sins that the Red Sox of [1990] are still paying for" that allegedly precluded the team from winning a World Series championship, as Dan Shaughnessy wrote in his book *The Curse of the Bambino*. "The Red Sox were punished with twenty-eight years of ineptitude after Ruth was sold [to the Yankees], but in the 1940s a new form of denial took hold, and it has proven to be a far worse strain on the fragile psyche of the New England region. The Red Sox have the best team, but still manage not to win."[20]

Despite the heart-breaking loss in New York, there were 3,000 "wildly cheering baseball fans" at the Back Bay train station on Sunday night to greet the "grim-faced" Red Sox players upon their return to Boston. "Boston fandom last night gave its unhappy Red Sox warriors a welcome such is usually reserved for only the conquering heroes," the *Boston Globe* reported. "If ever Boston fans proved their whole-hearted support of a team, it was this time."[21]

In a decided deviation in radio broadcast policy, WHDH broadcast the last six road games of the Red Sox that season, which included the decisive final game of the season at Yankee Stadium. Due to the whims of the playing schedule, there were no conflicts with the Braves home games during the five-day period September 26–30. For the last two games of the season on October 1 and 2, there were conflicts, but "the Braves relinquished their broadcast time." While this was a generous move by the Braves, in the spirit of the informal cooperative arrangement between the two Boston baseball clubs, the decision may have cost the Braves in the long run, as it planted the idea in Yawkey's mind to begin broadcasting all Red Sox road games in 1951.[22]

Like many young Boston baseball fans, 11-year-old Bart Giamatti learned that life is filled with disappointment, when he listened to Jim Britt broadcast that decisive game of the 1949 season from a radio in his parents' home in South Hadley, Massachusetts, 75 miles west of Boston. Giamatti, who would grow up to become the commissioner of baseball, listened to the radio a lot in 1949, where through Britt's words he visualized Fenway Park "in his mind every day as he listened to the games on the radio—as if he were actually there." The season-ending broadcast from Yankee Stadium was a special treat, even if Giamatti learned that "the path to Calvinism in modern America begins at Fenway Park." Those sad feelings from 1949 led to the opening of Giamatti's famous essay "The Green Fields of the Mind," which he penned a quarter-century later after yet another heart-breaking Red Sox defeat. "It breaks your heart. It is designed to break your heart. The game begins in the spring, when everything else begins again, and it blossoms in the summer, filling the afternoons and evenings, and then as soon as the chill rains come, it stops and leaves you to face the fall alone," Giamatti wrote. "Just when the days are all twilight, when you need it most, it stops."[23]

The Curse of the Bambino, "no joy in Mudville," and "wait till next year" all became mantras among multiple generations of Red Sox fans. This unyielding belief about their fate bound fans together as a community, which had to endure another half-century before the Red Sox finally broke through to win the 2004 World Series. All the promotional muscle in Boston could not enable the Braves to successfully compete with that much fan affection for a baseball team, as indicated by the crowd at the train station after the last ball game in 1949.

In the winter of 1950, the first tangible inkling of trouble with televised sports surfaced, when smaller audiences materialized at the Boston Garden for professional hockey and basketball games played there in the evening. Television was blamed for the drop in attendance. "It is not the televising of sports events themselves that is keeping people home, but televising, period. Sports in a rink are competing with difficulty against Hopalong Cassidy, Milton Berle, and Arthur Godfrey in the living room." Admitted Walter Brown, the president of the Boston Garden, "There's nothing we can do about it. We can keep television out of the rink, but we can't keep it out of the home."[24]

There was a spillover effect to baseball in the spring of 1950. Despite the poor picture quality and limited informative value from the announcers, televised baseball did appeal to intermittent fans because it relieved them of the hassle of traveling to the ballpark and the consequent "worry about getting a seat behind a post, near a noisy fan, next to a drunk, or in right field where [you] can't see the plate." One sportswriter expressed the opinion at the time that "there is strong suspicion, but no proof, that television has been hurting attendances of the Braves and Red Sox." He was correct.[25]

While baseball was challenging to follow on television, entertainment shows were much easier for viewers to digest. Television began to impact Boston baseball fans during the spring of 1950 when, for the first time, the three major TV networks (NBC, CBS, and ABC) had a full lineup of shows during the evening on Monday through Friday. Local programming, such as a televised baseball game, had to override scheduled network shows. In 1950 there were four times as many households with a TV set than in 1949, as about ten percent of American households now had access to television in their living room.[26]

The television uproar began in April 1950, with the scheduled baseball telecast by WNAC of the Braves–Dodgers game on April 24 from Braves Field. "Cameras will open up at 8:30 P.M.," television reporter Elizabeth Sullivan wrote in the *Boston Globe*. "What won't be seen are the following Monday night favorites: Arthur Godfrey's Talent Scouts, Candid Camera, the Goldbergs and Studio One. They are being pushed aside for the ball game." By July, both WNAC and WBZ were flooded with viewer protests when night baseball games consistently interrupted the showing of the Arthur Godfrey show on CBS as well as the highly popular *Texaco Star Theater*, hosted by Milton Berle, on Tuesday evening on NBC. When *Texaco Star Theater* did run on WBZ while WNAC telecast a night ball game, attendance at the ballpark dipped, as people stayed home to watch Berle on television.[27]

Because the Braves staged nearly triple the number of night games as did the Red Sox—39 to 14—television first impacted the Braves. Given the relative composition of the Braves fan base, with more intermittent fans, the television impact was felt more dramatically by the Braves than by the Red Sox, whose fan composition was more slanted to dedicated and general baseball fans.

Television coaxed many baseball fans including Dwight D. (near screen) and Mamie Eisenhower to watch entertainment at home, rather than go to the ballpark. Although TV was still in its infancy in 1950, with a black-and-white picture produced through a rabbit-ears antenna, TV shows featuring Arthur Godfrey and Milton Berle reduced ballpark attendance at night games (Library of Congress, Prints and Photographs Division, LC-DIG-ppmsca-03134).

Perini's emphasis on intermittent, or entertainment-oriented, fans might have proved devastating to Yawkey's Red Sox had the demand for public entertainment continued to flourish in the 1950s. However, television changed that mentality, as suburban residents preferred their entertainment to be delivered in private, through the living room of their ranch home in the suburbs. Even worse, in the fall of 1950, the TV networks began regular daytime programming for the first time. The advent of soap operas airing in the afternoon put a dent in the largely female audience for daylight ball games telecast by WBZ and WNAC, and broadcast by WHDH on radio.[28]

After watching Larry Doby's heroics for Cleveland against the Braves in the 1948 World Series and seeing Jackie Robinson lead Brooklyn to the National League pennant in 1947, Perini purchased the contract of Sam Jethroe, another black player in the Dodgers organization, to play for the Braves in 1950. Besides being a move to improve the prospects of the team, Perini may also have sensed a possible edge to convert some Red Sox fans into Braves fans. In an avowed racially unfriendly city like Boston, that was asking a lot. Even though Jethroe led the National League in stolen bases in 1950 and was named Rookie of the Year, his presence in the Braves outfield did not generate more spectators at Braves Field.[29]

Some scholars have postulated that the Braves' decline in Boston was due to the Braves employing black ballplayers, which "could be viewed as a backlash by Boston fans for integrating their team and thus the city ... [while] the Red Sox were able to maintain popularity because they continued a strict policy of no black players." If racial prejudice had any effect on Braves attendance, it was likely with men older than age 50 who had grown up near the South End Grounds in Roxbury and had stopped going to Braves Field because they now lived in the suburbs. Because Roxbury by 1950 had a majority black population, these older men would have been part of the "white flight" from that neighborhood to predominately white Boston neighborhoods like Hyde Park or to the outlying suburbs.[30]

Both clubs struggled with declining attendance in 1950. The Red Sox staged more Sunday doubleheaders and played two twi-night doubleheaders during August as promotions to bring more fans to Fenway Park. The Braves scheduled more than half of their home games at night, including five in mid–September when chilly evenings typically set in, and held more Ladies Day to prop up the dismal crowds at the few afternoon weekday games still played at Braves Field.

The Braves became the first major-league team to complete a day game under the lights on April 23, under the new National League rule that permitted such an action, primarily to facilitate twi-night doubleheaders. However, the Massachusetts Sunday baseball law overrode this league rule. This applied to the 8–8 tie in the second game of the Sunday doubleheader on June 18, which was ended by darkness since the 1946 modified law did not permit the continuation of a Sunday ball game under artificial lighting. This provision of the Sunday baseball law was not changed until 1954.[31]

By the middle of the 1950 season, the Braves had become concerned about the decline in attendance at night games and conducted a door-to-door survey to try to collect some insight why. The primary response to the question about how the homeowner decided which games to watch on television or which to go to the ballpark was poor weather conditions. That still left unclear why attendance was down for games played in clear, warm weather on summer nights.[32]

Two-thirds of the 0.9 million attendance at Braves Field in 1950 came from night games, signaling another disturbing trend beyond simply television networks pumping Milton Berle and Arthur Godfrey into suburban living rooms at night. Night-game attendance for the Red Sox represented just one-third of the overall 1.3 million in attendance in 1950, not only because the Sox averaged 30,000 for each of just 14 night games, but also due to an extensive base of fans for weekend games as well as a solid core of women and businessmen for weekday games.[33]

One draw at Fenway Park was the hard-hitting nature of the Red Sox teams, which in 1950 had an overall .302 team batting average. Williams, Dropo, Doerr, and Stephens all hit 25 or more home runs. Then there were the blowouts, such as the back-to-back games in June with the St. Louis Browns when the Red Sox won 20–4 and 29–4. The American League style of play was tough to match at Braves Field. Even when Williams made "vulgar gestures" at the patrons at Fenway Park in early May and described the fans to sportswriters via unpublishable expletives, the fans kept coming to Fenway. In many instances it was because of, not instead of, Williams, who continued to swing a potent bat even though the fans booed him heavily.[34]

Although the Braves fell just shy of one million customers in 1950, Perini went forward with his annual automobile giveaway just the same. Herbert Olson of Worcester won the convertible car given away at Appreciation Day in late September, when the Braves played a Monday doubleheader with the Phillies. Fewer than 10,000 people were in attendance. Olson was perhaps one of the last dedicated Braves fans. He attended two dozen games at Braves Field in 1950 and disliked the Red Sox because he preferred "inside baseball, as played in the National League." James Mulhern of Forest Hills won the raffle for the spring-training excursion. It was the last Appreciation Day at Braves Field, because in 1951 Perini had half as many fans to appreciate.[35]

Television has been often blamed for the demise of the Braves in Boston, whether due to televised ball games or just general entertainment shows. However, it was the older communication medium of radio that actually was the death knell for the Braves, when the Braves and Red Sox went their separate ways for radio broadcasts in 1951.

◆ 20 ◆

Road-Game
Radio Broadcasts

The eventual demise of the Braves in Boston accelerated when the Red Sox and Braves decided to have their own separate broadcasting staffs for radio and television for the 1951 season. This departure from 25 years of coordinated radio schedules between the two baseball clubs set in motion the destruction of Boston as a two-team city.

Lou Perini no doubt believed he had struck a coup in the summer of 1950 when he convinced announcer Jim Britt to work exclusively for the Braves during the 1951 season. Because Britt was an institution at the microphone, Perini believed that Britt would command the bulk of the listening audience among both general baseball fans and intermittent ones—in addition to the small number of dedicated Braves fans—for both home and road games, since the Red Sox couldn't possibly bring in another broadcaster who approached the stature of Britt.[1]

The decision to hire Britt exclusively exposed Perini's misunderstanding of the motivations underlying the general baseball fans of New England. There had never been live radio broadcasts of road games, except for a few Red Sox games in 1948 and 1949 during the stretch run for the pennant. Now, for the first time, the Braves would not have the undivided attention of general baseball fans for their home games at Braves Field, as they needed to compete with the radio broadcasts of Red Sox road games.

Perini may have believed that Britt's sidekick Tom Hussey would be tapped to do the Red Sox games, since Hussey was the only other local person with substantial baseball broadcasting experience. In the fall of 1950, though, Tom Yawkey hired Curt Gowdy, the number two man behind the microphone for the New York Yankees, to be the principal broadcaster of the Red Sox games. Gowdy didn't need an audition, since Yawkey, whose business office was located in New York City, had heard Gowdy broadcast the Yankees games. Yawkey hired then Bob DeLaney and Hussey to be the number two and three broadcasters.[2]

Gowdy easily won over not only dedicated Red Sox fans but also most general baseball fans, with the broadcasting skills he had learned from Mel Allen, the principal broadcaster for the Yankees. "Allen was the hardest-working broadcaster I ever knew," Gowdy wrote in his book *Cowboy at the Mike*. "He made me pay close attention to everything that happened, not only on the field but in the stands. He had the great faculty of picking up the side-lights that help give a listener the feel of the ballpark. Mel taught me to look everywhere in the ballpark for material, so that I could build a word picture of the baseball atmosphere, not just the game itself." Gowdy brought with him Allen's penchant for adding color to the game's atmosphere, such as "follow the ball into the stands and describe where it landed." Gowdy also had Allen's ability to smoothly deliver commercials.[3]

Not only did the Red Sox and Braves have different broadcast teams, but they also needed to have different radio networks, since there was a significant head-to-head overlap between Braves home games and Red Sox road games and vice versa. The Red Sox scored a coup by continuing the existing relationship with WHDH, which had a popular network of radio stations throughout New England as well as sponsors that were readily familiar to baseball fans, Narragansett beer and Atlantic gasoline.[4]

The Braves had to scramble to work a deal to return to WNAC and the Yankee Network, which had broadcast the games of both team before 1947. However, the new radio stations for Braves games didn't warm the hearts of New England fans, who were now a vital component of the business given the population growth patterns in Greater Boston. Additionally, few advertisers were willing to go against the Red Sox package, so the Braves had a difficult time locating a sponsor and had to settle for Ballantine, a New Jersey brewery, to be the broadcast sponsor. Ballantine was also the radio and television sponsor of New York Yankees games. For many Boston baseball fans, the brewery substitution of outsider Ballantine for local Narragansett left a bitter taste.[5]

Both teams began to lose some of their listening audience in Connecticut and western Massachusetts, as the New York Yankees and the New York Giants both extended their radio networks northeast of New York City. The Yankees radio network included stations in New Britain and New Haven, Connecticut, and Springfield, Massachusetts; the Giants network included Meriden, Connecticut, and Providence, Rhode Island.[6]

In February 1951, the Red Sox divulged the fairly well-known secret that Gowdy would be the announcer for both home and road games; the Braves followed suit a few weeks later with the confirmation that Britt would also do double duty. Britt would be assisted by Bump Hadley and Les Smith.[7]

The television deal continued to be shared by both teams, since only home games were telecast, with CBS-affiliate WNAC and NBC-affiliate WBZ dividing the games. Interestingly, though, the Braves decided to cut back on televised night games in 1951, with just 14 of the scheduled 32 to be shown on television. This attempt to maximize attendance at some night games was a big negative from the fan's perspective.[8]

By 1951, nearly one-quarter of American households owned a television, a ten-fold increase from just two years earlier; one year later in 1952 television ownership exceeded one-third of households. Television wasn't just a new technology, though, but also an instrument of a broader social transformation. "People seemed to go out less for entertainment once they bought a television," Richard Butsch wrote in *The Making of American Audiences: From Stage to Television, 1750–1990*, as steady attendance declines occurred in the 1950s not just at the ballpark but also at movie theaters and other places of amusement. For people who moved to the outer suburbs, the impact of television was even greater, as the automobile substituting for mass transit reinforced the emphasis of home as a place for family leisure in a private space, replacing the prior emphasis on leisure activities in the community space.[9]

Suburbanization hurt the Braves the most. General baseball fans were more inclined to tolerate the two-fold problem of driving into Boston and then parking their automobile, compared to the intermittent fans that the Braves tried to attract. Finding a convenient parking space for a car was difficult at both Fenway Park and Braves Field, but was incrementally more challenging at Braves Field given the proximity of the residential neighborhoods of Brookline. But driving to Boston, especially for a night game, could be even more frustrating since there were no highways yet built for easy access into Boston. For example, driving from the Brockton area, 20 miles south of Boston, fans took Route 138 through the towns of Easton, Stoughton, and Milton, past the Blue Hills Ski Area onto Route 28 (Blue Hill Avenue) past Franklin Park, turned onto Seaver Street to Columbus Avenue, then took side streets towards Fenway Park; if continuing on to Braves Field, drivers also had to navigate traffic through Kenmore Square onto Commonwealth Avenue.[10]

Baseball fans were clearly moving to the suburbs, and it seemed obvious that the exodus would continue for many years to come. By 1950, the towns in the outer suburbs (more than 15 miles from downtown Boston) were the fastest growing portion of Greater Boston, as Boston proper and the inner suburbs had stagnant growth. The city of Boston represented just one-third of the overall population of Greater Boston. During the 1950s, the outer suburbs would experience phenomenal population growth (55 percent), while Boston would shrink by more than 10 percent to contain just one-fourth of the population of Greater Boston.[11]

Another gaffe by the Braves was the new policy in 1951 to ban the serving and drinking of beer in the stands at Braves Field. Fans could only consume their alcoholic refreshment underneath the stands, and thus could not follow the game at the same time. For many male fans, the prohibition of beer was reason enough to stop going to Braves Field and more frequently patronize Fenway Park where beer drinking continued to be allowed in the stands.[12]

The banning of beer in the stands at Braves Field, under the guise of responding to complaints by women and children that the constant passage of beer down the aisles disturbed their viewing pleasure, alienated many male fans in the general baseball fan base. It must have been awkward for the Braves to ban beer from the stands when the radio/television sponsor of its games was Ballantine beer. Ballantine did drop the sponsorship after the 1951 season.[13]

The new beer policy signaled a problem with Perini's strategy to cater to women at the ballpark—he was trying to convert intermittent fans into dedicated Braves fans, or at least into general baseball fans that leaned toward the Braves. This was a tall order for intermittent fans of either gender. During the chauvinistic times of the 1950s, the Braves did not help themselves when they reportedly considered hiring a female radio broadcaster to team with Britt. "The public has even forgiven the Braves for those fried clams of two years ago," Gerry Hern of the *Boston Post* wrote, "but this female baseball announcer deal may be pushing the people too far. This is even harder to take than Appreciation Day."[14]

Perini greatly underestimated the desire of dedicated and general baseball fans in Boston for "real baseball" as opposed to his brand of baseball as entertainment. Removing the signage on the outfield fences at Braves Field in 1951, to mirror the conditions at Fenway Park, did little to encourage fans to forsake their attendance on the slugging Red Sox. Perhaps the biggest gaffe by the Braves was not having a quality product on the field to attract at least general baseball fans, if not the few dedicated fans among the Braves fan base. Red Sox general manager Joe Cronin summed up his club's focus on a quality product on the field, contrasted to the Braves' need for promotion, when he quipped, "There are our publicity men—on the field."[15]

What had been a slight attendance drop for the Braves in 1950 became a staggering decline in 1951 when just 487,000 customers went to Braves Field, about one-half of the count in 1950. Fan disinterest began immediately, when only 6,081 showed up for the season-opener on April 17 and just 12,682 attended the Patriots Day holiday doubleheader on April 19. The radio broadcast of the Red Sox road games at Yankee Stadium was powerful competition. It didn't take long to determine the preference among the Braves-leaning general baseball fans who followed both teams. Given the choice between (a) attending a Braves home game, listening to the game on radio, or watching it on television, and (b) listening to a Red Sox road game on radio, most of the dual-supporting fans picked option (b) to tune into the radio. This was devastating to the Braves, as the voice of Gowdy doing Red Sox road games on the radio siphoned off general baseball fans, Braves-leaning and pure ones, to devote more time to following the Red Sox.

This siphoning occurred even though Gowdy got off to a rough start in his first broadcasts for the Red Sox, when the Wyoming native butchered the pronunciation of several towns in New England. Gowdy received a lot of negative mail and even got a phone call from broadcast-sponsor Narragansett informing him that "guys in bars are complaining to our distributors that you're murdering the names of their home towns." Yawkey also asked to speak to him, not to complain, but to reassure him. Yawkey told Gowdy: "This is probably the most intelligent baseball town in the country. Its fans know the game better than the fans anywhere. You can't kid them. Just give them their baseball straight. Don't try to phony anything up. All they want you to do is tell them what's going on."[16]

The contrast in delivery between Britt and Gowdy was all that was needed to persuade Braves-leaning general baseball fans to switch radio allegiance to the Red Sox. While Britt had a patrician approach to calling ball games, Gowdy had an effervescent, everyman style. But Gowdy also elevated his delivery. He hired Joe Costanza to be his statistician and provide him with details that he could add to the broadcast to appeal to his well-informed audience. This aspect of his broadcasts set him apart from the just-the-ball-game approach of Britt. Gowdy intrigued radio listeners, not just informed them, which increased his appeal.[17]

A telling moment during the 1951 season regarding fan division was the twi-night doubleheader the Red Sox played in Chicago on July 12. After the Red Sox had won the first game, the second game went 17 innings as the radio broadcast stretched into the early morning hours back in New England. "It seemed everybody in New England lost sleep listening to that doubleheader," Gowdy recalled. "Edison reported that its customers used the highest number of kilowatt hours in history for that time in the morning." Because the night game at Braves Field was rained out that evening, even die-hard Braves fans tuned in to listen to Gowdy broadcast the doubleheader. A short anecdote in the next day's *Boston Globe* epitomized the difference between the followers of the two teams who had stayed up to hear the Red Sox win the second game. "It's another pennant sure," the Red Sox fan would shout, while "Ho Hum. Time for bed," the Braves fan would mutter.[18]

To try to jumpstart attendance for the late April series with the defending-champion Philadelphia Phillies, the Braves resorted to a Ladies Day and a Sunday doubleheader. However, the Saturday game drew only 9,038 spectators, just 7,848 paid admissions with the other 1,140 going through the gates as Ladies Day guests, and the Sunday doubleheader drew only 18,500 to see the first-place Braves play. Even night games at Braves Field had lost their appeal. While more than 15,000 came to the first night game of the season to see the Cardinals on May 1, the night game two days later against the Chicago Cubs drew a dismal 4,700 tally at the gate. In 1950, the Braves never had an audience of less than 10,000 for any night game before Labor Day.

The May 3 night game with the Cubs was not televised either, under the new policy established by Perini to put only 14 night games on television, in order to eliminate an excuse for people to stay home and not attend a night game. However, the decision to televise fewer night games at Braves Field failed to stimulate attendance figures. While the Wednesday evening game against Cincinnati on May 9, televised by WBZ, drew a paltry 4,900 fans, the non-televised game the night before, also with the Reds, generated just a slightly higher 6,300 attendance. While Perini was said to be "mystified"

Women, such as these four sitting in box seats at Braves Field, were important fans for the Braves, beyond their patronage at Ladies Day. Since women brought families to night games, the Braves catered to women and children, which resulted in the banning of beer sales at seats in 1951 (courtesy Boston Public Library, Leslie Jones Collection).

about the reason for the drop in attendance at night games, the answer was simple. More people were interested in watching the Milton Berle show on WBZ on Tuesday night and the Arthur Godfrey show on WNAC on Wednesday night. Televised baseball was not what kept people home, but rather unrelated televised entertainment.[19]

Unique promotions at Braves Field also had little impact on attracting full-pay fans to the ballpark. On Saturday, June 2, the Braves held a fete for the 1914 Miracle Braves team, as part of the 75th anniversary celebration of the founding of the National League. This game attracted less than 10,000 paid customers. There were, however, another 5,000 spectators who watched the game on discounted passes, between 3,000 Little League ballplayers and another 2,000 kids in the Knot Hole Gang. The spread of Little League baseball within Massachusetts, since its expansion from Pennsylvania to the state in 1950, contributed to a decline in weekend attendance, as families stayed closer to home to watch their children play Little League or participate in other family activities.

As night games became less popular, the Braves resorted to playing twinight doubleheaders, where spectators could watch two games for the price of one. These twin bills started at 6:00, rather than at the usual start time of 8:30 for a night game, now a relic of the past when there needed to be a distinction between day and night games. The non-televised twi-night doubleheader on August 17 against the first-place Brooklyn Dodgers drew a crowd of 15,448 people. This was a respectable audience by 1951 standards, but it paled in comparison to the expectations of just a few years earlier when a single night game with a pennant contender would generate 30,000 spectators.

Perini used this twi-night doubleheader to distribute a letter to every patron asking for their opinion on "how we can make your visits to Braves Field more enjoyable than ever." The survey asked for responses to five questions, the first of which asked "what factor would be the no. 1 medium of rebuilding fan interest?" Columnist Harold Kaese of the *Boston Globe* had an apt satirical response to that question: "Nothing except a pennant contender." Perini was much more interested in the intermittent fan, as indicated by the wording of the team's fan survey conducted in 1951. Nearly every question was couched in the context of making the visit to Braves Field more enjoyable, specifically about starting times and number of night games, rather than about the talent on the baseball diamond. Kaese summed up the Braves' attendance challenge in two short sentences: "Braves fans are no different than the fans anywhere. All they want is a winner." He could have added a second fix: an easier drive to the ballpark and a convenient parking spot.[20]

During 1951, the Red Sox continued to hit home runs, which excited and attracted spectators, while the Braves continued to pitch well, which bored spectators. The Braves' investment in young hitters in their farm sys-tem, which could replicate interest in the power-hitting Red Sox, was still a few years away. But even when slugger Eddie Mathews joined the team in 1952, Braves Field was still not a homer-friendly environment with its distant fences and blustery winds blowing off the nearby Charles River. Not surpris-ingly, the Red Sox drew 1.3 million fans to Fenway Park in 1951, more than double the 0.5 million people that went to Braves Field. Perhaps even worse, the Red Sox generated more radio listeners than did the Braves. Perini had few survival alternatives for the Braves by the conclusion of the 1951 season. A telling indication of the future was that there was neither an automobile giveaway nor Appreciation Day for fans at Braves Field in 1951.

By the fall of 1951, Perini likely seriously considered once again con-structing a new ballpark in the suburbs to replace aging Braves Field and be more convenient to the intermittent fans that lived in suburbia and others throughout New England who drove their cars to get to a ball game. Publicly, Perini stood by his announced plan to refurbish Braves Field, but privately he no doubt contemplated the suburban ballpark option again. Automobile traffic to and from Boston was increasingly congested, which deterred fans from going to Braves Field, which itself was considered by many to be "anti-quated and barny" with "hopelessly inadequate parking facilities" that made the ballpark "one of the hardest public places in Boston to reach."[21]

While the opening of the Mystic River Bridge in 1950 and Storrow Drive in 1951 helped a bit to improve traffic flow into and out of Boston, few of the highways in the 1948 state highway master plan were under construction that would significantly ease the traffic in the immediate vicinity of Boston. The most visible progress was the opening in 1951 of the Route 128 circumferential limited-access highway ten miles outside Boston, but this "road to nowhere" was of no assistance to Boston. Work did progress near Boston on the north-east and southeast expressways, which were completed later in the 1950s, as were the exurban portions of the northwest and western expressways, which both truncated at Route 128. The western expressway was eventually extended into downtown Boston (as the Massachusetts Turnpike), but not until the mid–1960s; the northwest expressway (Route 3) was never completed into Boston. The northern expressway into Boston, through the inner suburbs of Medford, Somerville, and Cambridge, took until the 1970s to be completed (as Interstate 93). Both the southwest expressway and the inner beltway never got off the planning board.[22]

Many in the baseball community saw Perini as a visionary executive, since in 1951 he had espoused the creation of two 12-team leagues to expand baseball across the continent by adding eight baseball clubs to the current crop of 16 clubs. He proposed adding four clubs in California (from the exist-ing Pacific Coast League that at the time was lobbying for major-league status) and one in Montreal, Canada. For the other three clubs, he suggested picking from among five cities: Baltimore, Houston, a third club in Chicago, a second club in Detroit, and "should Milwaukee be given due recognition?"[23]

Although there had been zero franchise relocations in major-league baseball since 1903, Perini surely considered that option by the fall of 1951. During the summer, he had been heavily involved in the Congressional hearings by the House Antitrust and Monopoly Subcommittee, which broached the topic of franchise expansion beyond the established 16 clubs. Perini thus had some political cover to consider the move of the Braves to another city, but for the times it was still a radical thought. But, as the old adage goes, desperate times require desperate measures.

At the beginning of the 1952 season, the diminutive "crowd" of 4,694 people at the home-opener at Braves Field followed by the even scantier assemblage of 4,042 two days later at the first night game, prophesized an unprecedented financial disaster for the Braves. By the end of the 1952 season, the attendance at Braves Field totaled just 281,000 people. That was about one-fourth of the 1.1 million fans who went to Fenway Park in 1952; the Red Sox audience would have been even larger if not for the absence of Ted Williams, who was recalled to active military duty to serve in the Korean War.

Perini announced that only one contingency would prompt him to sell the Braves, which was "if I felt it would be better for the Braves if someone else owned them." Portraying himself as a homegrown Boston guy, which he was, Perini went on to elaborate why he likely would not sell the baseball club. "I've always been a baseball fan—I was one long before I got into the game. When I had a chance to buy stock in the Braves, I bought. And, when it came time to take over the club, I took over. I did it for no other reason than the fact I enjoy being the president of a major-league club, and I enjoy the associations and excitement and all that goes with it." However, Perini never said he would not relocate the Braves to another city; he only said that he would not sell the Braves.[24]

Following the staggering financial loss in 1952, estimated to be more than half a million dollars, Perini again reiterated that he intended to keep the Braves in Boston. "But I'm not going to be stubborn about this thing," he said. "I don't intend to spend ten years here when people don't want to see the Braves." When a sportswriter turned the conversation to the potential expansion of major-league baseball to the West Coast, Perini conceded that "eventually it's going to happen," and added, as he had said in 1951, that there are cities not in the Pacific Coast League that can support major-league baseball. As an example, Perini noted the new stadium recently built for the Braves farm club in Milwaukee before remarking that "the Braves can't stand in the way of Milwaukee becoming a major-league city."[25]

By the summer of 1952 Perini seemingly had decided to move the Braves to Milwaukee for the 1953 season. Perini held a closed-door staff meeting in October 1952 at the Framingham headquarters of his construction company, to inform his inner circle about the move. Then he swore them to secrecy. "He told us not to say a word to anyone, not even our wives," recalled Chuck Patterson, Perini's administrative assistant. "He never even discussed it at the dinner table over that winter," said David Perini, Lou's son, who added that "as a business decision, it made sense, but I know it was the hardest decision of his life." The secrecy about the move to Milwaukee was necessary, because the decision required the approval of the other National League club owners. Accomplishing that was much more difficult than making the decision to leave Boston.[26]

At spring training in March 1953, most of the talk within baseball circles was about the possible relocation of the St. Louis Browns, not the Boston Braves. Bill Veeck, owner of the Browns, wanted to move the club to Milwaukee, which required Perini's approval, since the Braves still had their farm club there. Perini obviously rejected that request, which caused a political firestorm in Milwaukee. That was exactly the leverage Perini needed to effectively lobby the National League club owners to approve the Braves' move to Milwaukee. Perini went public with his decision on March 14 just before the Braves and Red Sox teams met in a spring training game. Veeck ultimately sought approval to move the Browns to Baltimore, but this transfer was rejected by the American League club owners on March 16. Two days later, on March 18, the National League owners approved the relocation of the Braves to Milwaukee.[27]

After the move to Milwaukee was announced, there was shock and indignation among the politicians in Massachusetts. Governor Christian Herter said: "I was shocked to learn of the plan to move the Braves franchise. It would certainly be a blow to the pride of Boston and Massachusetts to lose the Braves and become a one-team city." However, as Perini explained to the press after the National League approved the transfer, "I definitely feel that since the advent of television Boston has become a one-team city and the enthusiasm of the fans for the Boston National League club has waned."[28]

However, "only a minority of New England fans were outraged," Harold Kaese wrote in the introduction to his team history, *The Boston Braves*, and "they got little for their pains except the smirks of Red Sox fans who said, 'nobody will miss the Braves.'" A letter to the editor by baseball fan Dave Tavel, published in the *Boston Globe*, summed up the plight of the Braves: "When all we real fans wanted was good baseball, you [Perini] tried to get fancy with everything from door prizes to fried clams."[29]

Pitcher Warren Spahn was deflated, since he planned to open a diner near Braves Field in the spring of 1953. "Who can forget my diner on Commonwealth Avenue?" Spahn told Kaese. "I started work on it after I was assured by the front office that the team was staying in Boston. Needless to say, it opened adjacent to an empty Braves Field."[30]

Red Sox owner Tom Yawkey made no attempt to keep Boston as a two-team city. Perini said that Yawkey had offered him the use of Fenway Park for the 1953 season, but diplomatically Perini said that the offer had come too late in the process. That likely was on purpose, since Yawkey saw few, if any, benefits of Boston being a two-team city. Yawkey showed his hand here, when Perini tried an administrative maneuver for the major leagues to block Veeck's request to move to Milwaukee, which required approval of the executive council. Yawkey was a member of that council and was "unavailable" when the vote came up, so no action was taken.[31]

Yawkey also never made a public comment about the departure of the Braves from Boston. More visibly, at the April 12 city series game at Fenway Park, while Perini sat in the stands and chatted with Braves fans, Yawkey sat in his roof-top suite, "inconspicuous" in dark glasses, with just a few friends.[32]

Although the inaction by Yawkey seems harsh, the idea of the two-team city had become a quaint tradition by 1953. In a more complicated postwar world, many people no longer valued the ability to see major-league baseball every day of the six-month-long season, experience the vagaries of a different style of play in each league, and watch the unique players in each league.

The ruthless reality, though, was that the multiple-team city concept only worked in New York City, where the Yankees, Dodgers, and Giants had truly competitive teams. In the other two-team cities that remained for the 1953 season, the weaker clubs all finished in seventh- or eighth place in the standings and had a substantially lower fan following than the stronger franchise in that city. In regard to Boston, Perini diplomatically said: "I don't think we can ever take the town away from the Red Sox. Boston justifiably belongs to the Red Sox." Sportswriter Al Hirshberg exercised less restraint: "Boston was a Red Sox town ... and the Braves just got the overflow."[33]

Although there was some initial teeth-gnashing about Boston only having half a season of major-league baseball, the absence of the National League component of the two-team city was easily ameliorated by the smooth tones of radio announcer Curt Gowdy broadcasting the Red Sox road games. His radio audience had decimated attendance at Braves Field in 1951 to amply demonstrate that most fans wanted Boston to be a one-team city.

In 1953, the Red Sox settled into their newfound monopoly of Boston as a one-team city, while in Milwaukee the Braves drew 1.8 million fans to suburban County Stadium, as the Braves finished in second place in the National League standings. The Braves' relocation to Milwaukee was just the first of five franchise shifts in major-league baseball during the 1950s, which resulted in Chicago being the only remaining two-team city by 1958. At that point, the Braves were basking in the glory of their 1957 World Series championship.

Epilogue
Jimmy Fund Games

Following their sudden departure from Boston in March 1953, the Braves evaporated from the baseball consciousness of Greater Boston residents and the rest of New England. Most tangible connections to the Braves were soon forgotten, particularly Braves Field, which was sold to Boston University in July 1953. Boston rapidly became comfortable in its transformation from a two-team city into as a one-team city, since the Red Sox already had a virtual monopoly on the hearts of most baseball fans in the region.

The lasting legacy of the Boston Braves was the club's support for the Children's Cancer Research Foundation through the Jimmy Fund fund-raising campaigns. It was Braves president Lou Perini's devotion to the cause that resulted in the construction of the Jimmy Fund Building in 1951. With a dedicated space, Dr. Sidney Farber could now accelerate his research efforts to find a cure for cancer in children. However, it didn't take long for the Red Sox to supplant the Braves in the public eye as Boston's sporting proponent for cancer research.

In April 1953, the Red Sox announced their support for the Jimmy Fund, to replace the departed Braves in that effort. Four months later, Red Sox owner Tom Yawkey joined Perini as a member of the foundation's board of trustees. In 1954 Ted Williams joined Yawkey and Perini as a trustee, as he embarked on a lifelong effort to raise money for the Jimmy Fund. While Perini was a good fundraiser, Williams was even better. And Ted did it with little public recognition. "His most important [charitable] work was unheralded—the quiet visits Williams made to the bedsides of dying children, which he insisted could not be published," Ben Bradlee, Jr., wrote in his biography of Williams. "Without exception, the visits came with the same string attached: there could be no publicity. Williams's compassion was genuine, and if his visits were hyped in the press he worried that it could look self-serving."[1]

The impetus for a biennial Jimmy Fund Game likely began when the Braves played the Red Sox on July 25, 1955, in the annual Hall of Fame exhibition game in Cooperstown, New York. This game intertwined memories of the now-discontinued city series, which the two teams had contested in Boston for nearly three decades before the start of each regular season, with the idea of charity (which in Cooperstown was the Clark Foundation that operated the Hall of Fame). The timing was perfect too, since in the 1950s most teams were not scheduled to play on the date of the Hall of Fame induction ceremony, which coincided with the exhibition game.

Perini was likely the instigator of the nascent idea. In 1956 the Braves used their Hall of Fame day off to play an exhibition game in Toronto against an International League all-star team. Perini donated the Braves' share of the proceeds to the Canadian Cancer Research organization. Yawkey was probably warm to the idea by 1956, since the annual exhibition series between the Red Sox and the New York Giants to benefit hospitalized veterans had concluded in 1955 after a five-year run.[2]

Perini may have reminded Yawkey of the in-season exhibition game played by the two teams for charity in July 1949, when more than 36,000 fans jammed into Fenway Park to see the Braves and Red Sox square off to benefit the Community Fund. Yawkey may have recalled an even earlier charitable series between the two teams in the 1930s to benefit the unemployed in Boston during the Great Depression.[3]

The concept of a Jimmy Fund Game surely was discussed in April 1957 when Perini, Yawkey, and Williams all attended a Jimmy Fund dinner to honor Yawkey as the recipient of the Great Heart Award. Because Yawkey was in line to become the chairman of the board of trustees of the Children's Cancer Research Foundation, a post he assumed in July, a baseball game would be a perfect way to begin his expanded role in raising money for cancer research. Williams no doubt had a big role in creating the Jimmy Fund Game, since in 1957 he was the chairman of the Jimmy Fund campaign. It's easy to imagine that Williams had a strong hunch that a return to Boston of the Braves, now sporting slugger Hank Aaron, would excite baseball fans to contribute money to the Jimmy Fund.[4]

The logistics were perfect for an exhibition game on July 22, the day of the Hall of Fame induction ceremony in 1957. No games were scheduled that day in either league. Since the Braves would be winding up their series with the Giants in New York City on July 21, it was an easy trip to Boston, where the Red Sox would be ending a homestand.

The announcement of the first Jimmy Fund Game was made in early June, which spawned the following *Boston Globe* headline: "Braves Return

July 22—Play Sox for Charity." By the day of the game, the Braves were in first place in the National League standings and Hank Aaron was leading the league in home runs. Starting on the mound for the Braves would be Warren Spahn, who was well liked in Boston, not just for his pitching exploits at Braves Field but also sympathetically for his bad timing to open a diner across the street from it in 1953 just as Perini whisked the Braves away to Milwaukee.[5]

Boston newspapers published stories about the upcoming Jimmy Fund Game every day for a week preceding the actual game. "Too late, too late, five years too late," Harold Kaese wrote. "The Braves are again a big attraction in Boston. They will draw about five times as many people when they play the Red Sox at Fenway Park Monday night, in a Jimmy Fund Game, as they did five years earlier, when—unbeknownst to anybody—they were suffering through their last season in Boston." Kaese anticipated 35,000 fans at the Jimmy Fund Game, compared to the sparse crowd of 5,280 on July 22, 1952, at Braves Field.[6]

"This is no ordinary exhibition game. It's a contest designed to help swell the Jimmy Fund, an organization designed to help in the research and cure for cancer in youngsters," Bob Holbrook wrote. "The Braves—Boston Braves, that is—pitched in and helped push the Jimmy Fund into national prominence [in 1948]. And the Red Sox have done their part from owner Tom Yawkey to Ted Williams. Dr. Sidney Farber can tell you what it means to have Ted Williams walk through the Jimmy Fund Building, talking with the sick youngsters."[7]

There was a rush at the Fenway Park ticket office when tickets for the Jimmy Fund Game first went on sale. "They were all strangers," said a Red Sox staffer, "and they all wanted to sit behind the Braves dugout." As Kaese wrote, "The conclusion is inescapable: buried in our midst in the Red Sox hullabaloo remains a coterie of Braves fans." While some went to Fenway Park to root against the Red Sox, many had already forsaken their dedication to the Braves. One of the converts was Frances Soper, who "used to see all her baseball in Braves Field, but now is a Fenway Park regular."[8]

In the inaugural Jimmy Fund Game, the Braves crushed the Red Sox, 13–4, before 30,572 spectators at Fenway Park, while thousands of others watched the game on television. Ed Mathews and Del Crandall each hit two home runs, while Spahn pitched brilliantly for the Braves. This initial game raised more than $100,000 for the Jimmy Fund, nearly 20 percent of the total donations raised all year.[9]

There were huge challenges to playing the game in 1958. The Braves never played a regular-season game in New York City in 1958, since both the Giants and the Dodgers had relocated to San Francisco and Los Angeles, respectively. The Braves did play an exhibition game in May against the Yankees at Yankee Stadium, where Perini arranged for the Braves' share of the proceeds to go to the Jimmy Fund.[10]

The series resumed in Boston with a second game on July 20, 1959, when the Braves again defeated the Red Sox, 7–3, in a rain-shortened five-inning game before 26,953 spectators at Fenway Park. It rained again two years later at the third game on August 21, 1961, when the Braves continued their domination of the Red Sox with a 4–1 victory. This time the attendance dipped below 20,000, signaling a waning interest in seeing the Braves return to Boston. As fewer and fewer fans understood the Boston heritage of the Braves, many readers of the *Boston Globe* likely failed to understand the pun in the headline the next day: "Spahn and Rain, 19,773 Remain."[11]

Spahn had recently attained his 300th career victory. Those on hand at Fenway gave Spahn a rousing reception, wildly cheering him during the pregame announcement when his name was called as the ninth batter in the Braves lineup. Pitching just one inning, Spahn struck out two of the three batters he faced, including the highly touted rookie Carl Yastrzemski, who had replaced Ted Williams in left field for the Sox. The crowd roared as Spahn strode from the mound to the Braves dugout.

Spahn returned to Boston one more time to pitch in the fourth Jimmy Fund Game on June 3, 1963, as the Red Sox finally defeated the Braves, 5–2. There was a meager crowd to watch the 42-year-old pitching wizard throw the first inning for the Braves. In an odd reversal, the Red Sox were now drawing more spectators than the Braves did in Milwaukee. The attraction for the Braves had cooled after the team's phenomenal record through the 1960 season, with three first-place finishes (two pennants, one lost playoff), four second-place finishes, and one third-place.

Now ten years after Perini had moved the Braves from Boston, many wondered if the Braves would have actually succeeded in Boston given the team's success in Milwaukee. "What if the Braves had stayed in Boston?" Kaese mused. "If the Braves had stayed—ah, me, what a dream. If they had stayed, they would not have come close to their 17 million [attendance] in Milwaukee, would have missed the inspiration of such enthusiastic fans, could not have spent so much money on bonus players and farm teams, could not have paid the salaries deserved by Spahn, Aaron, Mathews and others. If they had stayed, no doubt they would still be lost in lonely Braves Field, their parking problems still unresolved by the city fathers, their status still secondary to that of the Red Sox."[12]

With the Braves on the brink of relocating from Milwaukee to Atlanta, there was no Jimmy Fund Game in 1965. The Atlanta Braves did return in 1966 for the fifth, and final, Jimmy Fund Game between the two teams, a somber affair on June 6 before 18,032 at Fenway Park as the Sox won, 5–3. "It used to be like meeting a lot of relatives at a clam bake," Cliff Keane wrote in the *Boston Globe*. "But now there is only one left—and the way things are going for Eddie Mathews it won't be long before that Braves' team that left town in '53 will be loaded with strangers." Mathews was the last remaining active Braves player who had worn a Boston uniform in 1952.[13]

By 1967, 14 years after the Braves had bolted from Boston to Milwaukee, Boston was solidly a Red Sox town. The concept of the general baseball fan who supported both teams in a two-team city, which had begun to die during the late 1940s, completely evaporated soon after that exodus. Since the exhibition game with the Braves had lost its philosophical foundation among Boston fans (as well as the owners of the now Atlanta-based club), the Jimmy Fund Game, which had commemorated the city's days as a two-team city, was discontinued.[14]

With the death of the Jimmy Fund Game in 1967 came the birth of Red Sox Nation during that year's Impossible Dream season, when the World Series returned to Boston for the first time since 1948. Boston baseball fans were now most appropriately categorized by the intensity—high, medium, or low—of their support for the Red Sox in a one-team city. The hierarchy of dedicated, general baseball, and intermittent fans, which had applied during the city's days as a two-team city, was now an ancient relic.

The Red Sox, and Ted Williams post-retirement, conducted many other events to raise money for the Jimmy Fund. In 1998, 50 years after the original 1948 fund-raising campaign, the Jimmy Fund came alive to many contributors. The real-life symbolic Jimmy shed his anonymity to reveal himself to be Einar Gustafson, who had grown up in Maine. Gustafson had beaten the low odds and was a cancer survivor.[15]

Today, the Red Sox and Braves remain intimately tied together in Boston, although not through baseball, but by the Jimmy Fund. While the 52-year-old reign of Boston as a two-team baseball city is now just a dim memory, nearly all Boston baseball fans do recognize the Jimmy Fund. This is a fitting conclusion, since Boston as a two-team city had been largely perpetuated, prior to 1934, by general baseball fans who followed the fortunes of both teams, rather than a body of dedicated baseball fans who rooted strictly for only one team. Contributors to the Jimmy Fund root for everybody stricken by cancer, not just for one single individual, just like those traditional general baseball fans in Boston.

Chapter Notes

Introduction

1. Daniel Wann and Nyla Branscombe, "Sports Fans: Measuring Degrees of Identification with Their Team," *International Journal of Sport Psychology*, January–March 1993.

2. John Davis and Jessica Zutz Hilbert, *Sports Marketing: Creating Long Term Value* (Northampton, MA: Edward Elgar, 2013), 93–95.

Chapter 1

1. *New York Clipper*, June 5 and 26, 1869; G.M. Hopkins & Company, 1873 map of Boston, plate Q.

2. Nancy Seasholes, *Gaining Ground: A History of Landmaking in Boston* (Cambridge: MIT Press, 2003), 6; William Newman and Wilfred Holton, *Boston's Back Bay: The Story of America's Greatest Nineteenth-Century Landfill Project* (Boston: Northeastern University Press, 2006), 46–47, 121–140.

3. Sam Bass Warner, Jr. *Streetcar Suburbs: The Process of Growth in Boston, 1870–1900* (Cambridge: Harvard University Press, 1962), 40.

4. G.M. Hopkins & Company, 1873 map of Boston, plate Q; *Boston City Directory*, 1872.

5. *Boston Daily Advertiser*, June 29, 1869.

6. William Ryczek, *When Johnny Came Sliding Home: The Post–Civil War Baseball Boom, 1865–1870* (Jefferson, NC: McFarland, 1998), 182–183.

7. *Boston Daily Advertiser*, January 20, 1871; George Tuohey, *A History of the Boston Base Ball Club* (Boston: M.F. Quinn, 1897), 61–62; *Boston City Directory*, 1869; U.S. federal census, 1870.

8. *New York Clipper*, May 21, 1870.

9. An April 7, 1870, article in the *New York Times* listed the Tri-Mountains as one of 18 professional teams starting the 1870 season, and one of the few clubs offering salaried compensation to its ballplayers. The July 16, 1870, issue of the *New York Clipper* reported that Bill Craver, a star player for the professional Troy Haymakers in 1869, was alleged to have jumped to the Tri-Mountains over the winter of 1870 and set up by club supporters to run a saloon; however, Craver fled back to Troy by spring.

10. Benjamin Dettmar, "Lowell Base Ball Club," in *Base Ball Founders: The Clubs, Players and Cities of the Northeast That Established the Game*, ed. Peter Morris et al. (Jefferson, NC: McFarland, 2013), 267–270.

11. Wright Mills, *White Collar: The American Middle Classes* (New York: Oxford University Press, 1951), 63.

12. Stuart Blumin, *The Emergence of the Middle Class: Social Experience in the American City, 1760–1900* (New York: Cambridge University Press, 1989) 83–84, 137.

13. Warner, *Streetcar Suburbs*, 53.

14. Mills, *White Collar*, 63.

15. David Surdam, *Century of the Leisured Masses: Entertainment and the Transformation of Twentieth-Century America* (New York: Oxford University Press, 2015), 46.

16. *Boston Daily Advertiser*, January 21, 1871.

17. Mansel Blackford, *A History of Small*

Business in America (New York: Twayne, 1991), 36.

18. A.J. Campbell, *Classic & Antique Fly-Fishing Tackle* (Guilford, CT: Globe Pequot Press, 1997), 246; Appleton obituary, *Boston Globe*, September 23, 1921.

19. Prescott Hall, *The Laws of Massachusetts Business Corporations* (Boston: Little, Brown, and Company, 1917), 1–2. The law was modified in 1874 to allow corporations to be formed for any lawful purpose, with only a few exceptions.

20. *Acts and Resolves Passed by the General Court of Massachusetts in the Year 1871* (Boston: Wright & Potter, 1871), chapter 131, page 508; *Boston Daily Advertiser*, March 2, 4, 13, 18, 20, 21, and 23, 1871.

21. *Boston Daily Advertiser*, September 5, 1871, advertisement for game against the Athletic club.

22. Richard Butsch, *The Making of American Audiences: From Stage to Television, 1750–1990* (New York: Cambridge University Press, 2000), 72.

23. *Acts and Resolves, Public and Private, of the Province of the Massachusetts Bay* (Boston: Wright & Potter, 1869), 1692 laws, chapter 22, pages 58–59; Charlie Bevis, *Sunday Baseball: The Major Leagues' Struggle to Play Baseball on the Lord's Day, 1876–1934* (Jefferson, NC: McFarland, 2003), 14–15.

24. Robert Tiemann, "Major League Attendance," in *Total Baseball*, 7th ed. (Kingston, NY: Total Sports Publishing, 2001); *Boston Daily Advertiser*, December 27, 1871, and September 22, 1872. All full-season attendance figures cited in this book are from the Tiemann source.

25. *New York Clipper*, December 21, 1872; *Boston Daily Advertiser*, December 4 and 15, 1873; James Cullen, *The Story of the Irish in Boston* (Boston: Cullen & Company, 1889), 415.

26. Leo Schnore and Peter Knights, "Residence and Social Structure: Boston in the Ante-Bellum Period," in *Nineteenth-Century Cities: Essays in the New Urban History*, eds. Stephan Thernsrom and Richard Sennett (New Haven: Yale University Press, 1969), 250.

27. *Boston City Directory*, 1872 and 1875.

28. James O'Connell, *The Hub's Metropolis: Greater Boston's Development from Railroad Suburbs to Smart Growth* (Cambridge: MIT Press, 2013), 71; Warner, *Streetcar Suburbs*, 86.

29. Terry Furst, *Early Professional Baseball and the Sporting Press: Shaping the Image of the Game* (Jefferson, NC: McFarland, 2014), 76.

30. *New York Clipper*, July 10, 1875; *Boston Globe*, May 31, 1876.

31. *Boston Globe*, June 3, 1876.

Chapter 2

1. *Directory of the Town of Newton*, 1871; Archives of Newtonville United Methodist Church, School of Theology Library, Boston University.

2. *Boston Daily Advertiser*, December 4, 1873, and December 7, 1876.

3. Walter Whitehill, *Boston: A Topographical History* (Cambridge: Harvard University Press, 1959), 137.

4. *Boston Globe*, August 19, 1881.

5. Richard Brown and Jack Tager, *Massachusetts: A Concise History* (Amherst: University of Massachusetts Press, 2000), 178.

6. *Boston Post*, March 15, 1879; *Boston Globe*, September 5, 1881.

7. *Philadelphia Inquirer*, January 24, 1873, and April 3, 1883; *A Record of the Streets, Alleys, Places, Etc. in the City of Boston* (Boston: City of Boston, 1910), 480; *Boston Globe*, November 16, 1881.

8. *Boston Globe*, December 23, 1888; *Boston Daily Advertiser*, August 29, 1879.

9. "Veteran Groundkeeper Knew All the Old Baseball Stars," *Boston Globe*, September 19, 1921; *Boston Globe*, May 22 and 29, 1881.

10. James Morgan, *Charles H. Taylor: Builder of the Boston Globe* (Boston: James Morgan, 1923), 85–89; Louis Lyons, *Newspaper Story: One Hundred Years of the Boston Globe* (Cambridge: Harvard University Press, 1971), 47, 65.

11. Jerry Nason, "A Century of Globe Sports: The W.D. Sullivan Years, 1884–1910," *Boston Globe*, March 13, 1972; William Harris, "Sketches of Baseball Writers," in *Athletic Sports in America, England and Australia*, ed. Henry Clay Palmer (Philadelphia: Hubbard Brothers, 1889), 602–603. In his early history of baseball writers, Harris provided historians with a perspective on the craft in an age when bylines were mostly pseudonyms and actual names were just beginning to be published. Articles written by Sullivan in the *Boston Globe* were attributed to "Featherweight" and those in *Sporting Life*

were bylined "Mugwump." Sullivan was quickly promoted to sports editor in 1884 and then to city editor in 1888.

12. Barbara Miller Solomon, *Ancestors and Immigrants: A Changing New England Tradition* (Cambridge: Harvard University Press, 1956), 44, 46.

13. Paula Kane, *Separatism and Subculture: Boston Catholicism, 1900–1920* (Chapel Hill: University of North Carolina Press, 1994), 50–54; Cullen, *The Story of the Irish in Boston.*

14. *Boston Globe,* February 21, 1884; *New York Clipper,* April 26, 1884; advertisement in *Boston Globe,* September 5, 1884.

15. *Boston Globe,* April 3, 1884; *Sporting Life,* July 21, 1886.

16. *New York Clipper,* November 29, 1884; *Boston Globe,* December 7, 1884, and February 8, 1885.

17. Schnore and Knights, "Residence and Social Structure," 249–250.

18. Edwin Bacon, *Boston Illustrated* (Boston: Houghton Mifflin, 1886), 153– 154.

19. Paul Dickson, ed., *Dickson Baseball Dictionary* (New York: W.W. Norton, 2009), 224.

20. "At the Ball Grounds: The Cranks, So-Called, Both Male and Female, Who Love the Sports," *Boston Globe,* June 7, 1885.

21. *Boston Globe,* May 29, 1886, and May 10, 1887; Dixwell obituary, *Boston Globe,* September 17, 1924.

22. *Boston Globe,* May 10, 1887.

23. *Boston Globe,* March 14, 1886.

24. *Boston Globe,* July 29, 1886, and September 9, 1887.

25. *Boston Globe,* May 31, 1886.

26. Charlie Bevis, *Doubleheaders: A Major League History* (Jefferson, NC: McFarland, 2011), 32–33.

27. *Boston Globe,* August 19–20, 1887.

28. *Boston Globe,* May 25, 1888.

29. Michael Kimmel, "Baseball and the Reconstitution of American Masculinity, 1880–1920" in *Baseball History From Outside the Lines,* ed. John Dreifort (Lincoln: University of Nebraska Press, 2001), 58; "Critics of the Game," *Boston Globe,* July 31, 1888.

30. *Boston Globe,* June 2 and 11, 1889.

Chapter 3

1. *Boston Globe,* December 11, 1889, and February 23, 1890.

2. *Boston Globe,* November 30, 1889.

3. *Boston Globe,* December 22, 1887; *Boston Daily Advertiser,* October 8, 1888.

4. *Boston Globe,* January 1, 1890, and April 19, 1890.

5. *Boston Globe,* May 4 and June 6, 1890.

6. Jean Hastings Ardell, *Breaking into Baseball: Women and the National Pastime* (Carbondale: Southern Illinois University Press, 2005), 31.

7. *Boston Globe,* January 17, 1891.

8. *Boston Globe,* March 18, 1891.

9. *Boston Globe,* March 13, 1891.

10. Charlie Bevis, "Rocky Point: A Lone Outpost of Sunday Baseball in Sabbatarian New England," *NINE: A Journal of Baseball History & Culture,* Fall 2005, 79, 84; *Boston Globe,* June 10 and 22, 1891.

11. *Boston Globe,* July 19–22, 1891.

12. *Boston Globe,* July 22, 1891.

13. *New York Times,* June 1, 1893; *Boston Globe,* June 1, 1893.

14. *Boston Daily Advertiser,* June 3, 1893; *Sporting Life,* July 22, 1893.

15. Alumni file of Prince, Harvard University Archives, Pusey Library, Harvard University.

Chapter 4

1. *Boston Globe,* April 22, 1892.

2. *Second Annual Report of the West End Street Railway Company, 1889* (Boston: Blodgett, 1889), 5; *Boston Globe,* November 14, 1889.

3. *Record of the Streets,* 480.

4. *Boston Daily Advertiser,* June 29, 1888.

5. *Boston Daily Advertiser,* September 14, 1888.

6. *Boston Globe,* December 23, 1888.

7. *Boston Globe,* September 3, 1889, and December 22, 1889.

8. *Boston Globe,* October 5, 1892.

9. *Boston Globe,* June 24, 1894, and March 17, 1895.

10. Warner, *Streetcar Suburbs,* 61–64.

11. "Elevated Routes in the New Rapid Transit Bill," *Boston Globe,* July 17, 1894.

12. Charles Cheape, *Moving the Masses: Urban Transit in New York, Boston, and Philadelphia, 1880–1912* (Cambridge: Harvard University Press, 1980), 142.

13. "Elevated Routes in New Rapid Transit Bill"; Matthew Edel, Elliott Sclar, and

Daniel Luria, *Shaky Palaces: Homeownership and Social Mobility in Boston's Suburbanization* (New York: Columbia University Press, 1984), 65.

14. "A New Car Route," *Cambridge Tribune*, April 11, 1896.

15. David Nasaw, *Going Out: The Rise and Fall of Public Amusements* (New York: Basic, 1993), 101.

16. *Sporting Life*, November 18, 1899.

17. *Record of the Streets*, 50, 123; *Boston Globe*, January 5, 1895.

18. *Boston Daily Advertiser*, March 15, 1895.

19. *Boston Post*, May 23, 1897; Dickson, *Baseball Dictionary*, 304–307.

20. *Boston City Directory*, 1897; Lavis obituary, *Boston Globe*, August 13, 1939.

21. Stephen Hardy, *How Boston Played: Sport, Recreation, and Community, 1865–1915* (Knoxville: University of Tennessee Press, 2003), 188; *Boston City Directory*, 1890, 1894, 1897, 1901; Peter Nash, "Mike 'Nuf Ced' McGreevey," in *New Century, New Team: The 1901 Boston Americans*, ed. Bill Nowlin (Phoenix: Society for American Baseball Research, 2013).

22. *Boston Globe*, September 24, 1897.

23. *Boston Globe*, September 25 and 28, 1897.

24. *Boston Globe*, October 5, 1897.

25. *Boston Globe*, October 7, 1897.

26. *Boston Globe*, October 21, 1898.

27. *Boston Globe*, April 20, July 20, and October 4, 1900.

28. *Boston Daily Advertiser*, November 4, 1899.

29. *Ibid.*

Chapter 5

1. Art Ballou, "Hub Fan Sees All Openers Since '94: Jack Dooley, 90, Boston Baseball's Close Friend," *Boston Globe*, June 30, 1963; Paula Kane, *Separatism and Subculture: Boston Catholicism, 1900–1920* (Chapel Hill: University of North Carolina Press, 1994), 53; *Boston Globe*, May 27, 1901; Marie Daly, "The Prendergast Family in America," in *The Prendergast Letters: Correspondence from Famine-Era Ireland, 1840–1850*, ed. Shelley Barber (Amherst: University of Massachusetts Press, 2006), 182–188.

2. *Boston Globe*, January 18, 1901.

3. *Sporting Life*, January 26, 1901.

4. *Boston Globe*, March 8 and May 9, 1901.

5. Charlie Bevis, *Jimmy Collins: A Baseball Biography* (Jefferson, NC: McFarland, 2012), 73–74; Tim Murnane, "His Winter Pastime Collecting Rents," *Boston Globe Magazine* section, *Boston Globe*, January 15, 1905.

6. Bevis, *Jimmy Collins*, 83–84.

7. *Buffalo Express*, February 9, 1901; *Boston Globe*, February 24, 1901.

8. Bevis, *Jimmy Collins*, 85–86.

9. *Sporting Life*, March 16, 1901.

10. *Chicago Tribune*, March 3, 1901.

11. *New York Times*, March 2, 1901.

12. *Boston Globe*, March 10, 1901.

Chapter 6

1. *Boston Globe*, February 3 and March 3, 1901.

2. *Boston Globe*, May 10, 1901.

3. *Boston Globe*, May 9, 1901.

4. *Boston Globe*, June 10–11, 1901; Ardell, *Breaking into Baseball*, 33. Additional Ladies Day games were staged in 1901 on June 14, July 5, July 10, and August 10.

5. *Boston Globe*, June 20, 1901.

6. *Acts and Resolves Passed by the General Court of Massachusetts in the Year 1895* (Boston: Wright & Potter, 1895), chapter 434, pages 480–482.

7. *Boston Globe*, May 11 and September 23, 1901; *Boston Post*, September 7, 1903.

8. Brian Cudahy, *Change at Park Street Under: The Story of Boston's Subways* (Brattleboro, VT: Stephen Greene Press, 1972), 19.

9. Bevis, *Jimmy Collins*, 91–92.

10. *Boston Globe*, August 11, 1901.

11. *Sporting Life*, March 15, 1902.

12. *Boston Globe*, October 7, 1903.

13. *Boston Globe*, October 14, 1903.

14. *Boston Globe*, April 19, 1904.

15. *Sporting Life*, April 2 and 30, 1904.

16. *Boston Journal*, October 6–10, 1904.

17. Ed Linn, *The Great Rivalry: The Yankees and the Red Sox 1901–1990* (New York: Ticknor & Fields, 1991), ix.

18. *The Sporting News*, December 12, 1907.

19. *Boston Globe*, October 23, 1904, and March 29, 1905.

20. *Macon Telegraph*, March 13, 1905.

21. *Boston Globe*, April 3, 1906; March 2, 1907; March 2, 1909; March 2, 1911.

22. Schaeffer and Sclar, *Access for All*, 75; Robert Woods and Albert Kennedy, *The Zone of Emergence: Observations of the Lower Middle Class and Upper Working Class Communities of Boston, 1905–1914* (Cambridge: Harvard University Press, 1962), 89; Edel, Sclar, and Luria, *Shaky Palaces*, 181.

23. *Boston Globe*, February 17, 1907; *Cambridge Tribune*, October 12, 1901.

24. Cudahy, *Change at Park Street Under*, 24, 27.

25. O'Connell, *The Hub's Metropolis*, 77–79.

26. U.S. Department of Transportation, "Highway Statistics Summary to 1995," *Federal Highway Administration* website, accessed April 17, 2016.

27. *Boston Globe*, April 18, 1906.

28. Edel, Sclar, and Luria, *Shaky Palaces*, 140; Schaeffer and Sclar, *Access for All*, 84.

29. Blackford, *History of Small Business*, 36.

30. Maury Klein, *The Genesis of Industrial America, 1870–1920* (New York: Cambridge University Press, 2007), 131, 133, 137, 145.

31. *Boston Globe*, November 29, 1906, and March 12, 1907.

32. *Boston Globe*, December 19, 1907.

33. Melville Webb, "Why Are You a Baseball Fan?" *Boston Globe*, August 31, 1913.

34. *Ibid.*

35. *Ibid.*

36. *Boston Globe*, August 4, 1909; Prevost obituary, *Boston Globe*, March 13, 1925.

37. Arthur Cooper, "Winter League Unique Among the Societies of Boston," *Boston Post*, January 19, 1913.

38. *Boston Globe*, April 5, 1908; August 26, 1909; May 5, 1910.

39. Alumni file of Morse, Harvard University Archives, Pusey Library, Harvard University; F.C. Lane, "The Greatest Problem in the National Game: The Critical Situation in Sunday Baseball," *Baseball Magazine*, October 1911.

40. *Boston Globe*, April 7, 1911; *Sporting Life*, March 11, 1911.

41. *Sporting Life*, August 12, 1911; Glenn Stout, *Fenway 1912: The Birth of a Ballpark, a Championship Season, and Fenway's Remarkable First Year* (Boston: Houghton Mifflin, 2011), 15; *Boston Globe*, September 15, 1911.

Chapter 7

1. *Sporting Life*, April 22, 1911; Cudahy, *Change at Park Street Under*, 38 41; *Boston Globe*, May 2 and June 28, 1911.

2. Stout, *Fenway 1912*, 16, 29.

3. *Boston Globe*, October 15, 1911, and March 17, 1912; Stout, *Fenway 1912*, 20–21.

4. Stout, *Fenway 1912*, 15.

5. *Boston Globe*, December 21, 1911; Oliver Allen, *The Tiger: The Rise and Fall of Tammany Hall* (Reading, MA: Addison-Wesley, 1993), 5–6, 210.

6. Stout, *Fenway 1912*, 215–216.

7. *Boston Globe*, August 14 and September 26, 1912.

8. *Boston Globe*, October 8–10, 1912.

9. *Boston Globe*, October 15–16, 1912.

10. *Boston Globe*, October 18, 1912.

11. *Boston Globe*, April 24, 1911; September 30, 1911; January 9, 1913.

12. Elizabeth Dooley, "Rooting for the Red Sox," in *Red Sox Century: One Hundred Years of Red Sox Baseball*, by Glenn Stout and Richard Johnson (Boston: Houghton Mifflin, 2000), 254.

13. *Boston Globe*, January 1, 1914.

14. *Boston Globe*, January 31, 1913.

15. *Boston Globe*, February 25, 1913.

16. *Boston Globe*, August 4 and September 7, 1914.

17. *Boston Globe*, October 10, 1914.

18. *Boston Globe*, October 3 and 12, 1914.

19. *Boston Globe*, December 5, 1914.

20. *Boston Globe*, August 15, 1915.

21. F.C. Lane, "The World's Greatest Baseball Park," *Baseball Magazine*, October 1915.

22. *Ibid.*

23. *Boston Globe*, June 26, 1915.

24. *Boston Globe*, August 2, 1914.

25. *Boston City Directory*, 1915; *Boston Globe*, November 10, 1916.

26. "Highway Statistics Summary."

27. *Boston Globe*, August 19, 1915.

28. Webb, "Why Are You a Baseball Fan?"

29. *Sporting Life*, September 25, 1915.

30. *Boston Globe*, October 11–12, 1915.

31. *Boston Globe*, October 9 and 12, 1915.

32. *Boston Globe*, February 1, 1916.

33. William Phelon, "The Return of Baseball Enthusiasm," *Baseball Magazine*, August 1916.

Chapter 8

1. *Acts and Resolves Passed by the General Court of Massachusetts in the Year 1918* (Boston: Wright & Potter, 1918), chapter 134, page 109.

2. *Boston Globe*, April 29 and May 6, 1918.

3. *Boston Globe*, May 26, 1918.

4. *Boston Globe*, July 24 and September 1, 1918.

5. *Boston Globe*, July 2, 1918.

6. *Boston Globe*, June 7, 1918.

7. Kerry Keene, et al., *The Babe in Red Stockings: An In-Depth Chronicle of Babe Ruth with the Boston Red Sox, 1914–1919* (Champaign, IL: Sagamore, 1997), 187; David Vincent, *Home Run: The Definitive History of Baseball's Ultimate Weapon* (Washington: Potomac Books, 2007), 38.

8. *Boston Globe*, August 27, 1918.

9. Charles Murphy, "The Pros and Cons of Sunday Baseball," *Baseball Magazine*, June 1919.

10. *Boston Globe*, August 3, 1919.

11. Glenn Stout, *The Selling of the Babe: The Deal That Changed Baseball and Created a Legend* (New York: Thomas Dunne, 2016), 60, 62.

12. *Boston Globe*, July 6 and September 21, 1919.

13. Leigh Montville, *The Big Bam: The Life and Times of Babe Ruth* (New York: Doubleday, 2006), 90; Stout and Johnson, *Red Sox Century*, 144.

14. James Szalontai, *Small Ball in the Big Leagues: A History of Stealing, Bunting, Walking, and Otherwise Scratching for Runs* (Jefferson, NC: McFarland, 2010), 1.

15. Stout, *The Selling of the Babe*, 150.

16. Vincent, *Home Run*, xxi–xxii.

17. *Boston Globe*, January 6, 1920.

18. Stout, *The Selling of the Babe*, 151.

19. Michael Lynch, *Harry Frazee, Ban Johnson and the Feud That Nearly Destroyed the American League* (Jefferson, NC: McFarland, 2008), 47.

20. *Ibid.*, 106.

21. *Acts and Resolves Passed by the General Court of Massachusetts in the Year 1920* (Boston: Wright & Potter, 1920), chapter 240, pages 259–260.

22. *Boston Globe*, April 2, 1920.

Chapter 9

1. Mills, *White Collar*, 63; Schaeffer and Sclar, *Access for All*, 86.

2. Schnore and Knights, "Residence and Social Structure," 250; O'Connell, *The Hub's Metropolis*, 109.

3. Schaeffer and Sklar, *Access for All*, 89; "Highway Statistics Summary."

4. Nasaw, *Going Out: The Rise and Fall of Public Amusements*, 241; Cotton Seiler, *Republic of Drivers: A Cultural History of Automobility in America* (Chicago: University of Chicago Press, 2008), 12, 39.

5. Bevis, *Doubleheaders*, 108–109.

6. *Boston Globe*, July 2, 1923; August 16, 1923; May 4, 1925.

7. *Boston Globe*, October 28, 1923; Bevis, *Sunday Baseball*, 220.

8. *Boston Globe*, September 22, 1924; Doe obituary, *Quincy Patriot Ledger*, October 6, 1938.

9. *Boston Globe*, February 6, 1925.

10. *Boston Post*, August 4, 1925.

11. *Springfield Union*, April 14, 1925.

12. "Baseball Broadcasts," *Boston Globe*, July 7, 1925; "Radio Broadcasts," *Boston Globe*, July 20, 1925; "Coming on the Radio," *Boston Globe*, August 24, 1925.

13. Curt Smith, *Mercy! A Celebration of Fenway Park's Centennial Told Through Red Sox Radio and TV* (Washington: Potomac, 2012), 24.

14. Richard Butsch, *The Making of American Audiences: From Stage to Television, 1750–1990* (New York: Cambridge University Press, 2000), 205; Christopher Sterling and John Kittross, *Stay Tuned: A Concise History of American Broadcasting*, first edition 1978 (Belmont, CA: Wadsworth Publishing, 1990), 656; Lynn Spigel, *Make Room for TV: Television and the Family Ideal in Postwar America* (Chicago: University of Chicago Press, 1992), 29.

15. *Boston Globe*, June 19, 1925; June 27, 1925; August 19, 1928.

16. *Boston Globe*, May 9, 1926; Stout and Johnson, *Red Sox Century*, 168; Fred Lieb, *Boston Red Sox* (New York: G.P. Putnam's Sons, 1947), 196.

17. *Boston Globe*, May 28, 1926; June 9, 1926; September 18, 1926.

18. James Walker, *Crack of the Bat: A History of Baseball on the Radio* (Lincoln: University of Nebraska Press, 2015), 7.

19. Alexander Russo, *Points on the Dial:*

Golden Age Radio Beyond the Networks (Durham: Duke University Press, 2010), 54.

20. "What's on the Air?" *Boston Globe*, April 12, May 2, and May 14, 1927.

21. Curt Smith, *Voices of the Game: The First Full-Scale Overview of Baseball Broadcasting, 1921 to the Present* (South Bend, IN: Diamond Communications, 1987), 20, 24.

22. Smith, *Mercy*, 26, 31; Hoey obituary, *Boston Globe*, November 17, 1949.

23. "Radio Broadcasts," *Boston Globe*, May 22 and June 1–26, 1928.

24. *The Sporting News*, November 1, 1928.

25. *Primaries and Elections, 1928* (Boston: Office of the Secretary of the Commonwealth, 1929); Ford Sawyer, "Bay State's Plans for Sunday Sports," *Boston Globe*, March 24, 1929.

26. *Acts and Resolves Passed by the General Court of Massachusetts in the Year 1928* (Boston: Wright & Potter, 1928), chapter 406, pages 583–584.

Chapter 10

1. Bevis, *Sunday Baseball*, 230. See Chapter 13 in *Sunday Baseball* for a more complete examination of the bribery scandal hearings.

2. *New York Times*, January 5, 1929.

3. *Boston Globe*, January 5, 1929.

4. *The Sporting News*, November 15, 1928.

5. *New York Times*, November 9 and December 28, 1928; *Boston Globe*, December 20, 1928.

6. *Boston Globe*, January 15 and 18, 1929.

7. *Boston Herald*, February 8, 1929.

8. *Boston Globe*, February 12–15, 1929; *New York Times*, February 19, 1929.

9. *Boston Globe*, February 19–20, 1929.

10. *Boston Globe*, May 13, 1929.

11. Harold Kaese, *The Boston Braves, 1871–1953*, first edition 1948 (Boston: Northeastern University Press, 2004), 207; Fuchs obituary, *Boston Herald*, December 6, 1961.

12. *Boston Globe*, April 29, 1929.

13. Russo, *Points on the Dial*, 54; Smith, *Mercy*, 24.

14. *Boston Globe*, May 19, 1930.

15. *The Sporting News*, February 11, 1932; *Boston Globe*, June 21, 1931.

16. *Boston Globe*, July 13, 1930; Sterling and Kittross, *Stay Tuned*, 656.

17. *Boston Post*, July 14, 1930.

18. *Acts and Resolves Passed by the General Court of Massachusetts in the Year 1931* (Boston: Wright & Potter, 1931), chapter 174, page 153.

19. Bevis, *Doubleheaders*, 119; *New York Times*, May 8, 1931.

20. *The Sporting News*, May 25, 1933.

21. James Palmer, "Economic and Social Aspects of Chain Stores," *Journal of Business of the University of Chicago*, July 1929.

22. Susan Currell, *The March of Spare Time: The Problem and Promise of Leisure in the Great Depression* (Philadelphia: University of Pennsylvania Press, 2005), 2.

23. *Boston Globe*, May 18, 1931.

24. *Boston Globe*, January 3, 1928, and May 29, 1930.

Chapter 11

1. *Acts and Resolves Passed by the General Court of Massachusetts in the Year 1932* (Boston: Wright & Potter, 1932), chapter 257, page 326.

2. *Boston Globe*, May 17, 1932; Peter Richardson, *The Boston Religion: Unitarianism in Its Capital City* (Rockland, ME: Red Barn Publishing, 2003), 116.

3. Leverett Saltonstall, *The Autobiography of Leverett Saltonstall: Massachusetts Governor, U.S. Senator, and Yankee Icon* (Lanham, MD: Rowman & Littlefield, 2015), 53.

4. Ballou, "Hub Fan Sees All Openers"; Richardson, *Unitarianism*, 202.

5. Wail Hassan, *Immigrant Narratives: Orientalism and Cultural Translation in Arab American and Arab British Literature* (New York: Oxford University Press, 2011), 88; Abraham Rihbany, *A Far Journey* (Boston: Houghton Mifflin, 1914), 197.

6. Entry dated April 23, 1930, "Records of the Business Meetings of the Church 1930 to 1941," Church of the Disciples, Andover–Harvard Theological Library, Harvard Divinity School, Cambridge, MA.

7. Entry dated January 24, 1930, "Records of the Business Meetings of the Church."

8. Margaret Bendroth, *Fundamentalists in the City: Conflict and Division in Boston's Churches, 1885–1950* (New York: Oxford University Press, 2005), 165–166.

9. Sterling and Kittross, *Stay Tuned*, 656; *The Sporting News*, December 17, 1931.

10. Surdam, *Leisured Masses*, 46; Smith, *Mercy*, 26.

11. *Boston Globe*, May 25 and 28, 1932.
12. *New York Times*, March 20, 1933; Rick Huhn, *Eddie Collins: A Baseball Biography* (Jefferson, NC: McFarland, 2008), 272; *Boston Globe*, February 26, 1933.
13. *Boston Herald*, May 23, 1932.
14. *Boston Globe*, August 7, 1930; F.C. Lane, "The Romance of Night Baseball," *Baseball Magazine*, October 1930.
15. *Boston Globe*, August 2, 1932.
16. *Boston Globe*, December 8, 1932.
17. *The Sporting News*, May 4, 1933; August 16, 1934; and May 7, 1936.
18. *The Sporting News*, February 25, 1929.

Chapter 12

1. *Boston Globe*, February 26, 1933.
2. *Boston Globe*, April 12 and April 30, 1933.
3. *Boston Globe*, October 24 and December 31, 1932.
4. *Boston Globe*, January 7, January 25, and March 26, 1933.
5. *Boston Globe*, April 7, 1933.
6. *Boston Globe*, May 14–15, 1933
7. *The Sporting News*, May 25, 1933.
8. *Boston Globe*, June 12–16, 1933.
9. Bevis, *Doubleheaders*, 127.
10. Paul Jesep, *Rockingham Park, 1933–1969* (Portsmouth, NH: Peter E. Randall, 1998), 6.
11. *Boston Globe*, May 10, 1933
12. *The Sporting News*, August 31, 1933; *Boston Globe*, August 21, 1933
13. *Boston Globe*, August 31, 1933
14. *Boston Globe*, September 2, 1933
15. *Boston Globe*, September 3, 1933.
16. *Boston Globe*, September 19, 1933.

Chapter 13

1. Stout and Johnson, *Red Sox Century*, 186, 189.
2. *Boston Globe*, April 15 and 18, 1934.
3. *Boston Globe*, April 17–18, 1934.
4. *Boston Globe*, April 23, 1934.
5. *Boston Globe*, August 13 and 20, 1934.
6. *Boston Globe*, September 23, 1935.
7. *Ibid.*
8. Surdam, *Century of the Leisured Masses*, 46, 218.
9. Schnore and Knights, "Residence and

Social Structure," 249–250; Edel, Sclar, and Luria, *Shaky Palaces*, 65–67.
10. "New 'Freeway' Plan for State," *Boston Globe*, July 6, 1937.
11. Henry Harris, "Why a City Goes Baseball Crazy," *Boston Globe*, September 4, 1938.
12. *Boston Globe*, April 17, 1934.
13. Red Barber, *The Broadcasters* (New York: Dial Press, 1970), 96; Edgar Brands, "Fred Hoey Moved to the Radio Booth From Usher, Player, Reporter Roles," *The Sporting News*, May 7, 1936.
14. Russo, *Points on the Dial*, 57.
15. *The Sporting News*, December 31, 1936; Walker, *Crack of the Bat*, 125.
16. Sterling and Kittross, *Stay Tuned*, 656; Henry Berry, "Happiness Is a Red Sox Victory," *New York Times*, September 2, 1979.
17. Al Hirshberg, *What's the Matter with the Red Sox?* (New York: Dodd, Mead, 1973), 124.

Chapter 14

1. T.D. Thornton, *Not By a Long Shot: A Season at a Hard-Luck Horse Track* (New York: Public Affairs, 2007), 31.
2. *Boston Globe*, July 12, 1935.
3. *Boston Globe*, December 11–12, 1934; January 11–14, 1935.
4. *Boston Globe*, February 6, 1935.
5. Montville, *The Big Bam*, 337.
6. *The Sporting News*, August 15, 1935.
7. *Boston Globe*, November 28, December 9, and December 29, 1935; Quinn obituary, *Boston Globe*, March 17, 1954.
8. *Boston Globe*, February 16, 1935; F.C. Lane, "Will the Major Leagues Adopt Night Baseball?" *Baseball Magazine*, October 1935.
9. *Lowell Sun*, June 9, 1934; *Springfield Union*, June 8, 1934.
10. *Boston Globe*, August 12 and October 1, 1936.
11. *Boston Globe*, January 31, 1936.
12. Brands, "Fred Hoey."

Chapter 15

1. J.G. Taylor Spink, "'I Won't Mess Around With a Loser,'" *The Sporting News*, January 30, 1936.
2. *Ibid.*

3. *Boston Globe*, July 4, 1936.
4. *Boston Globe*, March 10, 1936; *New York Times*, April 10, 1936.
5. Harold Kaese, "Even in Boston a Fan's a Fan," *New York Times*, September 29, 1946.
6. Harris, "Why a City Goes Baseball Crazy."
7. *Ibid.*
8. *Boston Globe*, August 9, 1936, and January 1, 1937; *The Sporting News*, April 22, 1937.
9. *The Sporting News*, April 21, 1938.
10. Blackford, *History of Small Business*, 108; Mills, *White Collar*, 63–64.
11. Cindy Aron, *Working at Play: A History of Vacations in the United States* (New York: Oxford University Press, 1999), 238–240; Surdam, *Century of the Leisured Masses*, 46.
12. *Boston Globe*, August 27, 1938; Harris, "Why a City Goes Baseball Crazy."
13. *Boston Globe*, August 20, 1939.
14. Letters to the editor, *Boston Globe*, April 7 and 14, 1941.
15. Ben Bradlee, Jr., *The Kid: The Immortal Life of Ted Williams* (New York: Little, Brown and Company, 2013), 134–135.
16. Franklin Roosevelt, *FDR's Fireside Chats*, eds. Russell Buhite and David Levy (Norman: University of Oklahoma Press, 1992), 150.
17. *Boston Globe*, September 4, 1939; Linn, *Rivalry*, 141. The president of the American League eventually reversed the forfeiture decision and ruled that the game ended in a tie due to the application of the Sunday curfew.
18. *Boston Globe*, November 8, 1939; *The Sporting News*, May 16, 1940; Ray Fitzgerald, "Voice from Hub's Past Is Stilled," *Boston Globe*, January 6, 1981; Mort Bloomberg, "Jim Britt," in *Pitching to the Pennant: The 1954 Cleveland Indians*, ed. Joseph Wancho (Lincoln: University of Nebraska Press, 2014), 281.
19. Radio program listing, *Boston Globe*, May 8, 1940; Betty Pesa, "Youngsters Are Top Scorers in Jerry O'Leary's Baseball Quiz," *Boston Globe*, August 1, 1948; O'Leary obituary, *Boston Globe*, May 25, 1980.
20. *Boston Globe*, September 25, 1939.
21. Bradlee, *The Kid*, 142; *Boston American*, August 13, 1940.
22. Leigh Montville, *Ted Williams: The Biography of an American Hero* (New York: Doubleday, 2004), 68; Bradlee, *The Kid*, 157.

23. Ted Williams, *My Turn At Bat* (New York: Simon and Schuster, 1988), 9–10, 132.
24. Bradlee, *The Kid*, 147–148.
25. *Boston Globe*, April 21, 24, and 30, 1941.
26. *Hartford Courant*, June 16 and July 9, 1941; *Lynn Telegram–News*, August 16, 1941.
27. *The Sporting News*, January 30 and February 6, 1941.
28. *Boston Globe*, February 5, 1937
29. *Boston Globe*, February 27, 1935.
30. *Boston Globe*, August 20, 1939.
31. *New York Times*, December 10 and 20, 1941.

Chapter 16

1. *The Sporting News*, January 22, 1942.
2. *Boston Globe*, January 20, February 4, and February 18, 1942.
3. *Boston Globe*, August 21–22, 1942.
4. Harold Kaese, "'Megaphone Lolly' Enlivens Games of Sox and Tribe," *Boston Globe*, August 2, 1943; Dan Daniel, "Mary, Lollie, Hilda—Loudest Fans in Stands," *The Sporting News*, February 2, 1963; Hopkins obituary, *Boston Globe*, September 25, 1959.
5. Kaese, "Megaphone Lolly."
6. Elizabeth Dooley, "Rooting for the Red Sox," in *Red Sox Century*, 254; "Team Is Hit With Loss of Grandest Fan," *Boston Globe*, June 20, 2000.
7. William Mead, *Even the Browns: The Zany, True Story of Baseball in the Early Forties* (Chicago: Contemporary, 1978), 82.
8. *Boston Globe*, May 27–28, 1943.
9. *Acts and Resolves Passed by the General Court of Massachusetts in the Year 1943* (Boston: Wright & Potter, 1943), chapter 303, page 319.
10. *The Sporting News*, May 27, 1943.
11. *Boston Globe*, July 19 and September 14, 1943.
12. *Boston Globe*, August 2 and September 26, 1944.
13. Russo, *Points on the Dial*, 75; *The Sporting News*, May 6, 1943; *Boston Globe*, June 14, 1942; October 25, 1942; May 2, 1943.
14. Radio program listing, *Boston Globe*, August 26, 1943; Barber, *Broadcasters*, 107–108; Smith, *Voices*, 81.
15. *Boston Globe*, January 22, 1944.
16. *Boston Globe*, July 14 and September 20, 1944.
17. *Boston Globe*, February 15 and July 19, 1945.

Chapter 17

1. *Boston Globe*, February 14, 1946.
2. Harold Kaese, "They're Digging a Pennant in Boston," *Saturday Evening Post*, June 28, 1947; *Boston Globe*, May 3, 1946.
3. *Boston Globe*, February 12, 1946.
4. *Boston Globe*, April 22 and May 18, 1946; *Acts and Resolves Passed by the General Court of Massachusetts in the Year 1946* (Boston: Wright & Potter, 1946), chapter 318, page 311.
5. *Boston Globe*, April 16, 1946.
6. *Boston Globe*, July 3, 1946; Al Hirshberg, *The Braves: The Pick and the Shovel* (Boston: Waverly, 1948), 178–179.
7. Kaese, "Even in Boston, a Fan's a Fan."
8. *Boston Globe*, May 14, 1946.
9. *The Sporting News*, April 18, 1946; *Boston Globe*, April 6, 1946.
10. *Boston Globe*, May 22 and 26, 1946.
11. *The Sporting News*, October 2, 1946; *Boston Globe*, January 23, 1947.
12. Harold Kaese, "Ted's Long Homer Pierces Straw Hat on Head 450 Feet Away," *Boston Globe*, June 10, 1946; Harold Kaese, "Longest Homer by Williams Was Felt, Not Seen," *Boston Globe*, July 26, 1953; Dan Shaughnessy, "Long Ago It Went Far Away," *Boston Globe*, June 9, 1996.
13. *Boston Globe*, August 16, 1946.
14. *Boston Globe*, September 10 and 13, 1946.
15. *Boston Globe*, October 8–10, 1946.
16. *Boston Globe*, October 16, 1946.
17. *Boston Globe*, November 27, 1946, and January 31, 1947.
18. *Boston Globe*, November 27, 1946.
19. *Ibid.*
20. Bevis, *Doubleheaders*, 154.
21. *Boston Globe*, April 9, 1947; *The Sporting News*, August 20, 1947; *Boston Globe*, June 12 and July 22, 1947; Hirshberg, *The Braves*, 184; *Boston Globe*, August 14, 1947.
22. *Boston Globe*, July 18, 1947; *Acts and Resolves Passed by the General Court of Massachusetts in the Year 1947* (Boston: Wright & Potter, 1947), chapter 627, page 657.
23. *Boston Globe*, April 11 and December 31, 1947.
24. Dan Shaughnessy, "The Wall Is an Icon of More Than Just Fenway," *Boston Globe*, April 1, 2012; Bob Sales, "Grass Roots," *Boston Globe*, April 7, 1968; Nathan Cobb, "This Company's Green Paint Is Always a

Hit at Fenway," *Boston Globe*, April 26, 2003; David Kiefaber, "Now Your Whole House Can Be a Shrine to Fenway's Green Monster," *Adweek*, August 13, 2014.
25. *Boston Globe*, August 20, 1946; *The Sporting News*, April 16, 1947; *Billboard*, September 20, 1947.
26. Radio program listing, *Boston Globe*, May 9, 1947.
27. *Boston Globe*, June 13–14, 1947.
28. *Boston Globe*, June 24, 1947.
29. *Boston Globe*, August 21, 1947.
30. *Ibid.*
31. *Boston Globe*, September 28, 1947; Hirshberg, *The Braves*, 182.

Chapter 18

1. *Boston Globe*, December 31, 1947, and April 15–18, 1948.
2. Siddhartha Mukherjee, *The Emperor of All Maladies: A Biography of Cancer* (New York: Simon and Schuster, 2010), 97–98; *Boston Globe*, May 23, 1948.
3. "Whole State Goes to Bat for 'Jimmy' in Cancer Drive," *Boston Globe*, June 27, 1948.
4. Sterling and Kittross, *Stay Tuned*, 656; DiPesa, "Jerry O'Leary's Baseball Quiz."
5. *Boston Globe*, May 12 and June 15, 1948.
6. *Boston Globe*, June 15 and July 11, 1948; *The Sporting News*, April 20, 1949.
7. *Boston Globe*, June 15, 1948; Spigel, *Make Room for TV*, 100.
8. *Boston Globe*, July 2, 1948.
9. *Boston Globe*, August 9, 1948; *The Sporting News*, August 18, 1948.
10. *Boston Globe*, August 9, 1948.
11. *Boston Globe*, April 29, 1946, and May 27, 1949.
12. *Boston Globe*, June 15, 1948.
13. *Boston Globe*, January 25, 1948.
14. K.S. Bartlett, "Women Fans Become More Excited," *Boston Globe*, June 25, 1950.
15. Russell Collins, "Mrs. Grace Coolidge Rootin' Our Red Sox Home," *Boston Globe*, September 11, 1949.
16. *The Sporting News*, September 15, 1948.
17. *Boston Globe*, April 14 and July 27, 1948.
18. *Boston Post*, September 14, 1948.
19. *Boston Globe*, September 20–23, 1948.
20. *Boston Globe*, September 30, 1948.

21. Radio program listing, *Boston Globe*, September 16, 20, and 24, 1948.

22. *Boston Globe*, October 4, 1948.

23. Elizabeth Watts, "Dave Stein, 14, Souvenir Seller, Braves' Fan, but Thinks Williams Tops," *Boston Globe*, October 12, 1948.

24. *New York Times*, September 29 and October 5, 1948.

25. James Walker and Robert Bellamy, Jr., *Center Field Shot: A History of Baseball on Television* (Lincoln: University of Nebraska Press, 2008), 73–75.

Chapter 19

1. Roger Birtwell, "Braves Buy Own Park, Blueprint Expansion," *The Sporting News*, February 2, 1949; Henry Harris, "Baked Beans for Saturday and More Seats at Boston Ball Parks," *Boston Globe*, April 17, 1949.

2. "Think of Those Expressways as a Hub with Eight Spokes," *Boston Globe*, February 26, 1948.

3. Birtwell, "Braves Buy Own Park."

4. Birtwell, "Braves Buy Own Park"; Kaese, "Digging a Pennant in Boston"; Harold Kaese, "The Quinns: Front Office Dynasty," *Boston Globe*, June 11, 1972.

5. Stephen Herrig, *South Middlesex: A New England Heritage* (Northridge, CA: Windsor, 1986), 125.

6. Barbara Miller Lane, *Houses for a New World: Builders and Buyers in American Suburbs 1945–1965* (Princeton, NJ: Princeton University Press, 2015), 123; James Jacobs, *Detached America: Building Houses in Postwar Suburbia* (Charlottesville: University of Virginia Press, 2015), 113, 120.

7. O'Connell, *The Hub's Metropolis*, 138; Joe Dineen, "Shoppers' World Opens Thursday," *Boston Globe*, September 30, 1951.

8. Susan Rosegrant and David Lampe, *Route 128: Lessons from Boston's High-Tech Community* (New York: Basic Books, 1992), 107.

9. Yanni Tsipis, *Building the Mass Pike* (Charleston, SC: Arcadia, 2002), 32, 49, 52.

10. John Hilliard, "Framingham Red Sox? It Was More Than a Passing Thought," *Framingham Tab*, February 1, 2008.

11. Harris, "Baked Beans."

12. Sterling and Kittross, *Stay Tuned*, 657; Walker and Bellamy, *Center Field Shot*, 26.

13. Elizabeth Sullivan, "Telecasters Don't Look at the Diamond When Describing the Game," *Boston Globe*, July 11, 1948.

14. *Boston Globe*, September 25, 1949.

15. *Boston Globe*, April 1, 1949.

16. *Boston Globe*, April 10, 1949.

17. *Boston Globe*, April 21, May 12 and June 11, 1949.

18. *Boston Globe*, August 31 and October 3, 1949.

19. David Halberstam, *Summer of '49* (New York: William Morrow, 1989), 250.

20. Dan Shaughnessy, *The Curse of the Bambino* (New York: Dutton, 1990), 89.

21. *Boston Globe*, October 3, 1949.

22. Radio program listings, *Boston Globe*, September 26 to October 2, 1949; "Sox Game to Air," *Boston Globe*, October 2, 1949.

23. Halberstam, *Summer of '49*, 112, 247–248, 277–278; A. Bartlett Giamatti, *A Great and Glorious Game: Baseball Writings of A. Bartlett Giamatti*, ed. Kenneth Robson (Chapel Hill, NC: Algonquin, 1998), 7.

24. *Boston Globe*, February 22, 1950.

25. *Boston Globe*, May 25, 1950.

26. Sterling and Kittross, *Stay Tuned*, 310, 657.

27. Elizabeth Sullivan, "Night Baseball on TV Tomorrow," *Boston Globe*, April 23, 1950; "Baseball Games TV on the Wane?" *Billboard*, July 8, 1950.

28. Spigel, *Make Room for TV*, 77.

29. Rick Swaine, *The Integration of Major League Baseball: A Team by Team History* (Jefferson, NC: McFarland, 2009), 92.

30. Michael Civille, "The Brave Departure: How the Boston Braves' 1953 Migration to Milwaukee Reflected the City of Boston and a Changing American Landscape," in *Cooperstown Symposium on Baseball and American Culture, 2007–2008*, ed. William Simons (Jefferson, NC: McFarland, 2009), 234, 241.

31. *Boston Globe*, April 24 and June 19, 1950; *Acts and Resolves Passed by the General Court of Massachusetts in the Year 1954* (Boston: Wright & Potter, 1954), chapter 132, page 78. The lighting restriction was removed, but was replaced with the provision that the first game of a doubleheader needed to start at or before 2:00 in the afternoon, or a single game needed to start at or before 3:00.

32. *The Sporting News*, November 1, 1950.

33. *The Sporting News*, January 31, 1951.

34. *Boston Globe*, May 12, 1950.

35. *Boston Globe*, September 26, 1950.

Chapter 20

1. *Boston Globe*, September 19, 1950, and March 20, 1953.

2. *The Sporting News*, November 8, 1950.

3. Curt Gowdy, *Cowboy at the Mike* (Garden City, NY: Doubleday, 1966), 101; Stephen Borelli, *How About That! The Life of Mel Allen* (Champaign, IL: Sports Publishing, 2005), 93.

4. *The Sporting News*, October 25, 1950.

5. *The Sporting News*, November 8, 1950, and March 21, 1951; Al Hirshberg, "Mistakes Helped Lose Braves from Hub," *The Sporting News*, March 25, 1953.

6. *The Sporting News*, April 18, 1951.

7. *Boston Globe*, February 15 and March 7, 1951; *The Sporting News*, April 18, 1951.

8. *Boston Globe*, March 7 and April 15, 1951.

9. Sterling and Kittross, *Stay Tuned*, 657; Butsch, *The Making of American Audiences*, 246–247; Surdam, *Century of the Leisured Masses*, 81.

10. Author's older brother, Bob Bevis. His recall of a 1950s trip to the ballpark was encyclopedic because it was the same route traveled by the Almeida bus line in 1959, where he first met his future wife on a commute home from college.

11. Schnore and Knights, "Residence and Social Structure," 249–250.

12. *Boston Globe*, April 13, 1951. Five years later the Red Sox also banned beer sales in the stands at Fenway Park (*Boston Globe*, August 17, 1956).

13. *The Sporting News*, January 30, 1952.

14. *The Sporting News*, April 11, 1951.

15. *Boston Globe*, April 16, 1951, and April 18, 1952.

16. Gowdy, *Cowboy at the Mike*, 112–113.

17. Jack Barry, "How Gowdy's Statistician Figures 'Em," *Boston Globe*, October 24, 1954.

18. Curt Gowdy, *Seasons to Remember: The Way It Was in American Sports, 1945–1960* (New York: Harper Collins, 1993), 141; *Boston Globe*, July 13, 1951.

19. *The Sporting News*, April 18 and May 23, 1951.

20. *The Sporting News*, August 29, 1951; *Boston Globe*, August 20, 1951.

21. Hirshberg, "Mistakes Helped Lose Braves."

22. "Roads of Metro Boston" and "Maps and History," *Boston Roads* website, accessed January 23, 2015.

23. *The Sporting News*, April 25, 1951.

24. *The Sporting News*, May 28, 1952.

25. *Boston Globe*, September 22, 1952.

26. Marvin Pave, "Fans, Former Players Nostalgic as Braves Return to Boston," *Boston Globe*, August 29, 1997.

27. *New York Times*, March 4, 14, 17, and 19, 1953.

28. *New York Times*, March 17 and 19, 1953.

29. Kaese, *Boston Braves*, xiii; *Boston Globe*, April 21, 1953.

30. Kaese, *Boston Braves*, xi.

31. *Boston Globe*, March 15, 1953; Hirshberg, "Mistakes Helped Lose Braves"; *New York Times*, March 11, 1953.

32. Edgar Driscoll, "Tom Yawkey, Red Sox Owner, Dies at 73," *Boston Globe*, July 10, 1976; *Boston Globe*, April 13, 1953.

33. *Boston Globe*, March 16, 1953; Al Hirshberg, "Lou Perini: Villain or Visionary?" *The Sporting News*, April 1, 1953.

Epilogue

1. Bradlee, *The Kid*, 369, 465.

2. *The Sporting News*, August 1, 1956; the five games between the Red Sox and Giants to benefit hospitalized veterans were played on June 25, 1951; August 4, 1952; June 29, 1953; August 16, 1954; and May 23, 1955.

3. *Boston Globe*, July 12, 1949; the four games between the Red Sox and Braves to benefit the unemployed were played on September 23, 1931; June 29, 1932; September 27, 1933; and August 31, 1934.

4. *The Sporting News*, April 24, 1957; *Boston Globe*, August 29, 1956.

5. *Boston Globe*, June 10, 1957.

6. *Boston Globe*, July 16, 1957.

7. *Boston Globe*, July 21, 1957.

8. *Boston Globe*, June 14, 1959.

9. *Boston Globe*, July 21, 1957, and January 1, 1958.

10. *New York Times*, May 13, 1958.

11. *Boston Globe*, August 22, 1961.

12. *Boston Globe*, June 4, 1963.

13. *Boston Globe*, June 7, 1966.

14. The Atlanta Braves did eventually return to Boston to play a ball game, in August 1997, when interleague play during the regular season was instituted between the two leagues.

15. Mukherjee, *The Emperor of All Maladies*, 395–396.

Bibliography

Alexander, Charles. *Breaking the Slump: Baseball in the Depression Era*. New York: Columbia University Press, 2002.

Ardell, Jean Hastings. *Breaking into Baseball: Women and the National Pastime*. Carbondale: Southern Illinois University Press, 2005.

Aron, Cindy. *Working at Play: A History of Vacations in the United States*. New York: Oxford University Press, 1999.

Bevis, Charlie. *Doubleheaders: A Major League History*. Jefferson, NC: McFarland, 2011.

_____. *Jimmy Collins: A Baseball Biography*. Jefferson, NC: McFarland, 2012.

_____. *Sunday Baseball: The Major Leagues' Struggle to Play Baseball on the Lord's Day, 1876–1934*. Jefferson, NC: McFarland, 2003.

Blackford, Mansel. *A History of Small Business in America*. New York: Twayne, 1991.

Bloomberg, Mort. "Jim Britt." In *Pitching to the Pennant: The 1954 Cleveland Indians*, ed. Joseph Wancho. Lincoln: University of Nebraska Press, 2014.

Blumin, Stuart. *The Emergence of the Middle Class: Social Experience in the American City, 1760–1900*. New York: Cambridge University Press, 1989.

Bradlee, Ben, Jr. *The Kid: The Immortal Life of Ted Williams*. New York: Little, Brown, 2013.

Brands, Edgar. "Fred Hoey Moved to the Radio Booth from Usher, Player, Reporter Roles." *The Sporting News*, May 7, 1936.

Brown, Richard, and Jack Tager. *Massachusetts: A Concise History*. Amherst: University of Massachusetts Press, 2000.

Butsch, Richard. *The Making of American Audiences: From Stage to Television, 1750–1990*. New York: Cambridge University Press, 2000.

Cheape, Charles. *Moving the Masses: Urban Transit in New York, Boston, and Philadelphia, 1880–1912*. Cambridge: Harvard University Press, 1980.

Civille, Michael. "The Brave Departure: How the Boston Braves' 1953 Migration to Milwaukee Reflected the City of Boston and a Changing American Landscape." In *Cooperstown Symposium on Baseball and American Culture, 2007–2008*, ed. William Simons. Jefferson, NC: McFarland, 2009.

Cooper, Arthur. "Winter League Unique Among the Societies of Boston." *Boston Post*, January 19, 1913.

Cudahy, Brian. *Change at Park Street Under: The Story of Boston's Subways*. Brattleboro, VT: Stephen Greene Press, 1972.

Currell, Susan. *The March of Spare Time: The Problem and Promise of Leisure in the Great Depression*. Philadelphia: University of Pennsylvania Press, 2005.

Davis, John, and Jessica Zutz Hilbert. *Sports Marketing: Creating Long Term Value*. Northampton, MA: Edward Elgar, 2013.

Dickson, Paul. *The New Dickson Baseball Dictionary.* New York: Harcourt Brace, 1999.
Edel, Matthew, Elliott Sclar, and Daniel Luria. *Shaky Palaces: Homeownership and Social Mobility in Boston's Suburbanization.* New York: Columbia University Press, 1984.
Gowdy, Curt. *Cowboy at the Mike.* Garden City, NY: Doubleday, 1966.
Halberstam, David. *Summer of '49.* New York: William Morrow, 1989.
Harris, Henry. "Why a City Goes Baseball Crazy." *Boston Globe,* September 4, 1938.
Herring, Stephen. *South Middlesex: A New England Heritage.* Northridge, CA: Windsor Publications, 1986.
Hirshberg, Al. *The Braves: The Pick and the Shovel.* Boston: Waverly, 1948.
_____. Lou Perini: Villain or Visionary?" *The Sporting News,* April 1, 1953.
_____. *What's the Matter with the Red Sox?* New York: Dodd, Mead, 1973.
Hochfelder, David. *The Telegraph in America, 1832–1920.* Baltimore: Johns Hopkins University Press, 2012.
Huhn, Rick. *Eddie Collins: A Baseball Biography.* Jefferson, NC: McFarland, 2008.
Jackson, Kenneth. *Crabgrass Frontier: The Suburbanization of the United States.* New York: Oxford University Press, 1985.
Jacobs, James. *Detached America: Building Houses in Postwar Suburbia.* Charlottesville: University of Virginia Press, 2015.
Kaese, Harold. *The Boston Braves, 1871–1953.* First edition 1948. Boston: Northeastern University Press, 2004.
_____. "Even in Boston a Fan's a Fan." *New York Times,* September 29, 1946.
_____. "They're Digging a Pennant in Boston." *Saturday Evening Post,* June 28, 1947.
Kane, Paula. *Separatism and Subculture: Boston Catholicism, 1900–1920.* Chapel Hill: University of North Carolina Press, 1994.
Karr, Ronald. *The Rail Lines of Southern New England.* Pepperell, MA: Branch Line, 1995.
Keene, Kerry, et al. *The Babe in Red Stockings: An In-Depth Chronicle of Babe Ruth with the Boston Red Sox, 1914–1919.* Champaign, IL: Sagamore, 1997.
Klein, Maury. *The Genesis of Industrial America, 1870–1920.* New York: Cambridge University Press, 2007.
Lane, Barbara Miller. *Houses for a New World: Builders and Buyers in American Suburbs 1945–1965.* Princeton: Princeton University Press, 2015.
Lane, F.C. "The Greatest Problem in the National Game: The Critical Situation in Sunday Baseball." *Baseball Magazine,* October 1911.
_____. "Will the Major Leagues Adopt Night Baseball?" *Baseball Magazine,* October 1935.
_____. "The World's Greatest Baseball Park." *Baseball Magazine,* October 1915.
Lieb, Fred. *Boston Red Sox.* New York: G.P. Putnam's Sons, 1947.
Linn, Ed. *The Great Rivalry: The Yankees and the Red Sox 1901–1990.* New York: Ticknor & Fields, 1991.
Lovett, James D'Wolf. *Old Boston Boys and the Games They Played.* Boston: Riverside Press, 1907.
Lynch, Michael. *Harry Frazee, Ban Johnson and the Feud That Nearly Destroyed the American League.* Jefferson, NC: McFarland, 2008.
Miller, Raymond. "A Biography of Braves Field." In *Braves Field: Memorable Moments at Boston's Lost Diamond,* eds. Bill Nowlin and Bob Brady. Phoenix: Society for American Baseball Research, 2015.
Mills, Wright. *White Collar: The American Middle Classes.* New York: Oxford University Press, 1951.
Montville, Leigh. *The Big Bam: The Life and Times of Babe Ruth.* New York: Doubleday, 2006.
_____. *Ted Williams: The Biography of an American Hero.* New York: Doubleday, 2004.
Morris, Peter, et al., eds. *Base Ball Founders: The Clubs, Players and Cities of the Northeast That Established the Game.* Jefferson, NC: McFarland, 2013.
Mukherjee, Siddhartha. *The Emperor of All Maladies: A Biography of Cancer.* New York: Simon & Schuster, 2010.
Nasaw, David. *Going Out: The Rise and Fall of Public Amusements.* New York: Basic, 1993.

Nash, Peter. *Boston's Royal Rooters*. Charleston, SC: Arcadia, 2005.

Newman, William, and Wilfred Holton. *Boston's Back Bay: The Story of America's Greatest Nineteenth-Century Landfill Project*. Boston: Northeastern University Press, 2006.

O'Connell, James. *The Hub's Metropolis: Greater Boston's Development from Railroad Suburbs to Smart Growth*. Cambridge: MIT Press, 2013.

O'Connor, Thomas. *The Hub: Boston Past and Present*. Boston: Northeastern University Press, 2001.

Palmer, James. "Economic and Social Aspects of Chain Stores." *Journal of Business of the University of Chicago*, July 1929.

Pesa, Betty. "Youngsters Are Top Scorers in Jerry O'Leary's Baseball Quiz." *Boston Globe*, August 1, 1948.

A Record of the Streets, Alleys, Places, Etc. in the City of Boston. Boston: City of Boston, 1910.

Redmond, Patrick. *The Irish and the Making of American Sport, 1835–1920*. Jefferson, NC: McFarland, 2014.

Riess, Steven. *City Games: The Evolution of American Urban Society and the Rise of Sports*. Urbana: University of Illinois Press, 1989.

Rihbany, Abraham. *A Far Journey: An Autobiography*. Boston: Houghton Mifflin, 1914.

Russo, Alexander. *Points on the Dial: Golden Age Radio Beyond the Networks*. Durham: Duke University Press, 2010.

Russo, Bob. "South End Grounds." In *The Miracle Braves of 1914*, ed. Bill Nowlin. Phoenix: Society for American Baseball Research, 2014.

Ryczek, William. *When Johnny Came Sliding Home: The Post–Civil War Baseball Boom, 1865–1870*. Jefferson, NC: McFarland, 1998.

Saltonstall, Leverett. *The Autobiography of Leverett Saltonstall: Massachusetts Governor, U.S. Senator, and Yankee Icon*. Lanham, MD: Rowman & Littlefield, 2015.

Sammarco, Anthony. *Boston's South End*. Charleston, SC: Arcadia, 1998.

Schaeffer, K.H., and Elliot Sclar. *Access for All: Transportation and Urban Growth*. New York: Penguin, 1975.

Schnore, Leo, and Peter Knights. "Residence and Social Structure: Boston in the Ante-Bellum Period." In *Nineteenth-Century Cities: Essays in the New Urban History*, eds. Stephan Thernsrom and Richard Sennett. New Haven: Yale University Press, 1969.

Seasholes, Nancy. *Gaining Ground: A History of Landmaking in Boston*. Cambridge: MIT Press, 2003.

Seiler, Cotton. *Republic of Drivers: A Cultural History of Automobility in America*. Chicago: University of Chicago Press, 2008.

Shaughnessy, Dan. *The Curse of the Bambino*. New York: Dutton, 1990.

Smith, Curt. *Voices of the Game: The First Full-Scale Overview of Baseball Broadcasting, 1921 to the Present*. South Bend, IN: Diamond Communications, 1987.

_____. *Mercy! A Celebration of Fenway Park's Centennial Told Through Red Sox Radio and TV*. Washington: Potomac, 2012.

Spigel, Lynn. *Make Room for TV: Television and the Family Ideal in Postwar America*. Chicago: University of Chicago Press, 1992.

Sterling, Christopher, and John Kittross. *Stay Tuned: A Concise History of American Broadcasting*. First edition 1978. Belmont, CA: Wadsworth Publishing, 1990.

Stout, Glenn. *Fenway 1912: The Birth of a Ballpark, a Championship Season, and Fenway's Remarkable First Year*. Boston: Houghton Mifflin, 2011.

_____. *The Selling of the Babe: The Deal That Changed Baseball and Created a Legend*. New York: Thomas Dunne, 2016.

Stout, Glenn, and Richard Johnson. *Red Sox Century: One Hundred Years of Red Sox Baseball*. Boston: Houghton Mifflin, 2000.

Surdam, David. *Century of the Leisured Masses: Entertainment and the Transformation of Twentieth-Century America*. New York: Oxford University Press, 2015.

Swaine, Rick. *The Integration of Major League Baseball: A Team by Team History*. Jefferson, NC: McFarland, 2009.

Szalontai, James. *Small Ball in the Big Leagues: A History of Stealing, Bunting, Walking, and Otherwise Scratching for Runs.* Jefferson, NC: McFarland, 2010.

Tiemann, Robert. "Major League Attendance." In *Total Baseball.* 7th ed. Kingston, NY: Total Sports Publishing, 2001.

Tuohey, George. *A History of the Boston Base Ball Club.* Boston: M.F. Quinn, 1897.

U.S. Department of Transportation. "Highway Statistics Summary to 1995." *Federal Highway Administration* website (accessed April 17, 2016).

Vincent, David. *Home Run: The Definitive History of Baseball's Ultimate Weapon.* Washington: Potomac Books, 2007.

Voigt, David Q. "Out With the Crowds: Counting, Courting and Controlling Ball Park Fans." *Baseball History*, 1989.

Walker, James. *Crack of the Bat: A History of Baseball on the Radio.* Lincoln: University of Nebraska Press, 2015.

Walker, James, and Robert Bellamy, Jr. *Center Field Shot: A History of Baseball on Television.* Lincoln: University of Nebraska Press, 2008.

Wann, Daniel, et al. *Sport Fans: The Psychology and Social Impact of Spectators.* New York: Routledge, 2001.

Warner, Sam Bass, Jr. *Streetcar Suburbs: The Process of Growth in Boston, 1870–1900.* Cambridge: Harvard University Press, 1962.

Webb, Melville. "Why Are You a Baseball Fan?" *Boston Globe*, August 31, 1913.

Whitehill, Walter. *Boston: A Topographical History.* Cambridge: Harvard University Press, 1959.

Williams, Ted. *My Turn at Bat.* New York: Simon & Schuster, 1988.

Wisnia, Saul. "From Yawkey to Milwaukee: Lou Perini Makes His Move." In *That's Joy in Braveland! The 1957 Milwaukee Braves,* ed. Gregory Wolf. Phoenix: Society for American Baseball Research, 2014.

Baseball Periodicals

Baseball Magazine
Sporting Life
The Sporting News

General Newspapers

Boston Daily Advertiser
Boston Globe
Boston Herald
Boston Post

Index

Numbers in *bold italics* indicate pages with illustrations

241